FELIM MOUNTAINS
SCARTEEN HUNTING COUNTRY
DEAD RIVER
TO DUBLIN
DUNDRUM
OOLA HILLS
OOLA
PENNY-IN-THE-SLOT!
CULLEN
MONARD
LIMERICK JUNCTION
GRENANE HOUSE
KILFEACLE
GOLDEN
CASHEL
LATTIN
SHRONELL
TIPPERARY
KILSHANE HO.
AUGHNAGAWER CROSS
MOUNT BRUIS
BANSHA
LISMACUE
KILROSS
SLIEVE NA MUCK
AHERLOW RIVER
GLEN OF AHERLOW
ROSSADREHID
CAHIR
CLONMEL
CARRICK-ON-SUIR
WATERFORD
WEXFORD
GALTEE MOUNTAINS
Claudia Reidy '01

THE DERRYDALE PRESS

FOXHUNTERS' LIBRARY

MY PRIVILEGED LIFE

With the Scarteen Black and Tans

THADY RYAN, M.F.H.

THE DERRYDALE PRESS

LANHAM, NEW YORK, AND PLYMOUTH, UK

THE DERRYDALE PRESS

Published by The Derrydale Press
An imprint of the Rowman & Littlefield Publishing Group, Inc.
4501 Forbes Boulevard, Suite 200, Lanham, Maryland 20706
http://www.rlpgtrade.com

Estover Road, Plymouth PL6 7PY, United Kingdom

Distributed by National Book Network

Library of Congress Cataloging-in-Publication Data

Ryan, Thady, 1923–
My privileged life : with the Scarteen black and tan / Thady Ryan.
p. cm.—(Derrydale Press foxhunters' library series)
Includes bibliographical references (p.).
ISBN 978-1-58667-096-2 (cloth : alk. paper)
1. Ryan, Thady, 1923– 2. Hunters—Ireland—Biography. 3. Fox hunting—Ireland. I. Title. II. Derrydale Press foxhunters' library.
SK17.R93 A3 2002

2002004741

∞™ The paper used in this publication meets the minimum requirements of American National Standard for Information Sciences—Permanence of Paper for Printed Library Materials, ANSI/NISO Z39.48-1992.
Manufactured in the United States of America.

I dedicate this book unreservedly to my family.

CONTENTS

ABBREVIATIONS

ACB	Ampleforth College Beagles
Co.	County
IMFHA	Irish Masters of Foxhounds Association
MFH	Master of Foxhounds
MSH	Master of Staghounds
OTC	Officers Training Corps
RDS	Royal Dublin Society
TBA	Thoroughbred Breeders Association

RYAN FAMILY TREE

John Ryan brought Family from Ballykeveen to Ballyvistea in 1755.

Thaddeus Ryan m. Helen Howley. Brought Family to Scarteen in 1798.

John Ryan, Scarteen, m. Alicia McKnight Hartigan

- Thaddeus The General m. Gwendoline Power
  - John m. Anita Purcell. Burton Park
    - Thaddeus m. Anne Peter. New Zealand
      - Rachel
      - John
      - Hugh
      - Christopher
      - Mark
      - Claire
    - Gwendaline m. Ernest Pearson M.F.H.
    - Jean m. Claude Thompson M.F.H.
      - Claudia
      - Helen
      - Maria
      - Geoffrey
    - John Ryan-Purcell (Burton Park) m. Rosemary Ronan
      - Oliver
      - Eliza
      - Anita
      - Charles
      - Walter
      - Hilda
  - James
  - Tha
  - Willie Distiller
    - Jim Kenya
      - Pip Kenya
      - Mark Kenya
      - Michael
      - Charles
      - Isobel
      - James Ballytrent
    - John Banker
    - Clem Distiller
    - Margaret m. Harry Roche M.D.
    - Veronica
  - Janey Edermine
  - Alice Nun
  - Hugh S. Africa
  - Frank M.C. The Colonel
  - Clement (killed WW I) m. Blanche Maguire (Aunt B) m. (2nd) Willie Wilson - Lynch Belvoir
- Jack Australia
- William L.L.B.
- Hugh Jesuit India
- Alice Nun
- Clement M.S.H. Emly m. Elizabeth Bianconi
  - Jack Emly
  - Helen Nun
  - Clem V.S.
  - Alice I.C.A.
  - Grace m. Nicolas Grene
    - James O.S.B. Abbot
    - Lily
    - Almary
    - Clement Grene Park
    - Grace
    - Helen
    - Nicholas
    - Francis
  - Charles
  - Hugh Trainer
  - Amy m. Tom Mangan
  - Tony Kenya
  - Betty
- Richard Australia
- Charles M.D. m. Mary Parkes
  - May Nun
  - Hilda
  - Phil m. Carlon Markes
  - Moira
- Arthur Mons.
- Walter
- Helen "Auntie"

John Power

- m. Gwendoline Power
- Fanny Power m. Joseph R. O'reilly
  - Harry
  - Bertie
  - Herbie
  - Charlie, M.D. m. Dorothy
    - Frank m. Tessa Williams
    - Maimes
    - June
  - Janey
- Thomas
- Sir James Edermine

FOREWORD

Thady Ryan tells his story of *My Privileged Life*, marked by generous service to many good causes, with a vivid description of a life passionately devoted to the many facets of country life in Ireland, and later in New Zealand, of his time. When grandchildren ask what rural life was like, this account of a life lived to the full will provide that information and entertain them as well.

The themes in the book: the importance of the family, the need to preserve the balance of nature in which the hunter and the hunted coexist to provide continuity, the leavening effect of sport in society, and strong religious faith are portrayed aglow with energy.

In his life with horse and hound, he lived through a period when the horse gave way, as a widely-used source of motive power, to the machine age. He had a unique opportunity, provided by the continuity of his forbears in hunting with hounds, of understanding the importance of that noble animal, the horse, as a medium of sport. Thus, we see his involvement in the Irish Horse Board in its beginning and his voluntary contribution to the equestrian activities of the Royal Dublin Society. From his experience in the hunting field, the greatest test of the all-around athletic ability of the horse, he sourced the innovative ideas that led to the hunt chase competition at the Dublin Horse Show and shows abroad. Many stories are related of how his expert knowledge of the horse led to a wide range of activities: as a respected judge, as well as his involvement with the Irish Horse Trials Team at many international events, including the Olympic Games.

He brings to life the rich pattern generated by the sport of hunting from Scarteen in his native Limerick/Tipperary country, populated by the many local characters that abound in the book devoted as they were, and still are, to rural pursuits. They are not alone; they are joined by a great number of the visitors that were hospitably entertained in his home and by local society at all levels. Then we are taken with equal interest to the other side of the world, to a new beginning in New Zealand.

His devotion to his family is told with great confidence, in places intensely personal, occasions where he had to face great sorrow with faith and courage. He expresses a deep faith, which from his observations he has clearly woven into the pattern of life within the local and wider community.

I feel sure that this entertaining book of Thady's will be of great interest to many people, from the wealthy to those less well off, who are somehow bound together by their common interest in that noble animal, the horse, and who have an interest in sport with horses. In this energetic and engaging story is a fascinating account of a committed life as a Master of Foxhounds, which revived many memories for me founded on a long friendship based on our mutual love of the horse.

Colonel W. A. (Bill) Ringrose
President
Royal Dublin Society

ACKNOWLEDGMENTS

Pride of place in the long list of those I must recognize here must go to my family for their long-suffering hard work, patience, and encouragement. Working with them has been a joy and has resulted in a unique family achievement. Among endless friends, I must mention especially Mairéad Bateman for instilling perseverance and confidence during my early writing days. I have been fortunate in having a multitude of superb photos for which I thank Barbara and Michelle Thompson in New Zealand and, closer to home, Mary Tarry and Catherine Power in Ireland. A special "thank you" to Catherine: many a happy evening my sister, Gwen, and I spent with her and her husband, Dickie, combing through her excellent collection. Thank you Ger O'Ríain for your beautiful and nostalgic "Ode to a Fox"—a real heart-tugger—and to Tanya Tremewan, my editor in New Zealand, for her rapid assimilation of a foxhunter's life. Who knows, she may follow hounds one day! A special tribute also to June Brilly for capturing brilliantly in crayon the momentous occasion when Chris presented the brush to his father. Finally, I thank sincerely Derrydale editor Norman Fine and his wife, Joan, for all their help and understanding. Too many years have slipped by since we hunted together. Now we can relive memories—this time in double harness!

PREFACE

Many friends have suggested that I should write a book so that the stories and experiences of my privileged but simple life might not be lost. So, after much persuasion, I decided to have a go. This book is the result. It is not a chronological account loaded with dates and statistics—I could not remember them even if I tried! Nor is it limited to hunting. (When I began, I could imagine people saying, "Thady Ryan writing a book? You must be joking—he will bore you stiff with his horses and hounds.") On the contrary, I have written *My Privileged Life* with the idea that it should be readable, entertaining, and a personal record of my experiences from an early age, richly coloured by the multitude of great characters with whom I have been fortunate to share my life.

Some of the anecdotes scattered throughout the book may embarrass some of my greatest friends. To my friends: if they have this effect, I beg your forgiveness. I relate them because of our mutual understanding and sincere friendship, and I hope that you will view them as I do in the spirit of fun and sportsmanship to which they belong. In some cases I have purposely used fictitious names. Inevitably some of you will recognise yourselves as these individuals. Again I crave your forgiveness for the same reasons!

And so, as my Dad used to say at the start of a journey—be it to a hunt or elsewhere—"We're off, in the Name of God!"

Thady Ryan. Barbara Thompson photo

ONE

LOOKING BACK WITH PRIDE

ONE

THE HILL OF HOWTH

As the ferry from Britain approaches Dublin, Howth Head is a welcome sight, particularly if the Irish Sea has been unkind. It commands a fine view across Dublin Bay to the distant Wicklow Mountains.

In the 1920s, taking a bumpy ride in the tram around the Hill of Howth was the standard advice that Dr Bethel Solomons, Master of the Rotunda, gave to mothers "nearing their time". It was, he said, an effective way to accelerate matters. The rank of Master of the Rotunda, the largest maternity hospital in Dublin, was (and is still) regarded as the highest honour a gynacologist can achieve in Ireland. Dr Solomons was a big man in every sense of the word: well over six feet tall, he had a loud voice, a commanding manner, and a love of sport. He hunted regularly with the Ward Union Staghounds—the reason, I suspect, why Dad chose him to deliver all four of us. On many an occasion among friends in later years, he would remind me with mischievous glee, "I was the first man to smack your bottom!"

And so it was that on 25 September 1923, in Hatch Street Nursing Home in Dublin (what an appropriate address!), I was born. After two lovely daughters in a row the arrival of a son and heir for Scarteen must have caused great relief and celebration. So I like to think—but I don't remember!

TWO

A LEGACY TO HONOUR

To be born into an old Irish Catholic family with long sporting traditions was certainly the greatest privilege of my life. Such a privilege also comes with serious obligations. Our forebears down the years have left us a legacy of loyalty to our religion, complete trust in God's mercy, and an unwavering devotion to His and our Blessed Mother. What a legacy to honour!

Dad gave us a simple recipe for success. "There are three priorities in life—strictly in this order: pray hard, work hard, play hard." I wish I could say truthfully that I have observed them wholly, but in all truth I have tried.

Grandfather, General Thaddeus Ryan of Scarteen—"The General"—was the eldest in a family of eleven. As a professional soldier in the Royal Artillery, his first commission was in India at the start of the Indian Mutiny. On one occasion, his duty was to fire his cannon at a specified time. Exhausted by long hours and intense heat, he was pressed by his aide-de-camp to continue resting while the aide de camp would fire the cannon for him.

General Thaddeus Ryan of Scarteen was a professional soldier in the Royal Artillery. By marrying Gwendaline Power, Grandfather united two old Catholic families of Ireland.

"No", said Grandfather. "It is my duty."

He left his tunic by a tree with his watch in a pocket, went forward, and fired his cannon. On returning to his tunic on which he had been resting, he found that an enemy cannonball had landed on the tunic and smashed his watch. We were often told this story—the moral is obvious.

After he had retired to Scarteen, Grandfather was helping his workmen in Finn's yard, as they raised a hand-pump with its long heavy pipe. Their grip failed and he was left holding the pump. It strained his heart and he died shortly afterward at the early age of sixty-eight.

THREE SWALLOWS

By marrying Gwendaline Power, Grandfather united two old Catholic families. The Power family seat was Edermine House in County Wexford. A magnificent stately home, it has an unrivalled view down the River Slaney—noted for its excellent salmon fishing.

Among the notable buildings close to the house was a beautiful chapel, designed by Pugin, who was a friend of the family and one of the best-known church architects of his day. Later the Benedictine Monks leased Edermine for a number of years and the chapel was fitted with stalls. Also erected nearby was a large and most unique conservatory, steel-ribbed and curved in the style of the Crystal Palace. Sir James Power asked Philip Pierce of Wexford to build it. Although at first Pierce said he could not do it, Sir James insisted, "Of course, you can". Pierce did a great job of it and then started manufacturing the famous range of Pierce Farm Machinery.

Probably the Power family's greatest claim to fame arose when John Power started distilling whiskey in 1791. It sparked fierce rivalry with the Jamesons, the other big distilling family. It is said that if a Jameson man spotted a Power coming towards him on the pavement, he would cross to the other side of the street so that he would not have to salute him!

Another contender in the distillery fray was the Williams family who produced the popular Tullamore Dew. There was amusing consternation when my cousin Frank O'Reilly married Tessa Williams. More recently, all the family firms were amalgamated to form Irish Distillers. Powers Gold Label (or, in full, Powers Gold Label Three Swallows Pure Pot-Still Whiskey) is still the favourite whiskey in Ireland today.

Frank O'Reilly's clan had joined the Power family when Fanny Power married Joseph R. O'Reilly of Sans Souci, Booterstown, Co. Dublin. It was in his honour that the magnificent Joseph R. O'Reilly Memorial Cup was presented to Fairyhouse Racecourse. Fanny Power's sister, Gwendaline, was our grandmother. The O'Reilly family were closely involved in Powers Distillery.

Frank's parents were Dr Charlie O'Reilly and his wife, Dorothy. I was fond of them. Whenever they visited Frank at our prep school Killashee and later at Ampleforth College, they would take me out also. On a visit to

Exhibition at Ampleforth one time, they brought me out to dinner at the Railway Hotel, York—a big treat. At the time there was a measles epidemic in the school and I knew I was getting it—all feverish, flushed, and pimply, but determined not to miss my dinner out! The next morning I was rushed to infirmary where Miss Jordan, the Irish matron, gave me blazes for not reporting earlier.

For a number of years Dr Charlie and Dorothy lived at Roseboro—a beautiful house near Johnstown on the main Dublin Road. Some years after Dr Charlie's death, the Kildare County Council decided to alter the road and thus cut a corner off the property. The assistant engineer was detailed to explain the situation to Mrs O'Reilly.

"Does that mean", she asked him, "that the beautiful beech trees will go?"

"Oh yes, madam", the assistant engineer replied.

"I will not allow those trees to be destroyed", she said firmly.

"But this is a Compulsory Purchase Order, madam."

"I don't care. Those trees are not going. My late husband would never have allowed it."

The assistant engineer reported the case to his boss who simply said, "It is your job to enforce the order."

"But I can't get any change out of that . . . woman", said the assistant engineer and he persuaded his boss to come with him. Together they still failed to change Dorothy's stance. An alternative route was decided on and those beech trees are still standing. I think that the incident epitomises the O'Reilly family's indomitable will and judgement!

The General's daughter, my Aunt Jean, eventually came to live in the Power family home of Edermine (where we would join her for holidays: see chapter nine). She soon had to come to terms with the water supply for the house, which came from a large circular ornamental pond surrounded by gunnera. (I used to think it was rhubarb!) In the pond was a big, round island accessed by an ornate wrought iron bridge. Mown lawns and a bed of strongly scented wallflowers completed the picture. The water was conducted along a small stream to drive the huge waterwheel, which in turn drove the generators, but this water was not suitable for drinking. Aunt Jean, anxious to know where the drinking water came from, asked Lady Power.

"From the pump in the yard, my dear", Lady Power replied. Aunt Jean searched the yard but had to come back and report her failure to find a pump.

"I think you had better ask Sir James", said Lady Power.

Sir James was puzzled. "Is it not in the yard? Ah, of course not—it's in the backyard", he explained. It was not there either. "Then you had better ask Dwyer", said Sir James, directing her to one of the workmen.

On enquiry, it turned out that every morning a workman walked several hundred yards away across the road, to draw a bucket of cold fresh water from a spring. This had been the routine for years and the family did not know it!

THE CRICKET 11

Among Grandfather's ten brothers and sisters, Hugh was a Jesuit in Bangalore, India, where his name is still remembered fondly. Canon Arthur was president of St Patrick's College in Thurles for sixteen years—the longest spell in the history of the college. He then came to Tipperary where he ministered as parish priest for the rest of his life. During World War I, he visited the Western Front in France to show his concern for and solidarity with his parishioners in the fighting line. He was dearly loved by all in Tipperary and by many further afield.

Canon Arthur Ryan, Grandfather's brother, was president of St Patrick's College in Thurles.

Dr Charlie Ryan also served his time with the armed forces, in the Sudan. However, he spent most of his life as a respected general practitioner in Tipperary. Stories of Dr Charlie abound. In one such story, a young chap of dubious character asked him for a reference so that he could get a gun licence from the barracks. Dr Charlie wrote the reference as follows:

"I have known Jim Clancy for a few years and I am convinced that he would not shoot anyone without the gravest necessity."

Another story begins with an old lady calling to the surgery.

"What ails you Mrs Hogan?" asked Dr Charlie.

"Och . . . it's me legs, Dochter."

"What age are you, missus?"

"I'll be ninety-four next April."

"Weren't they great oul legs!"

Among Dr Charlie's four daughters was Phil, a keen fisherwoman and masculine in appearance. Although she was a familiar figure on her motorbike with her rods over her shoulder, a policeman who did not recognise her stopped her one day and addressed her in coarse language. Taking off her helmet and goggles, she said, "Young man, you might be more polite to a lady." She rode off, leaving the officer with his mouth wide open!

Phil became engaged to Carlon Markes, a charming officer in the British Army. He came over to meet the family at Scarteen and to be "vetted". At rather a formal dinner party, the General (my grandfather) sat at the head of a long table and Grandmother and most of the family were present. One can picture the occasion—everyone in evening dress to make a good impression! Grandfather was strict, but Dad was allowed to have his terrier Nettle on his knee—even at table. During the meal, Dad spotted a rat's tail between the floor and skirting board. Leaving his terrier on the chair, he grabbed the rat's tail, passed it along to the hole in the corner, pulled the rat out, let it off and put his toe in the hole. He then called Nettle who chased the rat under the table—screams, chaos, and eventually a kill. Phil's engagement was nearly called off! Sadly, as brigade major, Carlon was killed in the Battle of the Somme in World War I.

Two other Ryan brothers, Jack and Dick, emigrated to Australia. There Jack had a successful career as manager of the Horse Traffic Melbourne Omnibus Company for twenty years. He had eighteen hundred horses and one hundred drivers in his organisation and became known as an outstanding judge of horseflesh at all the big agricultural shows. He was killed when the horse he was driving shied and overturned the coach. His only son was drowned on his way to join his regiment in the Sudan.

Helen, the General's sister, was the youngest of the family. Fondly called "Auntie", she worked hard for most of her life caring for the destitute in London and Liverpool. She loved us dearly and we loved her. In her early days, she was a keen huntswoman and brilliant across country. She spent her final years in the care of Aunt Jean in Edermine.

I introduce one further sibling of the General's for his contribution to the hunting tradition of my family: Grandfather's younger brother, Clem.

CLEMENT RYAN, MSH

Yes indeed—MSH stands for "Master of Staghounds". It was my Great Uncle Clem, who, with Dad, decided to give up hunting the hare in favour of the carted stag.

It has been a family tradition that the eldest son of each generation has inherited Scarteen along with the responsibility for hunting the family pack of hounds. Although Grandfather inherited the estate, being a professional soldier, he did not farm it—nor did he hunt hounds; in fact, we have no record that he ever rode a horse. While his brother Jack ran the farm for a few years before going to Australia, Clem was the huntsman. He lived at Emly House, formerly the Church of Ireland Presbytery, where hounds were kennelled for a period. After Jack's departure, Clem took on the running of Scarteen and eventually moved the hounds back there.

Clem was an outstanding and dedicated huntsman as well as a fearless rider. Clem's sight was so sharp that he could follow a hare's track through a muddy gap at the gallop.

One of the many talents Clem is remembered for is his reliable knowledge of the time. On most days he would ride to Scarteen across the fields. However, on Saturdays he went by road via Emly Station where he set his watch by the clock in the signal cabin. He could then bring "railway time" to the household so that they could be in time for Mass on Sunday—no radio to check with in those days! On one occasion while out riding, he witnessed a man being attacked and killed. As witness in court later, he was asked by the judge what time the murder took place.

"It was exactly half past three in the afternoon, m'lord."

"How do you know that was the time?" asked the judge.

"Because I looked at my watch, m'lord."

"Are you sure you looked at your watch?"

"My Heavens man, of course I'm sure. I always look at my watch when hounds find!"

Another story associated him with "miraculous powers". For years and up to my time, the huntsman always carried a master key to open the farm gates over the railway—the main line from Dublin to Cork. When a visitor from England was hunting with him, they came to a railway crossing. Clem put his hand in to his pocket and pulled out the master key, which was tangled up in his Rosary beads.

The visitor went home to England and told his friends, "I had an amazing experience when hunting in Ireland last week. The huntsman opened the railway gates with his Rosary beads."

Clem's intrepid courage was well demonstrated during a hunt when he had to jump off a road over a high demesne wall. Clem asked a county council worker, who had a "butt car" close by full of stones for road repairs, to bring the cart close to the wall. The horse changed on the load of stones and jumped over the wall.

Clem was a tall, handsome man, quietly spoken, deeply religious, kind, and extremely popular throughout Scarteen Hunt country. He loved his hounds. Dad asked him one day, "Uncle Clem, where did these hounds come from?"

Taking his pipe out of his mouth, Clem replied, "Don't be silly, boy, they were always here."

When he was stag hunting in later years, a tragedy occurred. Clem jumped into some scrub and came upon the stag unexpectedly. The stag attacked and with his antlers killed the horse under him. This remarkable event was recorded in the press of the time.

Clem married Lilly Bianconi—a great-granddaughter of Daniel O'Connell, the Liberator, and a granddaughter of Charles Bianconi. The latter built up and owned the hugely successful entire Mail Coach network in the south of Ireland. At its peak, one thousand people were employed and fourteen hundred horses travelled thirty-eight hundred miles per day. The business flourished until the advent of the railways.

Ourselves When Young . . .

Extracts From Our Issues of January 1875

CHARGED BY A STAG: A singular incident occurred the other day during a run with the Co. Limerick Staghounds. Hounds met at Kilmallock Hill and a splendid red buck which had been caught in the mountains of Killarney was enlarged for the occasion. After a run of four miles the quarry took refuge in a large brake of briars at the rear of Ashill Towers. Hounds passed him and had to be cast. While the field was waiting, the buck broke cover and dashed through a plantation. Straight in his path was a Mr. Clement Ryan of Scarteen, who was mounted on a splendid horse, 17 hands high and valued at 200 guineas. The old buck rose on his hind legs, lowered his antlers and struck the horse full in the chest. Mr. Ryan was thrown violently but fortunately escaped without a scratch. The horse reared, plunged and fell dead on the spot.

An Incident with the Limerick Staghounds.

Newspaper extract, 1875: Carted stag attacks and kills Clement Ryan's horse during a run with the County Limerick staghounds.

THREE

THE EMLY CONNECTION

In Clem and Lilly's family of ten, Jack was the eldest. We knew him as "Cousin Jack", although, of course, he was Dad's first cousin and many years younger. If ever there was an argument, Dad would remind him, "I was at your father's wedding!"

We knew Jack better than his brothers because he was secretary of the hunt for years. He was known to be a great shot (as recounted in later chapters). A religious man, too, he would never let a day pass without saying the Rosary. When the vet pronounced that a cow owned by a chap in the village was beyond recovery and should go to the kennels, it was decided that Mr Jack should be asked to shoot the cow. So Jack came up with his gun.

"Will I hould her for you, sir?" asked one of the spectators. At this stage, the cow was stretched out.

"Shure nobody houlds the snipe for him", said another.

Jack's brother Clement was a veterinary surgeon and served in World War I. Later he worked for the Department of Agriculture. At the time of the foot-and-mouth outbreak in Meath, his job was to reach an agreement with stock owners on a compensation value. One farmer was distressed; he had home-bred his herd of dairy cows over years of hard work and they were excellent milkers—now the entire herd had to be destroyed. Calling to see him, Clement told him to work out a fair figure for compensation and Clement would do the same. Clement returned the next morning to discover the gross figure that the farmer had come up with was far lower than his own figure. With a similar philosophy, Jack always said that if you succeeded in making a deal in your favour, but left the farmer unhappy, you had wasted your time and money and made an enemy rather than a friend.

Jack's sister, Alice, was devoted to her work in the Irish Country Women's Association, of which she was President for many years. Brother Tony joined Walter Trench (of Castle Oliver) farming in Kenya.

Their brother Hugh trained racehorses on the flat at Emly for some time. He would gallop his horses in the middle field in Ballyhoulihan. Later he moved to the Curragh. Quiet spoken and kind, he was immensely popular in the racing world and had a reputation as the best feeder in the business.

Dear Betty was the "saint in the family". Sadly she contracted tuberculosis in the spine and was taken to Switzerland for treatment. She spent ten years on the flat of her back in great pain and eventually improved, although she almost lost her sight. Through it all she radiated courage and holiness. For years she cared for retired clergy in France and finally came home to Emly. Her greatest joy was to go on pilgrimage to Lourdes caring for the invalids. She had the most wonderful happy countenance and always a cheerful word for everyone.

When Betty came with us to Lourdes, there was an incident I shall never forget. At lunch in a restaurant she spotted a young Irish couple having difficulties making themselves understood to the waitress.

Betty went over to them and said, "I can speak French, can I help you?"

"Oh yes, please", they replied. "She does not understand us—all we want is spuds in their jackets!"

Jack's sister, Grace, married Nicholas Greene of Greenepark in Co. Tipperary. Their son James became Abbot of the Benedictine College Fort Augustus in Scotland. Happily, a grandson, Patrick Farrell, now lives with his family in Emly House, keeping it in the clan. He is the image of his Great Uncle Hugh, but without the moustache and the cigarette fixed between his front teeth!

Their sister, Amy, married Tom Mangan, a big landowner in Co. Meath. Their son "Junior" was a key member of the Ward Union Hunt. He had the responsibility of capturing the stag at the end of the run—a duty carried on today by his son Simon.

The Meath ditches are still as deep and challenging as they always were. On his first day out with the stag, a visitor who came on one of them asked a local standing by, "Is there a bottom to this ditch?"

"Oh, there is, sir", the local replied.

The horse failed to clear, came back into it and started to sink. The visitor shouted, "I thought you said there was a bottom to this."

"Oh, there is, sir, but you haven't reached it yet!"

So much for now on the Emly Ryans.

FOUR

THE POPE'S OAK

Among Dad's eight brothers and sisters, my Uncle Willie was the distiller, producing the famous Powers Gold Label Three Swallows Whiskey for most of his life. On his honeymoon in Rome, while strolling with Aunt Mena through the Vatican Gardens, Uncle Willie spotted an oak seedling growing as a weed by the side of the path. He pocketed it, later transferring it to his tooth mug in their hotel in London. While they were out sightseeing the maid cleaning the room threw out the precious plant. That evening Uncle Willie missed his little oak tree. Exploding in anger—he could be fiery—he demanded to see the hapless maid and discover the whereabouts of his treasure. He found it in the rubbish dump behind the hotel. Years later, on a visit to Scarteen, he planted the young tree alongside the avenue. Now it is a handsome tree known as the "Pope's Oak", and proudly bears a bronze plate inscribed *Pius X 1906*. We are privileged to have a tree from the garden of a saint!

Uncle Willie loved his hunting. When Dad was a prisoner of war, Uncle Willie would come down by train on Friday evening, hunt hounds on Saturday, and catch the train back to Dublin on Sunday. Aunt Jean would whip-in to him.

In those days foxes were scarce. If no fox could be found, a carted stag would be let off and hunted. At one meet at Derk a number of army officers from Tipperary Barracks were mounted. Uncle Willie was worried because he had only a small young fallow deer in the van. Hounds found in Derk, but unfortunately chopped in covert. By good luck they found again down the country, had a nice run and back to Derk covert where hounds marked to ground. In a moment of pride, Uncle Willie thought he would show his followers what a good huntsman he was by bringing out the first fox (pretending hounds had just killed) and letting hounds "break him up" in front of the field. He could not find the fox.

He furiously asked a local lad who had come into the covert, "Where is my dead fox?"

"We buried him, sir", the lad replied.

"Well, dig him up quick!" said the frustrated huntsman.

When Uncle Willie came down from Dublin for one hunt after World War I, Dad put him "on point" at the gate behind Kilteely Hill overlooking Richie Ryan's farm. Hounds found, great cry, all excitement—then a long silence. Uncle Willie eventually got impatient, left his post, and rode around to the north side of the hill to see hounds, Master, and field going like blazes over the top of Wonder Hill. He rode home in disgust and took the train back to Dublin. The two brothers did not speak for weeks!

All the same, Uncle Willie was devoted to his old home Scarteen and could never do enough for it nor for Dad. He gave Dad his first motor car—a second-hand Model T Ford. As I remember, it had a collapsible canvas roof that folded behind the back seat, cellophane windows that fitted with two spikes into the doors, a hand-operated windscreen wiper and no gears, but one pedal made it go forwards and another backwards. On the steering wheel column were two levers: one controlled the governor, the other set the timing of the spark. You had to be sure to hold the starting handle with your thumb outside the handle because the engine would backfire if the spark was too far advanced. The petrol tank was on top of the engine with gravity feed to the carburetor—frightfully dangerous.

Dad had that car for years. When it finally reached the end of its roadworthy life, Uncle Willie took it up to the distillery, where the mechanics mounted the engine on a solid timber bench and fitted a circular saw directly to the driveshaft. It could be ideal for cutting firewood—but at times it proved to be a nightmare. Sometimes, half way through a stubborn log, the saw would heat, buckle, and cut crooked. The governor would rev the engine into a frenzy with the extra load, and the whole bench would shudder and shake. You then had to rush and turn off the ignition—nothing else would stop that old car. And it was still dangerous. When Dad was showing off his new toy to Keith Reynolds and turned to pick up a light beech limb for cutting, he inadvertently touched the saw and lost the top of his finger.

Uncle Willie and his family lived at Thornhill—a beautiful house with spacious lawns and gardens across the road from Kilmacud Church, where they attended daily Mass. Aunt Mena trained young country girls for domestic duties; in those days, domestic service was a secure and rewarding career. When the family were out to dinner one evening, the young maid had occasion to leave the house. Before leaving, she left a note on the door handle: "Madam, you will find the key of the door under the mat!"

Jim was the eldest of Uncle Willie's children. He farmed in Kenya close to Tony Ryan (one in the "Emly connection") and Walter Trench. He was awarded the silver medal for the second best farm in Kenya; later, his son Pip achieved the gold. In their turn both men were Masters of the Molo Hunt. Dad sent out some hounds to Jim, but the heat was too much for them.

Pip's brother Michael has the disease real bad! He is just crazy on hunting. He is following in his grandfather's footsteps, coming down from his business in Wicklow at least once a week for a day's hunting. He occasionally rides second whip to Chris. A forceful rider, his enthusiasm is infectious and he revels in studying every move of hounds.

John A. was the banker. He served two terms as governor of the Bank of Ireland, as well as being a director of several companies, including the Electricity Supply Board and John Power and Son. He was also involved in many charities. I envied John's ability to be completely at ease discussing any matter under the sun.

John was patient with me whenever I approached him on the behalf of others. For example, a farmer would say to me, "I believe you have a cousin in the Bank of Ireland; my daughter is 'going for the bank' and maybe he could put in a good word for her." John always explained that the girl had to get in on her own merits, but if two applicants for the job had equal merits, he would recommend the girl in question. In those days, a job in the bank was a guaranteed career with a good pension—sadly those days are gone.

Clem, Uncle Willie's youngest son, stepped into his father's shoes and spent a lifetime in Power's Distillery. His responsibility was the staff and he was immensely popular. Traditionally there was a great family atmosphere among the staff. Many of them followed their fathers and grandfathers in the firm, and Clem was proud of their loyalty.

His sister Veronica, who had a love for children, started the first Montessori school in Ireland. The Children's House was built on the lands of Thornhill and is still going strong. On one occasion when staying with Veronica, my sister Jean joined her for a riding lesson at Burton Hall. The instructor asked her, "What aids do you use when you want your horse to go forward?"

Jean thought for a moment then replied, "My whip and spurs!" No one could live with Jean out hunting—she went through the country like a sparrowhawk—but higher equestrian education was not in her syllabus!

Another of Dad's brothers, Hugh, studied forestry and emigrated to South Africa. We looked forward greatly to his infrequent visits home. Coming from a warm climate, he hated haymaking in the rain. Out in the meadow Uncle Hugh composed the following line that features Dad's head man, Dan Hurley:

"Up spake Daniel Hurley, his hair blowing in the wynde; ten thousand million cocks in front and the divil a wynd behind!"

Uncle Hugh's other bête noire was corncrakes. When they kept him awake at night, he would go out in his pyjamas to the meadow cracking a hunting crop, but without success. Where have all the corncrakes gone? I believe that they have disappeared mainly because of the change from haymaking to silage, and the use of nitrogen to bring the meadows in earlier; formerly the young birds were strong before the hay season. The growth in the number of foxes has also taken its toll.

Like most old houses, Scarteen was built on bare ground—no such thing as a damp course. A space of about twelve inches lay between the floorboards and the clay—ideal habitat for rats, which moved in when the weather turned bad. There were several holes in the skirting boards in the dining room, pantry, and passages. Uncle Hugh arranged blocks of wood with strings attached so that the blocks would shut off the holes when the strings were pulled. The big problem was lack of light. Instead of electricity, we had candles and Uncle Hugh had a paraffin hand lamp.

After our evening meal we would put out some bread and scraps as "bait" in the pantry and then all gather in the sitting room, armed with hockey sticks and of course our four terriers. All the strings led out of the front door. We waited for about half an hour to give the rats a chance to get feeding. It was difficult to keep the terriers quiet as they were wild with excitement. My job was to pull the strings. Then the fun started—rats everywhere, terriers in full cry up the front stairs and down the back, everyone hollering and shouting. Uncle Hugh took a swipe at a rat and smashed the chimney of his lamp. When the last rat was accounted for, a dozen or so corpses were collected and we went to bed. We did not need any TV or wireless for entertainment—even if they had been invented!

Aunt Jean and Aunt Alice were great horsewomen who loved their hunting. Aunt Alice gave it all up to answer God's call and become a nun in the Sacred Heart Order. For many years she was Mistress of Novices in Mount Anville Convent in Dublin.

Aunt Jean ran the hunt while Dad was a prisoner of war. She was also active in the Irish Countrywomen's Association. When Dad returned home she moved to Edermine. Uncle Frank joined her there, and together they hunted with the Island hounds, after World War I. During the war he was a gunner (as was his brother Clem, who was killed in action). His men would always wait to return to base through enemy shell fire until they could come back with him; they knew they would be safe with him because he was such a good man.

Uncle Frank had a great sense of humour. As a junior officer in Woolwich, it came to his turn to take charge of the fatigue party doing chores in the barracks. One regular chore was to use the fire engine, operated by eight men, to wash down the windows of the commanding officer's office. In the previous week Uncle Frank had seen that the pressure in the delivery hose was feeble and realised that the pump was faulty. So now he said to the group, "Instead of washing down the windows today, we will overhaul the pump."

As he had suspected, they found a pebble firmly embedded under a valve; it had been there for years. He said to the lads, "Next week I will not be with you. You will have another junior officer in charge and I want you to pump like blazes!"

The time came. Excited, the lads pumped as hard as they could. The force of the water smashed the windows and drenched the commanding officer at his desk.

I never heard Uncle Frank swear. When frustrated, he would let off steam with "Godfrey-Daniels-Blasting-Powderworks". In World War II he commanded a Royal Artillery Training Depot at Marske, near Middlesborough in Yorkshire. When he arrived to referee some big training manoeuvre in Northern Ireland, he noticed that no provision had been made for alternative lighting in the event of a power failure. The manoeuvres were to start at 2 A.M. He privately arranged for the sappers to cause a vast explosion near the generating station and for the switchboard staff, on hearing the noise, to pull the main fuses. All went according to plan. The explosion awoke the camp. Generals and officers stumbled around in their pyjamas cursing and swearing in the confusion.

Uncle Frank had his powerful lamp and asked them, "Haven't you got a torch?"

He was not popular!

On his visits to us, which I loved, he would come on Cousin Jack's snipe-shooting parties. One day Jack positioned the two of us at points on the far side of the bog.

Uncle Frank, using the name he always called me, said, "Tha', would you go to the far bush. I don't feel too good."

I was worried. Shortly afterwards, riding home from a hunt with the Island Hounds, he toppled off his horse and I'm sure went straight to Heaven.

FIVE

MASTER JOHN

Now we come to the most important and beloved man in my life: Dad, widely known as "Master John" (or later, when I came on the scene, as "the old Master") and the eldest of his family of nine. Along with some other family members, he was educated at Oscott College, near Birmingham. His achievements in track-and-field events, performed in long grey flannels and tennis shoes, were phenomenal. With modern training techniques, I believe he could have been an Olympian. At the prizegiving for his final school sports, the Headmaster presented him with the Victor Ludorum Cup and called out, "Is there nobody here who can beat this Irishman?"

Dad spent a couple of years at Glasnevin Agricultural College, but used to say that the students were really farm workers. They spent most of their time on manual work: thinning root crops, picking potatoes, cleaning out sheds—all the usual farm chores. (In stark contrast, farming today is a prestigious and scientific business.) He then joined his Uncle Clem farming and hunting hounds. They both decided to give up hunting the hare. Foxes were still scarce in the country, so they started to hunt the carted stag, a huge undertaking. Some deer were donated by the Ward Union Hunt. In early years they used primarily the

Derk House meet: (l–r) Mary Webb, Lady Dorothy Moore, John J. Ryan, MFH, Thady, Jean, General Sir George Franks, 1928. The latter, from Ballyscaddane, lived across the road from Scarteen and commanded Dad's regiment in World War I.
Frank O'Brien photo

Master John J. Ryan (Dad) hunting hounds at Derk, 1940. He was the most important and beloved man in my life.

red deer. Later Dad changed to fallow—they were wilder compared to red deer, which sometimes ran the road for miles.

But Dad's dreams of hunting and farming were rudely interrupted by the Boer War in South Africa. Feeling it was their duty to help in the war effort, he and his brother Tha', along with his great friend and cousin Jerry Howley of Rich Hill, enlisted in the 7th Imperial Yeomanry. The journey out with their horses by steamship was long and hazardous. Once there, conditions were harsh. At times Dad was uneasy about the war. Many of the Boers were farmers like himself; nonetheless they were skilled fighters and took a heavy toll of the British forces.

There were also lighter moments. His mother sent them a tin box full of shamrocks for St Patrick's Day. On opening it all they found was a fat worm. They also had a spot of trouble when the commanding officer's mule suspiciously "broke loose" and was raiding the feed pots of the others in the lines. Living under canvas nearby, Tha' awoke and spotted the thief. With feed so scarce, he was furious. He flung his bayonet at the marauder: it stuck in the mule's buttock and he galloped madly down between the rows of tents, ripping the guy ropes and causing pandemonium. There was a brief court-martial the next day!

The greatest danger Dad faced in the three-year campaign was on the journey home. He went missing for two days and was thought to have fallen overboard in the rough seas. However, he was discovered in the fodder store below decks weakened by severe vomiting and dehydration and almost dead. To be easily prone to seasickness is the only thing I wished I had not inherited from him.

The next few years Dad spent on a life he loved; working on the farm, training and trading horses, and point-to-pointing. His mother would drive her pony and trap to local meetings to see him ride. If another horse overtook him, she would say as the leader jumped each fence, “I hope he falls, but I hope he won’t be hurt.”

They were true point-to-points in those days and a knowledge of the country was an advantage. In one race the rider of the hot favourite was told, “Stick to John Ryan’s tail ‘till the second last—then pull out and win.”

A thick fog came down, Dad won the race. The rider of the favourite came up to him and said, “Why didn’t you tell me when we came to the second last? I could have beaten you easily!”

Dad won many point-to-points and there are several beautiful cups at Scarteen. Probably, his sweetest triumph was the Munster Plate. The following letter describes the race and the atmosphere so well that I have included it unabridged. The cup is magnificent, 13.5 inches high and eight pounds of solid silver.

This is the letter Tha’ Ryan sent to his brother Willy.

The Munster Cup
National Point-to-Point Steeplechases
Kilmallock
County Limerick
21 March 1896
14 st 4 miles
Won by John J. Ryan’s BRATTON

My dear Willy

Last Saturday was a great day for Ireland! Father, Mother, Auntie, Jerry Murphy, John, Jerry, Dickie, Miss Murphy and self left Scarteen in a brake (from Tip) at 11.30 and got to Kilmallock at 1.

We were one of the first there, so consequently got the very best position on the hill. We walked part of the course before the race, which was timed for 2, but a desperate shower of hail delayed the start till after 2.30. John had on Mrs Murphy’s red coat and looked real business-like.

He has to carry about 5 lbs of lead, which he put underneath the straps of the girth and it was a perfect miracle that they were not lost. When he took off the saddle after the race, the lead fell all over the ground!! He had no saddle cloth!

It was a very safe course, good solid banks with very open ditches, with water in them on both sides.

They started at a very slow pace—some even trotted; but after the first few fields, the pace became a “cracker”! John immediately went into 3rd place and except for once when he led over a jump, he remained 3rd till the third field from home. At this point there were at least 4 or 5 all together, with the other 6 close up.

A short time before this, about 4 or 5 fields from home, they began to use their sticks, but John sat quiet and Bratton kept his place. John was first over the last fence and, as he had not “called upon” Bratton, he knew he was certain, bar accidents, of landing the cup.

He gave the old horse a few "skelps" as he neared the winning post and sailed out a winner by 3 lengths. He said he was not a bit excited till he knew that he had a chance of winning and as he was actually winning he was overcome with excitement and would just as soon as not have turned round and ridden in the opposite direction!!

To return to the brake on the hill. Auntie was next to me and kept on praying to the Angels in heaven etc while at every fence Mother would ask "is he over, has he fallen?" etc, etc. There were about 20 people in the brake; besides us there were Uncles Charley, Clem, Willy and other people I forget.

Now would you believe what I am going to tell you.

In the second field from home, someone said John was fifth, but as he passed the post Auntie let a scream and said "John has won—I know the bandages on the horse's legs"—she almost shoved me out of the brake there and then. I rushed as hard as I could down the hill. On the way down I could hear everyone asking "who's won?" but I had to wait in suspense till I was almost at the weighing-in tent, when I heard "John Ryan of Scarteen".

Then the "roars were something awful"; the first man I met was Tim and I hit his old brown hat almost down over his eyes! Owens rushed out after John had won and was nearly killed by the second horse.

When he appeared from the weighing-in tent there was a desperate scene. The people simply shouted, every second man you met came from our side of the country. They shouted "Good old Black and Tans, Well done Scarteen" etc.

John was carried away in a huge crowd up to the foot of the hill, they cheering most of the way and a fellow now and again all by himself would let an unearthly yell as if he felt horribly pleased that Bratton had won.

A swell chap asked old Paddy Creed who won and Paddy told him. Then he said "where is Scarteen?" whereupon Paddy said "Scarteen . . . Scarteen . . . Scarteen?" with slight pause between each, as much to say the fellow might just as well have asked him where Ireland was!!

Dan Hurley, John Reeves, Tom Ryan, Tim etc were simply intoxicated with joy and all came up to the brake and drank neat whiskey!!

Was it not a funny thing, not actually knowing for certain whether it was John or not. It was the most perfect course for seeing, but it is simply impossible to distinguish between one red coat and another—not like racing colours.

The course and hill were like this, going: good, nothing like as heavy as our country. Bratton looked as if he only came in after a mile of a gallop.

We all went to tea at Dr McNamara's and then drove home with Regan riding Bratton behind us and looking as pleased as punch!

When we got to the lodge, we saw a blaze—this was hay on the end of forks : bonfire! Bridget running about beating the gong! Could have heard shouts in Tipperary.

Uncle Clem was over on Sunday and told us that there were bonfires at Emly on Saturday night in honour of the event.

I think I may end in the same way as I began—It was a great day for Ireland.

Ever fond brother,
Tha Ryan

SIX

A MIRACULOUS SURVIVAL

Soon the horizon was darkening with storm clouds, this time World War I. Again Dad was off to do his duty. His age prevented him joining his old regiment, so he enlisted in the 16th Lancers. They were soon in the trenches in France, fighting in the most appalling conditions. Years later Dad still had nightmares about it.

His time in the trenches ended suddenly. In his trench he was aware of some vibration, but could not fathom what it was. Then the mine exploded. The Germans had tunnelled forward and planted the mine underneath the trench. All was black. He was buried for three hours under about two feet of clay. The Germans advanced, dug a new trench, and came across his feet. They pulled him out leaving the rest of his platoon buried alive. A couple of soldiers took him back behind German lines—a prisoner of war.

On the way a German officer stopped them and asked Dad, "Are you from England?"

Dad said, "No."

"Then where are you from?"

"I'm from Ireland."

"Oh", said the officer, "the best time of my life I have spent hunting in the south of Ireland. Is there anything I can do for you?"

"Try and get news through the Red Cross that I'm alive."

Back in the trenches, a desperate, bloody battle ensued with huge casualties. With other prisoners of war captured at the time, Dad was held that night in a Catholic church and was able to hear Mass and receive Holy Communion next morning. Meanwhile Dad's commanding officer sent a telegram to Grannie telling her the sad news that he had been killed: "no human being above ground could have survived that battle". Throughout Ireland people were in mourning and a Requiem Mass was being offered. In the mail train from Dublin one of the sorters, who knew of Dad (who didn't?), found a postcard with a German stamp. He turned it over and read:

"John Ryan is alive and well. A P.O.W. unwounded. A German Officer."

Although the mail train stopped at only the principal stations, as it rolled through Emly Station the sorter put his head out of the window and shouted, "John Ryan is alive!"

The porter hopped on his bike and sped up to Emly Church, where he burst into the huge crowd shouting, "He's alive! He's alive!"

Uncle Willie and Uncle Tha' whispered to the rest of the family, "Don't tell Mother. It can't be true—we have the telegram from his commanding officer."

Then the German postcard arrived at Scarteen. You can picture the excitement, the relief, the happiness, and the prayers of thanksgiving.

BEHIND BARS

For a long period, Dad was a prisoner in a camp near Danholm in Germany. The compound of the prisoners of war was within the military barracks and a high-wire fence separated them from the barracks square. What angered Dad most was the way the young German lads—many conscripted straight from the farms—were cruelly treated by their officers; this is what fired his hatred for the Germans.

When I was about eight, we went to a children's party at Kenmare Castle. On leaving, each of us was given a wee present—a lead toy animal (they are now worth a fortune). Mine was a beautiful Hereford bull. Back home, I dashed into the study where Dad was reading the paper by the fire.

"Daddy, Daddy, look what I've got!"

Dad said, "What a beautiful bull."

He examined it and found the words "Made in Germany". He paused for a moment, then threw it into the fire. I burst into tears—I didn't understand.

Dad never complained of the way he was treated: they got minimal rations, but could receive parcels from home via the Red Cross. After his mother sent him a parcel of wool and rug backing, over the long evenings he made a tan floor rug with black lettering:

> KRIEGSGEFANGENER
> (prisoner of war)
> Danholm
> 21-2-1915–?

Years later, Anne and I had a charming Austrian lady and her daughter as paying guests for a riding holiday. One evening at dinner, the lady turned to me, "Please forgive me, but what is the history of that rug under the sideboard?"

I felt a bit embarrassed, but told her the whole story and showed her the post card from the German officer. She looked at the rubber stamp and exclaimed, "This is extraordinary. My father was commanding the regiment next in line to this one. I hope they treated your father well."

I wondered to myself, "Is Dad smiling in Heaven?"

During his imprisonment Dad learned of an extraordinary coincidence. An elderly Russian Orthodox priest was a fellow prisoner of war. He and Dad had no language in common, but they became good friends. During exercise they sat on a bench in the sun. In the sand, using a stick from the wood, Dad sketched a picture of a horse. The old man turned to him and said "Galty-

While a Prisoner of War, Dad made this rug with materials sent by his mother via the Red Cross.
Catherine Power photo

more", the only non-Russian word he knew. Dad was flabbergasted. They quickly found an interpreter and learned the story.

Galtymore and Ardpatrick were both Derby winners and were reared at Knockainey Stud, about seven miles from Scarteen. A large and beautiful oil painting of the two famous horses hung for years in the dining room of Kilfrush (see chapter ten). Galtymore was exported as a stallion and stood at stud in the old priest's parish in Russia. While they were prisoners, he learned some English from Dad (I don't believe Dad learned any Russian!) and afterwards they corresponded for some years. Eventually his letters stopped—Dad thought he may have perished in the Russian Revolution.

Several wonderful postcards came from Dad in prison to his mother:

> "How are all the family? Give them my love."
> "How is the Hunting?"
> "Send me some of Hanna's brown scones."
> "Tell John Reeves (his herdsman) I can hear him shouting from here!"
> "I can get Mass and Holy Communion on Sundays."

Along with these came an official letter from King George V sending his deepest sympathy on the loss of her son, John J. Ryan, killed in action.

SEVEN

FREEDOM

About six months before the Armistice, the International Red Cross arranged an agreement acceptable to both the Germans and the Allies to relocate their prisoners of war to a neutral country. Dad, along with fellow prisoner and friend Ernest Pearson, was billeted on parole with a charming family in Holland. Madame Drury de Pallant, their hostess, was like a mother to them. With wholesome food and good care, she nursed them back to full strength. The two friends had a great time breaking and exercising the hackney ponies she kept. However, both felt something close to guilt for being "out of the fight". Dad, who knew that his brother Clem had been killed and that Frank was still in the heat of battle, felt especially uneasy.

When the war was over, Dad returned home to a tumultuous welcome from his family and a huge circle of friends from all over Scarteen Hunt country. He was back with his beloved hounds, back after four long and stressful years to a life he loved—hunting and farming, surrounded by family and friends.

CUPID AT WORK

Inevitably, Cupid got busy. The Harold-Barrys of Ballyvonaire succeeded in introducing him to the Purcell sisters of Burton Park. It might have put him

Burton Park was the home of the Purcell sisters. Dad married Anita, my mother. The Purcells were Normans who came to Ireland in the twelfth century.

in something of a dilemma: Maisie sang most beautifully while Anita was a virtuoso with her Stradivarius violin. However, without hesitation, Anita won the toss.

The Purcells are Normans, one of many families who came to Ireland from France in the twelfth century. They were Catholics, but apparently became Protestants during the Cromwellian persecution. They ruled as barons of Loughmoe up to the start of the eighteenth century.

Loughmoe was a very fine castle between Thurles and Templemore overlooking the river Suir. The name derives from the Irish LuachMhagh meaning "the field of reward", and there is a colorful legend as to how it got its name, which goes as follows:

Around the mid-1100s the parish of Loughmoe was plagued with a wild boar and sow who spread terror through the land, killing everyone in their path. Butler, King of Ormond, naturally wishing to be rid of these menaces, promised that the slayer of these creatures of gigantic size should receive, as reward, the hand of his only daughter in marriage, the castle, and as much of the adjacent land as he wished.

Tempted by this most generous offer, many men ventured forth on this fateful mission. At last a young man named Purcell arrived at the castle to seek permission to attack these boars. His request was readily granted. Purcell made his way tither in search of the boar and his mate, not by walking on the ground, but by stepping from branch to branch and tree to tree until he arrived over the spot where the sow lay with two young. Purcell carried with him a bow and arrows and on finding the sow proceeded to shower her with arrows. The skin of the sow was so thick that the arrows made no impression on it, but only succeeded in making her violently angry. Purcell bided his time and seized his opportunity by sending an arrow down the sow's open mouth. At this she gave one almighty roar and died. Hearing her cry of death, the boar raged savagely through the wood, flattening trees in its path until it came to the spot where the sow lay. Seeing Purcell in the tree, the boar made every attempt to uproot

Loughmoe Castle overlooks the river Suir between Thurles and Templemore. Ancient legend tells how young Purcell won the hand of the King's daughter by his bravery and became the baron of Loughmoe.

the tree. Again Purcell seized his opportunity and sent an arrow down the mouth of the roaring boar. At this, the boar turned on its heels, rushed off through the wood and died at some unnamed locality near Thurles. As proof, in the ruined church, the boar, the sow, and the two boneens are carved on a stone. This is the Purcell coat of arms.

Following this deed of bravery, the King kept his side of the bargain. Purcell won the prize and Loughmoe got its name. Because of the extent of the lands then owned by the Purcell family, the King granted them the title of baron.

Moving down several generations, we find that Sir John Purcell was knighted for bravery in 1811. His son was the Rev. Matthew Purcell, who bought Burton Park, a magnificent example from the late Georgian period set among beautiful mature hardwoods close to the village of Churchtown in Co. Cork. As pastor of Churchtown, he was revered and loved by his parishioners for more than fifty years. His grandson, Matthew-John married Anne Daly of Dalysgrove in Co. Galway. She was a deeply religious lady whose four brothers joined the Jesuit order. They had six in the family, including Margaret, who married Sir Maurice O'Connell, descendant of Daniel O'Connell, the Liberator (and keen hound breeder!) and Anita who was my mother.

On his frequent visits to Burton, Dad would say a prayer in Ballyhea Church. Eventually, at a shooting party at Castle Oliver and to the great joy of both families, they announced their engagement. They were married on 24 April 1919.

APOLOGIA I

If any of you, my readers, feel that I have dwelt too long on my forebears, I beg your forgiveness. I have done it for two reasons. First, I wished to remind myself to live the strong Catholic faith and high Christian principles that guided their lives, and to pass these values on to others. Second, I invite you to share my pride in their achievements.

TWO

A FORTUNATE CHILDHOOD

EIGHT

HOME SWEET HOME

It is said that "behind every successful man is an outstanding woman". My mother was just such a woman. With her huge and loving heart, she was truly an Irish mother. When she married Dad, she was welcomed instantly into the Ryan clan. Though shy by nature she readily took up the duties of a wife of an MFH. She knew hardship in the Depression years of the 1930s, to the extent that she was obliged to sell her treasured Stradivarius violin (to the regret of her children later). Mum was known and loved for her strong devotion to the Holy Family.

Dad and Mum were devoted to each other. They also sacrificed much—we shall never know the full extent—to give their children the best possible upbringing. Just over three years spanned the birthdays of my elder sister Gwen, Jean, and myself; our brother John arrived five years after I did.

Money, or rather the lack of it, had dogged the family for generations. The Great Depression bit deep. At one point the family was bankrupt. The bailiffs ordered all the livestock to be sold. Dad's men had the cattle on their way to the railway station in Knocklong. The men, along with all the neighbours, were in tears. Then word came through that Thomas Power and Colonel George Clarke had come to the rescue—Scarteen was saved. The men threw their hats into the air, turned the bullocks around, and drove them back to Scarteen at the gallop.

Jean, Thady, Mum, Gwen, 1926.

Thady's first mount is a stuffed bear, 1926.

However, gaining greater financial stability was not the reason for the happiness of our home. Instead, our sense of wellbeing stemmed from a wealth of love and confidence in the Will of God. Our parents practised true Christian living. Prayer was the backbone of their lives and they endeavoured to ensure that their children followed their example.

Towards the end of the eighteenth century, the family had moved to Scarteen from their previous home, Ballyvistea, about eight miles away in the parish of Emly. They moved in just after the front portion of the house had been completed, to create an ample home of great character. It is hard to imagine a better location in which to rear a family. The five hundred acres included some low boggy land—a great lie for snipe and other game—along with ample space for us to roam with freedom and safety. (Originally, Scarteen had about seven hundred acres, until the Land Commission took away about two hundred acres and "paid" for them with land bonds barely worth the paper they were printed on.)

As was the custom in those days, Mum had staff living in the house—a nanny, cook, kitchenmaid, parlour maid, and housemaid. Five live-in staff would seem an extravagance in modern terms, but in those days one was expected to give much-needed employment and adequate keep and lodgings. The wage was small but of secondary importance. For years our cook was Hannah, who lived near Burton and came to Scarteen with Mum. Hannah was short and squat with a look of wonder and kindness. Like another mother to us, she spoiled us thoroughly.

In those days a small wood was by the avenue (now in grass and known as the "Orchard Field"). The wood housed a multitude of crows' nests, as well as several herons' nests in the tall beech trees in the corner nearest the tennis lawn. We got endless enjoyment from watching the crows building in the spring time. Their call in the mating season was a soft, guttural "Khawh, khaah, khawh", quite distinct from the harsh winter call, "Caw, caah, caw".

Scarteen House in the 1920s. The Ryans moved there in the late–eighteenth century from Ballyvistea in the parish of Emly. By family tradition, the eldest son of each generation had the right to inherit Scarteen along with the responsibility of hunting the family pack of hounds.

We were entertained even more by the cranes (the local name for herons). During incubation the sitting bird was fed by its mate, who would come in, calling fondly, and alight gracefully on the edge of the nest with a fish or a frog. Hatching was shared by both parents, as was the task of feeding when the young were ready for food. Feeding time was bedlam, accompanied by the most bloodcurdling, raucous screeching, as if someone was being strangled. When the fledglings were almost ready to fly, they would be pushed out of the nest to land in a bed of nettles and twigs where, they were easy prey for foxes.

Hannah would tell us that after we had gone to bed, she would go up and spend the evening with Mrs Crane and we had better be good—because otherwise Mrs Crane would punish us. It never cost us a thought as to how Hannah climbed up to the nest—we believed every word she said!

In the summer, Hannah would take us for a walk down to the Well Field. She would be laden with a kettle, a basket of bread and jam, a frying pan, and a jam jar of pancake mix. We would light a fire on the big flat rock by Clancy's Wood river and have a right royal picnic. We loved to fish for sticklebacks and brinkeens with nets and glass jars, and feed our "catch" to Dad's Khaki Campbell ducks.

The big day came when Hannah got us two young donkeys from a farmer near Garryspillane. Brown Ivy and Flyaway became great pets and we had them for years. Flyaway did not like climbing, but Brown Ivy would come up the back stairs and into the nursery.

On Sundays, with Jack Dwyer, our kennel huntsman (the "unsung hero" in chapter 22), we would walk across country with our terriers to Glenefy—about three miles—and hunt rabbits. On the way home, we would stop at Jack's cottage, where Nora had a feed of homemade bread and jam and sweet tea for us.

Rat hunting with Dad down the river with our terriers was a favourite pastime. We would count the cattle on the way. Crossing the railway that ran through our farm, Dad would place a penny on the rail, then we watched the train squash it flat!

Thady on Brown Ivy, 1929. The donkey, a family pet, would climb the back stairs of Scarteen and visit the nursery.

Mum, Jean, Gwen, Dad, Thady, Brown Ivy and Flyaway, 1930. The two donkeys came to us from a farmer in Garryspillane.

Sometimes on Sundays we would cross the river and call to John Reeves. John was a small farmer in Lackelly who helped herd the cattle. He wore a bowler hat and leggings and smoked a pipe. While Dad discussed farming with him, John's sisters would treat us to fizzy lemonade.

For us, the hay season (in fine weather) was bliss. At first light, Dad would tackle up our two steady work horses, Sally (part Clyde) and Brown Bess (part Irish Draught), to the noisy old Woods mowing machine. Later Gwen would take over and give Dad a spell. Dad's head man, Jim Finn, would take over at 9 A.M. and another man would keep the knives sharpened. The sound of the mowing machine was soothing and music to our ears. The horses were rested when the sun got too hot and the horse flies tormented them.

Dad was the first person in the parish to get a Deering mowing machine. It had a gear box and ran silently. At first, the horses would not pull it: without the noise of the Woods, they sensed something must be wrong.

With unemployment high, people were desperate for work. The story is told of a lad from Kerry who went to London in the hope of getting work. He was prepared to do anything. He replied to an advertisement for a bus driver and went for an interview.

The foreman asked, "Have you ever driven a bus?"

"Well, no sur, but I've driven a big lurry."

"Well, of course, we have double decker buses in London."

"Shure that would be like a high load of hay on the lurry—I could manage that alright", says Paddy.

"Well now, we have one-man buses."

"Oh gor, sur, what's a wun-man bus?"

"Well, on a one-man bus, the driver collects the fares."

Dad, Jean, Gwen, and Thady picnic on the meadow. The hay season in fine weather was blissful.

"Och, I suppose I'd get used to that, too."

So, God help us, Paddy got the job. Next morning, Paddy was driving his bus bravely down Oxford Street. There was a ghastly smash and the bus ploughed its way through the huge plate-glass window of Selfridges store. The manager came storming out.

"What the hell is going on here?"

"Oh gor, sur, I don't know", says poor Paddy. "I was upstairs collecting the fares!"

Dad would hire extra men for the hay season. It was a common sight to see ten men in a line with pitch forks turning the swath. I enjoyed taking my turn with them. In broken weather, it was necessary to make small cocks; first, two swaths were turned into a row and the cocks were shaped to be rainproof. As soon as the weather allowed, the cocks were shaken out flat. When ready, the hay was rowed with the horse-drawn rake—a most satisfying machine to handle.

Then the gatherer (a machine also known as a "tumbler" or "skeeter") took over. Dad favoured the wooden variety. The horse walked the row while the driver, with the reins around his neck and two hands on the handles, guided the gatherer until he had a full "load", then drove to the point where the wynde was to be made. There he lifted the handles so that the points of the gatherer stuck into the ground and it tumbled over, depositing the hay in a heap. This was hard work. Jimmy Keefe, one of Dad's grooms, was the past-master at it.

For the next step, three men took over. They shaped the round base of the wynde, one man standing in the middle while the other two piked forkfuls to him.

"D'ye keep a heart in it", the old men used to say. They meant the man on top of the wynde should put the hay under his feet so that the centre always remained the highest point.

When the wynde was complete and shaped like an egg, the sugáns (pronounced "soogawn") would be attached. Dad was an expert at making sugáns. He would fluff up a small pile of hay, draw some out, and hook it on to the twister. One of us would twist the hay and step backwards, keeping an even tension, while Dad would pass the hay through his fingers. The resulting "hay rope" was of even thickness right through.

When the correct length was completed, the "rope" was rolled into an oblong ball, thrown over the wynde, and each end twisted on to a fist of hay that was secure in the base of the wynde. A field of wyndes of identical and perfect shape, placed in straight lines, was a joyful sight.

The wyndes would remain out in the meadow for maybe six weeks to season. They were then loaded on to a float (a broad, flat-bodied cart on small, wide, iron wheels) by means of a hand-levered winch, which "sang" a lovely song—"clink-clink-clink-clink, clonk-clonk-clonk-clonk". Next a man, standing on the barrel of the winch, drove the load to the hay barn.

We stood on the tail of the float and held on tight to the hay. Paddy was our favourite horse for this job—he liked to gallop home across the fields!

Family in hayfield with Tom Carroll sitting on the wynde of hay with Brown Bess, 1932. A field of wyndes of identical and perfect shape, placed in straight lines, was a joyful sight.

In the hay barn, the hay was stored in "columns". When the column was high, a ladder was used. Number 1 man on the ground would pass it to Number 2 on the ladder, who passed it to Number 3 (also on the ladder), who passed it to Number 4 on the stack, who passed it to two or three men spreading the hay evenly—all hard manual work. Later Dad bought an elevator, powered by a small petrol engine. I would sit up on a batten on a lump of hay, the elevator was put in gear, and I would have a joyride to the top. I don't think insurance companies today would agree to cover such a practice!

In those wonderfully happy and carefree days, we had our simple pleasures out in the countryside. We went for walks with Mum and Dad, reared chickens and ducklings in the yard under hens, rode our donkeys, played with the hound puppies, and collected blackberries and mushrooms as well as kindling for the fire. We were close to nature and learned how to forecast the weather. When the leaves of the trees turned upside down, dust in the yard would chase round in circles and the wind would whistle through the old windows and doors of the house, you could be sure that rain was on its way. Conversely, the *Sí gaoite* (pronounced "she geehe"—a fairy wind) that lifted and twisted the hay in the meadows up into the air out of sight was a sign of an oncoming heat wave.

NINE

HI BROTHER

When I was five years old, the arrival of our brother John was a great occasion. I remember looking on him in wonderment as he lay on the monk's bench in the hall, tightly wrapped in a soft white woollen shawl. It was going to be fun to have a brother.

At about this time, Kate came into our lives. Her family lived in a cottage in the townland of Ardmore, close to the Cross of the Tree, and were loyal friends of our family for generations. Her father, Mick Ryan, was a wonderful carpenter. The difference between him and Grandfather was that when Grandfather inserted a screw, he would put a drop of oil on it to make it easier to withdraw; when Mick put in a screw, he would spit on it to make it rusty and impossible to take out!

Kate's first responsibility was "Baby John," but she looked after the rest of us, too. She would drive Gwen and Jean to the convent in the village of Hospital, where the nuns were preparing them for their First Holy Communion. I

Dad, Gwen, Thady, Jean, and Mum on holiday at Ballytrent, 1924. After our holiday each year, Dad and Mum would go to Dublin where Dad served on the panel of judges at the Royal Dublin Society Horse Show.

would go along with them and play with toys in the parlour. The pony was stabled in the yard of Canon McCarthy, the parish priest.

For many years, Dad was on the panel of judges for the jumping in the Royal Dublin Society (RDS). Before going up to Dublin with Mum for Horse Show Week, he would drive us all to Ballytrent, where we had a wonderful three weeks by the sea with all our cousins. The long, safe beach gave us endless pleasure, but the water was usually cold and we did not learn to swim seriously. Lobsters caught by local fishermen were big, plentiful, and on the menu most days.

In alternate years, Dad would drive us to Edermine for our holiday. It was a whole day's drive—about 100 miles—and a big adventure. The old Ford was temperamental and frequently boiled with clouds of steam. We got to know all the convenient streams and hand pumps along the way. Once a back wheel came off and rolled down the road in front of us. We had no jack, so the three of us walked across the fields until we found a pole across a gap. We borrowed this and used it with a big stone to raise the car and Dad got the wheel back on. Auntie (our great-aunt Helen) meantime walked back along the road saying her Rosary and picked up all the nuts!

We loved Edermine. Aunt Jean looked after us as a mother would, but she was also strict. She taught us to be punctual (is this something I've forgotten?), to be polite always, to speak properly—even a brogue was frowned upon. Good manners, especially at mealtimes, were strongly enforced. A gentleman must always stand up when a lady enters the room; and juniors must give way to their elders and should address their elders as "sir" or "madam" until better acquainted. Although these matters might seem trivial, they are important, indicating a good family upbringing, and are sadly lacking in many young people today. Moreover, as with our parents at home, Aunt Jean stressed the importance of our morning prayers and of family Rosary in the beautiful chapel before bedtime—a habit I have always tried to observe.

Our greatest joy was an outing on the river in *Waterlily*—a small, but beautifully built rowing boat. Aunt Jean taught us to row, feathering the oars without "catching crabs". We would go upstream with the tide towards Enniscorthy, then left-handed up the Boro River—a wonderland of overhanging trees and bushes full of birdsong, the weed waving lazily in the peaty waters of the Boro. It was idyllic picnic country. Two elderly dear ladies, Miss Holmes and Miss Johnson, lived up there. They reared white angora rabbits for their fur. I can still smell them (the rabbits!).

Another memory is Auntie's little brown donkey called "Jet", which she drove in her chaise around the spacious grounds. When Aunt Jean was out shopping, Auntie would drive down the two grass slopes: she chuckled at being "Jet-propelled".

Another much-anticipated annual event was a visit after Easter to Belvoir near Six-Mile-Bridge in Co. Clare, the home of our Aunt B (Blanche) and cousin Willie Wilson-Lynch. Aunt B was my godmother, a special person to me, and a loving and caring soul. She had been married to my Uncle Clem, who was killed in World War I. Some years later she married Willie Wilson-Lynch, from an old Galway family, who was distantly related to my mother through the Dalys. He was tall, erect, and a kind, gentle man with a deep voice and big bushy moustache.

Belvoir was a handsome old house set in natural hardwood forest and bogland. Close by was a beautiful small private chapel where Mass was celebrated occasionally. The old house had been destroyed by fire many years before our time; the stables were converted to a delightful bungalow-style home of great character. There was a profusion of rhododendrons and other shrubs and a maze of paths through the woods.

What a fairytale situation for a treasure hunt, which was the highlight of our visit. First, we had a sumptuous lunch of roast lamb and all etceteras, followed by my favourite dessert—bananas, strawberry jam, and thick cream all mixed up. There was a large assortment of presents for everybody, along with a quantity of Easter eggs. Dad and Cousin Willie used their imagination in hiding the treasures. At the sound of a gong we were let loose! Inevitably one or two items were lost; I found one of my presents the following year—it was a small hand drill which I use regularly to this day.

Aunt B and Cousin Willie always came to stay with us "over the Christmas", as did Uncle Frank and Aunt Jean. Aunt B would bring a feast of fresh turbot—a great treat—and other goodies. A large box of crystallised fruit from Uncle Hugh in South Africa was also a regular feature of the family feast.

Our nearest and dearest neighbours, General Sir George and Lady Franks from Ballyscaddane—across the road from Scarteen—usually joined us for Christmas dinner, too. Their family had played a big part in the fortunes of the Ryans. In years gone by, the Ryans were tenants of the Franks; during the Troubles, when Catholics were not allowed to own horses or hounds, they took the hounds up to Ballyscaddane for a couple of years to save them. It was General Sir George who commanded Dad's regiment and sent the letter to Grandmother in 1915 with the sad (fortunately mistaken) news that Dad had been killed. In our youthful innocence we were always in awe of General Franks. We also thought him a bit pompous—he frequently quoted "When I was in Constantinople"—yet how wrong we were.

When dinner was over we would make our own entertainment—sometimes a play, individual sketches, miming, singing, or recitations. My lasting memory of Cousin Willie is of him standing erect in the drawing room and with his deep resonant voice reciting the entire poem, "Hiawatha". On one occasion Uncle Frank produced that ever popular after-dinner act, "The Flea". He made it land on the General, who unfortunately did not see the joke, took grievous offence, got up with Lady Franks, stamped out of the room and walked home—to poor Uncle Frank's huge embarrassment!

I have entertained countless parties down the years with "The Flea". The act goes like this. The presenter removes his coat and rolls up his shirt sleeves. From a small box he produces an "imaginary flea" called Paddy and allows him to feed on his bare left arm while he introduces him to the audience. He then holds out his bare right arm about a foot away and calls, “Jump”. He watches Paddy’s flight, then Paddy lands on his right arm. The “jump” is repeated and the gap between the arms is gradually widened. Meanwhile the presenter moves slowly towards a member of the audience. In the final jump Paddy fails to make a landing on the arm and is lost. Greatly upset, the presenter searches everywhere and “finds” the flea on the member’s head. Much relieved he coaxes the flea on to his arm. “Oh, this is not Paddy”, he cries in dismay, and returns the “new” flea to the member’s head!

One afternoon I was playing with croquet mallets with my little brother John, who was three or four years old at the time. Mum called us in for tea. I took one last swipe at the tennis ball and swung around, hitting John hard on the head and knocking him to the ground. I thought I had killed him. I ran up to my room straight away and wept bitterly for hours.

I was to make another inadvertent attempt on John’s life many years later. We were coming home from a party at the Wallers in Beechmount, Rathkeale. After a fog along the river at Bruree, followed by frost, the road, without warning, was a sheet of ice. I braked coming down the hill into the village, the car skidded straight on, knocking a piece of the bridge’s wall into the river, with the engine overhanging the water.

Seatbelts had not been invented in those days. John’s wife Rosemary was flung from the back seat to the front. I got away with light concussion and a split lip. Poor John went out through the windscreen with a severed nose and severe lacerations. Few people ever guessed that that was the reason why John wore a moustache.

By coincidence, some years later Lord Daresbury had an identical crash at the same site. It then became known as the “Masters’ Bridge”!

My brother, John R. Ryan-Purcell of Burton Park.

TEN

GETTING TO KNOW YOU, GETTING TO KNOW ALL ABOUT YOU—GREAT HUNTING FAMILIES

Throughout our hunting country numerous old family homes were in the hands of great sporting friends.

MOORESFORT

One of our favourites was Mooresfort, the home of Captain Charles and Lady Dorothy Moore. Mooresfort is a large estate with rolling parkland, beautiful trees—and four fox coverts! The house is a handsome mansion, set in ample lawns and shrubs with a fine stable yard and out offices, all maintained in immaculate condition. One of the most beautiful estates in the south of Ireland, Mooresfort features again in later pages.

The captain's tall stature and noble bearing held us in awe while Lady Dorothy's effusive warmth and sense of fun put us immediately at ease. Lady Dorothy was constantly involved in charitable works, helping anyone in distress (as does the family to this day). She loved her hunting, too: She rode sidesaddle, impeccably turned out complete with habit and veil, beautifully mounted and always up with hounds.

The mansion lent itself to hide and seek, sardines and all sorts of other games. Like their mother, the four daughters, who were about our own age, enjoyed their hunting. They also showed their talents in music and the arts. I vividly remember Ruth playing a xylophone (made of milk bottles with varying amounts of water) and young Tommy Barry, son of their steward, singing "Panis Angelicus" in a most lovely voice.

DERK

Mooresfort was the venue too for various events run for charities and for hunt funds. My first introduction to gambling was watching Captain Tolly Considine as master of ceremonies running the roulette table: "Faites vos jeux . . . Rien ne va plus." I always lost my money, probably for the best! Tolly was one of the Considines of Derk, distant cousins of ours. The name *Derk* derives from the Gaelic word for "a view"; in favourable weather one can see five counties from this magnificent and stately home.

Tolly, a close friend of Dad's, was treasurer of the hunt for many years. His vocabulary could be colourful to put it mildly. If you have ever watched rooks building their nests, you will have seen an old bird at the end of a high branch desperately trying to break off the end twig, bending it to and fro, mostly without success. Dad and his brothers were watching this performance from the front of the house one Sunday morning. One of them announced, "If that was Tolly, he would be saying, 'Goddam and blast this bloody stick'."

All the same, Tolly had a heart of gold. Occasionally out hunting he and Dad would go for the same hole in the bushes and he would curse Dad in heaps. Next morning without fail there would be a letter for Dad in the post, full of apologies.

Stories of Tolly abound. He was fearless and impetuous across country. On one stag hunt the deer took refuge in a small farmer's cow shed. The urgency was always to save the deer from the hounds who meant to kill. Tolly was first on the scene, to find the elderly farmer lying in the yard; the pack had knocked him down. Off his horse in a trice, Tolly bent over loosening the poor chap's collar when "the missus" appeared. She found a complete stranger in a black coat apparently throttling her husband.

She fetched a broom and was beating Tolly over the head shouting, "I'll larn ye ta kill me ole man", when cousin Jack appeared on the scene.

"Take her away, damn you", cried Tolly. "She's killing me." Jack was powerless with laughter.

Tolly's outbursts also had long-term effects. In the early 1930s the old kennels were in the farmyard at Scarteen. The only water supply was rain water collected in a big tank off the roof of the large hay shed. In dry weather, water for the hounds and for washing down the kennels was brought in buckets from the well in the stable yard, about 150 yards away. The Hunt Committee decided to install a hydraulic ram in the well field fed from a never-failing spring of purest water. The big day came. Tolly and committee members all turned up to see the ram started up, then went back to the kennels to see the water pouring into the tank. All they found was a small trickle.

Tolly exploded in fury, "Is this all we have got after spending all that bloody money and it so scarce?"

Of course next morning the tank was full and it remained so for years.

Another morning Tolly was selling a small dairy cow in the cattle fair in Old Pallas. An elderly woman in a shawl came up to buy the cow from him.

"Is she a good milker, captain?" she asked.

Tolly looked around to make sure nobody was within hearing distance. "Do you think I am a bloody fool to be selling a good milker? Now run away with yourself!"

His four sons were explosive, but fun like their father. Tolly reared the boys with a firm hand. He kept two pairs of boxing gloves in his desk; if a serious argument arose, he would put the gloves on the two contestants and let them settle the matter in fair play.

Sadly, two of the boys died while they were relatively young. The eldest, Heff, died from a poisoned finger. Anthony was killed in battle after he joined the Royal Air Force (RAF).

Like his brother, Peter fought in the RAF in World War II. After the war he took on the management of Derk, but his hunting was limited by hard work on the farm. The fourth brother, Neal, loved his hunting. A chain smoker as well, during one hunt he inadvertently put his cigarette into his coat pocket—and caught fire!

To our great sorrow, financial pressure finally necessitated the sale of Derk. Many shared the sense of loss with Peter; it was hard to accept Derk without the Considines. The place has since changed hands a couple of times. Happily the present owner, an industrialist from Germany, loves and cares for it. Importantly he also enjoys hunting with Chris when he can!

NEWTOWN ELLARD

Not far from Derk is Newtown Ellard, an attractive old house. It was formerly the home of Miss Ellard, who bred some great racehorses. Many years ago an English lady answered Miss Ellard's advertisement for a lady gardener. And so it was that Miss Tudor broke into the Scarteen hunting scene.

Soon gardening took a very poor second place to hunting, and Miss Tudor became one of the great characters in the hunt. She rode sidesaddle, preferred almost thoroughbreds (that were not always fully schooled!), being extremely light herself, and crossed the country fearlessly. She was a frequent winner point-to-pointing. Even at the end of a hard race all she would take was a glass of soda water.

In her later years her groom Fogarty accompanied her. However, as his nerve was weaker than hers, he was always saying, "Easy now, miss." One day hounds were drawing Cullen covert. "Tudor and Fogarty" were late arriving. As

Miss Tudor winning a point-to-point, followed by Tolly Considine, Dad, and Lady Dorothy Moore. Miss Tudor came to Newtown Ellard from England as a gardner, but her first love was hunting and she crossed the country fearlessly. Frank O'Brien photo

they entered the covert field, they headed a dog fox back into covert and gave a shout.

Dad came galloping up with his hounds, "Which way did he go?"

Tudor had rather prominent front teeth. "I'fe juss seen a ffox—he cave out here and he went vack again." Dad took a deep breath!

Her favourite plant in the garden was a flower. She did not know its name, but she knew its scent was just like that of a "ffox".

KILFRUSH

Kilfrush was another great bastion of hunting. The large late-Georgian house was set in beautiful grounds among exotic trees and shrubs, and a large area of clipped laurels and mown lawns, kept in immaculate order by a dedicated and numerous staff. On one side was a long conservatory dense with cinerarias and heady with their opulent scent. Catherine Gubbins, a dedicated gardener, took great pride in her successes with flowers, fruit, and vegetables in Limerick Show, the premier flower show in the south. Her husband Jack was a collector of antiques, so the walls of the Kilfrush hallway, stairs, and rooms were laden with priceless pictures and china. I used to be scared of brushing against them.

As neither parent was "horsey", their only child Maureen must have inherited her deep love and knowledge of horses from her grandfather. He had bred the two famous Derby winners Galtymore and Ardpatrick (as Dad's fellow prisoner of war from Russia knew). Within the large handsome stable yard adjoining the house, ample loose boxes and a tack room housed Maureen's super ponies and later a host of top-class hunters, all the domain of her devoted

Eileen and Keith Reynolds of Kenmare Castle on John Silver and Matt. The Reynolds supported Dad and me through thick and thin.

groom John Quigley. With a well-planted fox covert, Kilfrush was a sure find throughout the season—of which more anon.

KENMARE CASTLE

Supporting Dad and me through thick and thin were Eileen and Keith Reynolds. They lived in Kenmare Castle, Eileen's old home, at the end of the village of Hospital (the name stems from the Knights Hospitallers who cared for leprosy patients in days gone by) alongside the small river. For a while Eileen had lived in Malaya with her first husband, Dr Jimmy Rea, where they had one son Maurice. On Jimmy Rea's death, Eileen married Keith, a close friend and rubber planter. To their great sorrow, their one child died on board ship on their way home.

If anyone ever deserved the title "Matron of the Hunt," it surely was Eileen, a dedicated and intensely keen huntswoman. Eileen rode sidesaddle; she needed and had big, quality horses. John Silver (the grey) and Matt (the black) carried both Eileen and Keith for many seasons.

Being married to Eileen, of course, Keith had to hunt. He loved to watch hounds working, but he had never ridden before. Although, inevitably, he took the most unmerciful falls, he was determined to master it. A great hunting character, Jerry Callaghan—known as "the Lord Mayor of Hospital"—kept a pub in the village. He used to tell how Mrs Reynolds would burst her way out through the bushes over a huge double bank and call back to Mr Reynolds, "Come on, darlin'," sez she. And he had to go.

(A similar story is told of two big, hard-riding hunting folk. They came to this impenetrable horror of a big double. Jim had a go and the bushes closed after him. His friend shouted "What's on the other side, Jim?" There was a brief pause and the reply came back. "I am, thank God!")

Keith's gift was as a born naturalist. He had intriguing experiences working elephants in the Malayan jungle. Back in Ireland, he studied wildlife. He was also an expert fisherman and an excellent shot. He and Cousin Jack, who were like brothers, were the prime organisers of our weekly snipe-shooting parties. An important member of these parties was Tom Burke from Emly Station. Tom knew the lie of every fox in his area, and also had great terriers. He would beat the bogs and send the snipe upwind over the guns. Able to call the wild duck and golden plover without any aid or whistle, he took great pride in his work—a real "man of the country".

As a member of the Hunt Committee Keith was in charge of coverts. Many was the long day he put in fencing and planting. His "brief" also included settling fowl claims. The hunt's policy was to pay some small compensation for fowl killed by foxes. In those days hens, ducks, geese, and turkeys had free range, getting a "good fist of Indian meal" (cracked maize) thrown to them every day. They were easy prey for foxes. Keith would try to persuade the farmer's wife that the "hen was never yet hatched that did not die in debt". Nevertheless there were always one or two regular "chancers" putting in a claim for "twenty hens and five ducks and a turkey" every October. Such claims could not be ignored—as the hunting alphabet suggests:

> P is the price of a nate little hin
> that the foxes ate over and over agin.

KNOCKTORAN

Another great hunting stronghold was Knocktoran, the home of Napier (Napper) and Mary Webb. This attractive property contained "The Bog"—probably the best covert in Scarteen Hunt country. The Bog features in Peter Curling's excellent portrait, presented to me by members of the hunt. Mary Webb rode sidesaddle and hunted hard. She was a great disciplinarian so everyone respected her orders. Napper was hunt treasurer as well as Field Master for many seasons. He was always smartly turned out with hunting topper.

When her daughter's good pony hesitated at a fence, Mary called out, "Shout at him, Betsy, shout at him!"

Another day, when Mary herself took a toss, a young chap nearby came running to her.

"Do you want to get on to your horse again, madam?"

She shouted at him, "What do you think I want to do—sit in the middle of the field and sing a song?" Always colourful with her language, if she disliked someone, her favourite phrase was, "I'd like to get my nails into his liver."

ATHASSEL

Percy and Sheila Harris lived in Athassel, a charming small stud farm alongside the village of Golden, just inside Tipperary Hunt country. Percy was a most diligent hunt secretary for more than fifty years; during the last twenty years he was joint honorary secretary with my sister Gwen. Percy always caused great amusement at committee meetings when asked to read the minutes, as he could not read his own writing.

I want to recall many more great friends, but they will feature in later chapters. I must get back on track!

ELEVEN

KILLASHEE

In my time it was the norm for young boys to go away to boarding school (when top-class primary schools in Ireland were much rarer than they are now). I enjoyed my years at Killashee near Naas in Co. Kildare. Formerly a big private house, it was taken over by a French order of nuns, La Sainte Union de la Sacré Coeur, to become one of the best preparatory schools for boys.

Nonetheless, the wrench of leaving the security of home three times a year was always painful. Occasionally Dad would drive me back to school. When the time for parting arrived he was tearful, too. I would wonder why; when my turn came to leave my family back at school, I discovered the reason.

Normally, to return to school, I was put on the train at Knocklong Station. Waiting on the platform, I would spot the smoke from the engine appear in the distance and tears would flow again. After the journey the school car would meet the boys from the south at Sallins Station and bring us out to Killashee. Then we were back together with our friends and all was well.

Madam Patrick Clare was in charge of first form, Madam Mary Loyola of second form, and Madam Ita Magdalen (inevitably known as "Madam Eat A Maggot") of third form. Other nuns took us for art and music. Mr O'Neill—I think he was in the army—came once a week for gymnastics, when he drilled us with dumbbells, barbells, and clubs. My dread was the wooden vaulting horse. Even using a springboard, I could only manage a weak spring. I envied the real gymnasts among the boys, who could take flight over the horse like swallows.

The nuns were strict, but kind. Some rules were peculiar—for instance, we had to wear bathing togs when we had a bath! We looked forward to the autumn term, particularly the "conkers" that we collected on walks through the woods. There was a skill in drilling a hole with a nail and knotting the string so that the chestnut would not break.

The food was adequate, but plain. "Bread and scrape" was normal. Some days we would get a sausage for breakfast (after a plate of runny gruel). If a sausage or two were left over, the senior boy at the table would cut them into small pieces and square the solidified fat with a knife. Then the plate was passed around—all eyes following it hoping, a piece might be left. Black treacle helped us to swallow the thick slices of dry white bread. We were allowed "tuck boxes"; some boys would come back from holidays with a rich assortment of jams, biscuits, cake, chocolate, and other treats I could not afford.

As a convent school, it had a beautiful chapel. It was a joy to visit the Blessed Sacrament in free time. Senior boys were taught to serve Mass. I used to love the Mass in Latin—even though some of the responses were tongue twisters—the Confiteor was one of the hard ones.

I had a thrill when the Kildare hounds had a lawn meet at the school. A photo was taken of the boys seated on the front steps. In the middle sat the Master Lady Helen McCalmont in her sidesaddle kit. I remember feeling proud and rather special—I was probably the only boy there whose father was a Master of hounds!

One of the highlights of my time at Killashee was on 3 June 1932, the day of my first Holy Communion. In the atmosphere of the convent, prayer came easily; we were carefully prepared for our big day for weeks beforehand. That morning, we wore our best suits and had a beautiful badge and medals on our lapels. The joy of receiving Our Lord was supreme.

Coming down from the altar, I had a grievous distraction. I spotted my parents in one of the benches; they had not told me that they were coming. My heart jumped higher still! We all had bacon and eggs for breakfast together in the parlour.

I suppose I was about ten years old. After being sick one Saturday night, I could not go to Mass early on Sunday morning. As I recovered quickly, Reverend Mother told me to go to Mass in Naas. I expected that she meant me to go in the school car, so she found me waiting for the driver.

She was cross, "Certainly not; you will run."

So I had to run about one-and-a-half miles to Naas and try to find the church. And I got to Mass all right.

It was a lesson I shall never forget. It underlined forever for me the supreme importance of hearing Mass on Sundays.

As the end of July approached, excitement mounted. Exams were over, we were packing our trunks and counting the hours—and then home for the long summer holidays.

TWELVE

A FIRST TASTE

On those glorious holidays our great delight was to climb the Galty Mountains. Dad taught us to fish in the small streams coming from the lakes. A six-inch trout was a whopper; they were easy to catch (so were the overhanging bushes) and occasionally we would have one on each of the three flies at once. After wrapping them in grass and flaggers (wild irises), we would cook them in the embers of the picnic fire while the tea was brewing. Delicious.

We also tried to learn to swim in a couple of deep pools. Three strokes would cross the pools, but ouch the water was cold!

Then the big day came when we progressed from donkeys to ponies. Dad got two good ponies from Paddy Punch in Crecora, who also owned the pub at Punch's Cross in Limerick. Gwen rode Paddy, a plainish sort with strong mouth, but full of go. Jean rode Crecora, a bay or brown well-bred sort. Both ponies were brilliant across country. I rode Sylvia, a retired grey cob given to us by a cousin.

Dad would take us schooling over the ditches in the big field in front of the house. Although we were soon confident over them, our big dread was "the pole" in the side lawn. Dad was a brilliant rider across country, but he taught us the old hunting seat. He would tell us to lean well back coming in to the fence and then ask us why we fell off! He also put a sixpenny piece between our knees and the saddle. If it was still in place on landing, we could keep it—I never made any money.

Jumping down into a road or river, he would tell us to touch the horse's tail with the ribbon of our hunting cap. In later years the camera caught me doing this when my wife Anne and Tommy, my whip, were competing at the Limerick Hunt Hunter Trials. As the photo got published in a sporting paper, I had my leg pulled unmercifully! Soon afterwards during a hunt we came to a huge trench, too big to jump overall. I spotted Di Turner, honorary secretary of the Tipperary, following me, so I thought I had better do the right thing. I leaned forward, knees bent, and my horse dropped short into the trench. The clay bottom was soft and we took a right purler. From then on I followed Dad's advice.

Our ponies were for hunting: we had no pony clubs or organised competitions. How different from today, when children from an early age are taught to ride correctly right up through the grades. A huge variety of clinics and competitions in all disciplines are held throughout the year. My one small concern is that too much emphasis is laid on winning ribbons and parental pressure is taking the fun out of competing. For example, some years ago in Dublin Horse Show, two high-class ponies were neck-and-neck for the championship. The judges deliberated for a long time before arriving at a decision. The rider of the

Thady, wife Anne, and Tommy Dwyer at the County Limerick Hunter Trials, Kilballyowen, 1955. Dad told us to touch the horse's tail with the ribbon of our hunt cap when jumping off a bank. After this photo was published in a sporting paper, I was ribbed unmercifully! Ambrose O'Mullane photo

reserve came out of the ring and was set upon for not winning, first by her groom and then by her mother. She was reduced to tears.

For the first few weeks of cub hunting (autumn hunting—pardon me!), Dad always hunted hounds on foot. He felt that it developed a closer bond between hounds and himself. We would hunt up in the heather-clad hills and glens—Glenanaar, Darragh, Coolfree, Lonergan's Glen, and Slievereagh, magic-sounding names. In those days foxes were reasonably plentiful. They were also wild, living up in the heather, in contrast to nowadays, when they are semi-domesticated and prefer to frequent farm houses and villages down the country.

It was taking a big chance—hounds could riot on hare or whatever and one could not check them. But we always tried to start where we were sure there were foxes, and they could "enter" for certain first time out on fox. Another line from the hunting alphabet comes to mind:

N is for Nannygoat upon the hill.
Begorrah them puppies are hunting her still!

But more of that anon.

The first morning's "cubbing", usually about mid-July, was breathtaking. I would lose my breakfast behind a wynde of hay from sheer excitement! "Leu in there"—it still gives me goose pimples. The old hounds crashing into covert (not always silently), the entry (young hounds about eighteen months old starting their first season) rush in with them and a few minutes later a couple or more will come back to the huntsman bewildered: "What do you want us to do? All along you have made us stick close to you and now you are telling us to go away." But hark, an old hound has spoken down the glen, followed by a surge of celestial music, and the young 'uns are gone.

Wallis's Glen near Ballyorgan was, and still is, one of our favourite haunts. Many great sportsmen lived up there, including Mossy Wallis, Paddy Sweeney, Dan Hannigan and, of course Canon Manning, an Anglican Minister. Hounds and hunting were high on the list of the canon's loves—in the summer time a Colonel Pennefather would bring his Otter Hounds to work the Darragh River. In spite of having only one hand, the canon, who was also an ardent fisherman, would tie his own flies.

My sister Gwen sells poppies to canon Manning, a great sportsman. In spite of having only one hand, the canon, an ardent fisherman, would tie his own flies.

We were cub hunting on foot one morning at Darragh, between Mitchelstown and Kilfinane. Dad was hunting hounds and I must have been home from Ampleforth towards the end of the long summer holidays. Hounds got away on an old fox and disappeared over the top of Coolfree Mountain into the low cloud and out of sight. We had lost them "good and proper". Dad waited on the road by Dan Hannigan's house. He gave me the horn, sending me along with Jack Dwyer (the kennel huntsman) up into the fog, blowing and calling.

After some time hounds came trickling back, delighted to find us, and we came down to Dad with all hounds on. Dad was relieved.

Looking through the hounds, he said, "What is wrong with Starter? He has got something around his neck."

It was a fox's brush. We heard later that away down in the Duhallow Hunt country, which adjoined ours at this point, a farmer was ploughing with a pair of horses. A pack of strange-looking hounds (which he knew were not the Duhallow hounds) killed their fox in the open field where he was working. He thought that whoever owned the hounds would like to know what happened, so he cut off the fox's brush and tied it around a quiet hound's neck! Canon Manning found out later who the sportsman was. Dad wrote to thank the farmer for his thoughtfulness and sent an account of the incident to the *Field Magazine*.

The canon's great friend was the Catholic parish priest Fr O'Shea. I can see the father now in his "tub trap", a fat chestnut pony in the shafts, almost crossing the country after hounds. When during the season the canon's horse went lame, Fr O'Shea untackled his pony, put the canon's saddle on him, gave the canon a leg-up, and away they went.

Another favourite cubbing spot was Castle Oliver. Built in the time of the famine to give employment, it is a *huge* imposing red sandstone edifice with towers and battlements, terraced lawns, and even a folly on the hill. Inside there are about forty rooms, a magnificent hallway and banisters and a ballroom—it features later in the story.

Cub hunting on horseback started in early September so we would have about three weeks on our ponies—then back to school.

THIRTEEN

AMPLEFORTH

A monk from Ampleforth College was travelling back from London by train, reading his office (daily prayers). In the same compartment two elderly ladies were chatting.

One said, "I believe that the public school up in Yorkshire is a fine college. They say it is the Catholic Eton."

The monk took off his spectacles and turned to them. "Please forgive me, but I must correct you. Eton is the Protestant Ampleforth!"

This was one of the favourite stories of Fr Paul, the Headmaster.

Ampleforth was and still is a magnificent monastic school. Situated with its back to the high lands that lead on to the Yorkshire Moors, it has a splendid view across the broad valley to the woods around Fairfax lakes and Gilling Castle, once the home of the Earl of Feversham. Since the college acquired it, it has been the preparatory school for many years. It has a warm spot in my heart because the Ampleforth College Beagles were kennelled close by (more on them in the next chapter).

I believe there were three main reasons why I was sent to Ampleforth. First, it had a reputation as one of the leading Catholic public schools in England. Second, Uncle Willie's three sons, Jim, John, and Clem, were all there. Third, Uncle Willie helped Dad with the cost of my schooling. Maybe the beagles had a small influence, too! Jim was Master of them in his time.

There was one stumbling block. The entrance exam for the junior house in Ampleforth was a bit above the standard I had reached in Killashee, so Dad secured a tutor to give me a grind. Mr MacDonald might have come out of Oliver Twist—pinstriped trousers, black jacket, stiff collar, and bowtie. He was a complete city man from Dublin, and could not understand how houses in the country stood up without the support of houses alongside. We tried to teach him to ride, but that was a fiasco.

Because of, or in spite of, Mr MacDonald, and possibly with some string pulling, I was accepted for the junior house.

I travelled there with about thirty boys from Ireland. Fr Ignatius, and later Fr Hubert, would come over and meet us at Dun Laoghaire. I believe that the Headmaster of Glenstal College near Limerick, which was just starting as a public school, was "uneasy" that Ampleforth should be poaching his would-be pupils. My first year at "Shack", the boys' nickname for Ampleforth, overlapped Cousin Clem's final year.

On the Liverpool route we would share a cabin. More often than not the Irish Sea was unkind, with disastrous results. As the Scottish comedian Harry Lauder once said, "If there is any good in a man, the sea will get it out of him."

Shades of Dad's time, when he would send a telegram to his mother to put her mind at ease: "Arrived safe, good crossing, not ill, John." The catch was that he would send it from Dublin before going aboard!

Many folk groan about their miserable school days. Yet I can say honestly that, after the initial break from home, I was happy in all my time at Ampleforth. For me the Benedictine ethos is something special. I felt part of a new and enlarged family. All (almost all!) the monks were more than teachers; they were friends. I was fortunate to be a pupil during Fr Paul Neville's reign as Headmaster. Well over six feet tall, straight as a ramrod, with dark features and bushy eyebrows, his severe countenance concealed a warm-hearted and sincere character. Within three weeks of the start of the school year, he would know every boy by name. His appearance at the top of the Long Passage steps, with the whole school before him as he led us in prayer every morning before study, is a treasured memory. For many years he was president of the Headmasters Conference in England, a good indication of his calibre.

Fr Paul Nevill, Ampleforth Headmaster visits Thady and hounds at Scarteen.

On one occasion a boy was unhappy and ran away, causing great concern throughout the school. By good chance the stationmaster in York Station telephoned to say there was a boy on the platform who looked as if he might be from the college. Fr Paul asked him to keep the boy in conversation while he drove there at speed. He took the boy into the well-known Station Hotel, gave him a slap-up meal, regained his confidence, and brought him "home". The boy never had any further trouble.

Fr James was Fr Paul's popular private secretary. One of his resolutions was never to let a day go by without dealing with the huge correspondence of that day. It is a resolution I too have tried to follow, but mostly failed to achieve.

Under Fr Illtyd Williams, our house master in the junior house, discipline was strict, but just. He kept his flat whalebone ferrule in his desk and administered it on the hand when justified. It hurt! Friends had a basin of hot water ready in the washroom to relieve the pain. Fr Illtyd would distribute the letters at breakfast, flicking each one to the appropriate boy who was called by name. My mother's big generous handwriting meant her capital "T" looked like an "S". He called out my name "Shady Ryan"—it stuck with me for years.

I had the distinction of being in the same year as the late Cardinal Basil Hume. Every St Patrick's Day our (Irish) parents would send us sprays of shamrock, which we displayed proudly. One day, Hume and his good friend Haigh (we never used Christian names in those days) snatched our precious shamrock from our lapels and stamped it into the floor—just to make us furious. Years later when visiting the Cardinal, I reminded him of the incident and we had a good laugh. Fr Martin Hague, another monk of Ampleforth, is working hard on the English mission in a parish near Liverpool.

School certificate marked the end of junior house days and we advanced to the upper school. There were the seven "houses" in those days; I was posted to St Aidans, one of four based in the main building. (Another, St Cuthberts, could be called the "Huntin', Shootin', Fishin'" house—their housemaster, Fr Sebastian, was a great fisherman and would take his boys on fishing jaunts.) Fr John Maddox was my first housemaster. At our first meal in the new refectory block, after Fr John said grace, we sat down. For a joke, my friend Tony Hansen removed my chair. My head hit the partition hard and I saw stars. Tony got a lecture—yet he was to become an eminent doctor in later years.

Ampleforth Abbey Church. "A fine college . . . the Catholic Eton," said the lady. "Please forgive me but I must correct you," said the monk. "Eton is the Protestant Ampleforth!"

In those days the Abbey Church was only half built (in which state it stayed for many long years). There were many small chapels and altars, including about six in the crypt, to accommodate all the priests—this in the days before Concelebration. As at Killashee, I found it a great joy to get up an hour early and go down to serve Mass. My favourite was Our Lady's Chapel, where I loved to pray in free time.

Owen Hare, a classmate of mine, and I became close friends. We were similar in height and appearance and were frequently appointed acolytes and altar servers at High Mass on Sundays. On days when it was too wet for rugby, most of the boys would occupy themselves indoors. Owen and I would hit off across county with just a rugger shirt, shorts, and gym shoes kicking, a tennis ball as we went. We ran for miles. Occasionally I would stop and talk with a farmer.

After I had stopped for a chat a couple of times, Owen asked me, "Do you know all these people?"

I said, "No."

I suppose it was the Irish familiarity in me coming out. But this can sometimes lead to difficulties. I heard of a chap recently who was cycling down the road and leading a second bike with his right hand. As a car passed the driver waved a salute to the cyclist. Automatically the cyclist returned the greeting, and you can guess what happened—he took a helluva fall. Seeing the smash in his mirror, the driver stopped his car and ran back to see if the chap was all right. The cyclist was lying on the road with the two bikes on top of him and he furious.

Says the cyclist to the driver, "Do you know me? No. Do I know you? No. Don't you ever dare salute me again!"

Discipline in the school was strict and enforced by the school monitors. For a severe infringement of the rules, the head monitor of the house administered a tanning. For a very severe infringement, the head monitor of the school carried out the sentence, after consultation with the headmaster. In such cases the offender would be led from his dormitory at about 10 P.M. He would be accused of his crime in front of all the school monitors, his pyjama trousers would be lowered and he would receive the prescribed number of strokes with a cane, hard. Such punishment might seem cruel, but it was just. The rules were there to be observed and we knew what we were in for if we broke them, so we respected them and the people who were responsible for them.

Moreover, school tannings were reasonably rare. For minor faults, we would be given lines by the house monitors. One I shall never forget. I had to write it out 100 times: "In youth's bright harmony there is no such word as 'can't.'" It has been my motto through life!

The day of the terrible train tragedy must surely have been the blackest in the history of the college. On the special train bringing boys from Kings Cross in London to Gilling Station at the end of the holidays, nobody spotted a lighted cigarette slipping down between the seats. Fire took hold, fanned by the speed of the train. Someone pulled the emergency cord, but for some unexplained reason the engine driver decided not to stop until further down the track where there was a compulsory stop. Also unexplained was that the communicating doors to adjoining carriages were locked.

As a result of the tragedy six young lives were lost, including two sons of the Belgian Prime Minister. Owen Hare almost lost his life trying desperately to save others. This dire event, coupled with losing his elder brother in World War II, had a devastating effect on poor Owen.

After Fr John's retirement, Fr Terence Wright took over St Aidans. A man of iron and a great sportsman, Fr Terence commanded authority with firmness and understanding, and won the hearts of all his boys. He was determined to lead St Aidans to the top. When the school was grounded by bad weather, St Aidans would go for a house run.

Although Fr Terence had few disappointments, he encountered one during World War II. It was decreed that all the houses should manage a vegetable garden to supplement the meagre war rations. The St Aidans plot was half the quadrangle between the Long Passage and the science block. We dug furiously and planted as instructed. The miserable spuds and other veggies appeared and promptly died—we were attempting the impossible in pure heavy clay, originally dumped there from the foundations of the "new" classroom block. Fr Terence was furious!

One of the highlights of the summer term was Goremire Day. It saw the traditional exodus of the entire school—staff, pupils, the lot—to Sutton Bank on the edge of the moors towards Thirsk. Travel was by bicycle for sixth formers, by truck for the grub and picnic equipment, by bus for those unable to make it otherwise, and on foot for the majority. It was just a huge day out in the country, and a mighty picnic feast was enjoyed by all.

A big excitement on Goremire Day was launching the gliders. Sutton Bank was one of the best-known centres for the sport in the United Kingdom; the configuration of the cliff face was such that a west wind created a great updraught. About 100 boys would be spaced along a double rubber rope. On a signal from the pilot (a member of the local gliding club), we would start running. As the rubber expanded the glider would launch into the air and out over Sutton Bank—impressive!

But *the* event in the summer term was Exhibition. Parents came from far and near. All hotels, guest homes, and pubs over a wide area were booked out. Activities included Fathers vs School cricket matches, diving displays in the big outdoor pool, music and drama productions, prizegiving, and awards. Of course the main purpose of it all was to give masters and parents the opportunity to meet and discuss the future of the boys, and for the boys to show their parents around the college proudly.

Mum and Dad came one year along with Uncle Willie (planter of the "Pope's Oak" in chapter 4) and Aunt Mena. Cornering Dad, Fr Paul tried to persuade him to agree that I should be steered towards a career in the diplomatic corps.

Dad was adamant. "He must come home, take over the farm, and hunt his hounds!"

Needless to say my sights were firmly set on a future at Scarteen. Fr Paul was disappointed. Had I followed his wishes, how different my life would have been. But his judgement was vindicated: diplomacy is a necessary attribute for a Master of Foxhounds.

Returning home from Exhibition on a hot summer's day, Uncle Willie was at the wheel of his big open tourer with Dad alongside and the two ladies in the back. They were doing about sixty miles per hour through the beautiful English countryside when suddenly Mum discovered that Dad and Uncle Willie were both fast asleep. She woke Dad who put his hand on the wheel and woke the driver. Some guardian angels were perspiring that day!

Fr Hubert Stevenson (fondly known as "Popeye") was one of the real characters in the monastery. He was my chemistry master, and a crack shot with a piece of chalk to someone's ear if they made a mistake. For a more serious fault you would get the wooden duster on the back of the head—that hurt! His brother-in-law was Arthur Blake who trained horses on The Heath in

Co. Kildare. Occasionally after class he would whisper to me, "Arthur's filly is fancied in the 3:30 at Naas on Saturday—worth a couple of bob!"

Fr Anthony Ainscough was my biology master, as well as a close friend for years. Once when he was ill, Mr Watson, our botany master, took his place. He was, however, rather squeamish about animals. We were studying the blood vessels of the frog for an impending exam. Mr Watson had a euthanised frog beautifully skinned and pinned out on a board, legs outstretched. He had to leave the laboratory for a few minutes. For a joke one of the boys put a small drop of hydrochloric acid on the frog's legs. When Mr Watson returned, the dead frog was twitching furiously. We all shouted, "Ooh sir it's alive." The poor chap nearly fainted and class was abandoned!

I was not a strong swimmer. In the interhouse swimming sports, the tug o' war (back stroke) was the final event, in which every member of each house had to take part. On one occasion, in the excitement of the match, nobody spotted the dip in the rope—I was underwater and nearly drowned. I have been nervous of water ever since.

Cricket I enjoyed. I was put on to bowl once in a practice match. After taking three wickets in my first three balls, the fourth ball went out over the wicket keeper's head. I was not put on again! Rugby was great. I played in the back row of the scrum, but never achieved a first XV team. Ampleforth had a great name and achieved much success in interschool matches. It used to be said that the highest standard of rugby was seen in public school matches, where it was a real sport—far superior to a lot of international rubgy nowadays, which has become a dangerous professional battle.

Membership of the Officers Training Corps (OTC) was compulsory for all boys in the upper school. Once a week we would go on parade. Fr George Forbes was our commanding officer and some senior boys were promoted to noncommissioned officers. Three companies comprised several platoons. Each platoon was drilled on the "Square" between the main building and the theatre. We wore regulation battledress—a tunic with a (scratchy) high collar, knickerbockers, and puttees.

Puttees were a terrible invention. These broad, four-inch, khaki bandages, made of coarse wool, were carefully wrapped around the lower leg from the boot to the knee, where they were secured with tapes. If they were not wrapped tightly enough, they would unravel during drilling and a boy was in disgrace. If they were too tight, his legs ached.

Sergeant Higgins, a retired regular army soldier, trained the corps band. I joined the band as a bugler. This came easy to me due to my regular practice on Dad's hunting horn.

Once a year in the summer term, we had manoeuvres, which were mock battles in the valley over two days. We were issued with regular army rifles, Lee-Enfield Mark Three and blank ammunition; some platoons had a Brenn gun. Manoeuvres were fun, but serious. The OTC stood in great stead to those boys who were to enlist later in the armed forces.

AMPLEFORTH IN WARTIME

Shortly after the start of World War II the German U-boats were causing havoc. Our parents considered that the risk of being lost in the Irish Sea was too great, so they sent my cousin Frank O'Reilly and myself to St Gerards School near Bray in Co. Wicklow. We were senior boys there under Mr Murphy, the Headmaster. Our form was billeted in Glen Field, a small house across the road, under the supervision of Mr Reynold, a short, dapper little man, who was strict, correct, and a brilliant professor in English.

I had my lovely warm rug on my bed. Unwittingly it had been frequented by our big woolly schnauzer dog at home. After a few days back at school the other six boys in my dorm were being savagely bitten by fleas. The trouble was traced to *my* bed—that took a lot of living down!

One Saturday Frank O'Reilly and I got permission to go on bicycles to a meet of the Bray harriers at Newtownmountkennedy. Hounds had moved off, so I asked a local which way was the draw. He was unsure, but said they would finish the run at Murphy's Pub about five miles away. I realised at once that it was a drag and we rode back to school in disgust.

After my two terms at St Gerards, it seemed that the Royal Navy were doing a great job and the Irish Sea was relatively safe, so I returned to Ampleforth. I shall be eternally grateful to Fr Paul for allowing me back again after my "walking out on him".

Blackout! It was eerie travelling from York in the old Reliance bus operated by two sisters, one driving, the other welcoming everyone aboard with a chat, and not a light to be seen all the way. The blackout was observed thoroughly. Every one of the hundreds of windows was well fitted with black cloth frames at dusk.

Otherwise life carried on as normal. Meals were simpler; butter, meat, and tea were strictly rationed, but adequate. Training in the school OTC was stepped up for the senior boys in preparation for their military service. Beagling meets were limited to those within walking distance, as petrol rationing prevented use of buses.

Uncle Frank (then Colonel Ryan) took me to his headquarters in Marske, near Middlesborough, where he was in command of a Royal Artillery training base. A ride in a Matador—a huge troop-carrying, four-wheel drive truck, mounting and descending a precipitous cliff face was scary.

One night when Uncle Frank was returning along this route with Crotty, his trusty Irish batman, he was alarmed by something on the road.

He said to Crotty, "Do you see what I see?"

"Yessir", Crotty replied.

They stopped, got out and went forward cautiously to inspect . . . cats' eyes. These reflective road markers had just been invented and were being planted on all main roads!

On another night Colonel Ryan had an urgent request from the local county council. A fire on the moors—not uncommon in dry weather—was spreading rapidly. Please would he get a couple of hundred men out there to beat it out?

Furious, the colonel replied, "My job is to train my men to kill Germans, not to be domestic fire fighters."

It turned out that German bombers mistook the fire for factories, set alight by previous raids, and for several nights emptied tons of bombs on the moors.

In my fifth form years I shared a room in the "Barn" (the attic) with John David. At night we could hear the drone of "our lads"—the Royal Air Force planes heavy with bombs on their way to annihilate the enemy. On their return, we heard occasionally the sound of a damaged engine, but we did not count them.

We had one serious air raid. It is believed that the Germans were on their way to bomb Belfast, and must have had inside information. One plane broke formation and dropped a stick of incendiaries on a military camp at Gilling. They landed on the avenue, but thankfully caused no great damage or casualties. As air raid warden my job was to get St Aidans boys to the indoor firing range, our allotted shelter. On the way I could see the flames all around the kennel area. I could hardly wait to get over there the next day to see the situation, when I found that the bombs had missed the kennels by about 100 yards. When the ack-ack gunners on Oswaldkirk Bank ceased firing, they trained their search lights on to the college buildings to see if we were okay—making us a perfect target for attack. Fr Oswald, who was in command of air-raid precaution, phoned them and gave them blazes!

FOURTEEN

THE AMPLEFORTH COLLEGE BEAGLES

The Ampleforth College Beagles (ACB) date from October 1915. Probably some packs were disbanded during World War I and drafts were readily available. Whoever first put the pack together certainly did a good job—quality was their hallmark with good music and they hunted well.

Their first Master was Paddy Dunne-Cullinane (each Master thereafter was also a boy in the school). Years later I had the honour of serving with Paddy on the ground jury of the Royal Dublin Society Horse Show. When he was farming in Co. Meath, I would also meet him buying his store bullocks in Ballinasloe Fair.

In my time old Jack Welch was kennel huntsman. He loved his hounds, and they him. He was a genius in hound breeding, shy (partly due to deafness—how many huntsmen go deaf from constant use of the horn!) and silent when hunting hounds. As he was also a stickler for kennel routine, discipline, and management, the lodges and yards were always spotless. Walking out with Jack was a pleasure. We exercised down along the beautiful oak avenue to the lakes. On a hot day he would throw biscuit far into the water and the pack would swim out to get it. Occasionally hounds would riot on the numerous grey squirrels.

Jack was strict with his whipper-ins—always boys. Whatever I did not learn from Dad, I learned from Jack. He taught us the most important attribute of a good hunt servant: to try to anticipate the huntsman's intentions and be in the right place at the crucial moment to turn hounds to him. I went over there as often as I could. Jack's face would light up when I arrived and he enjoyed the opportunity to discuss hounds and hunting. He seemed to know the run of every hare. Up on the moors a strong hare would take us miles: Jack would take short steps, we ran our hearts out, and yet at the first check, there was Jack!

Imagine my delight when Fr Gerard Sitwell, who was in charge of the ACB, appointed me second whipper-in. I was now on the first rung of the ladder. To my joy he also took me down to Peterborough Hound Show, the premier hound show in the United Kingdom. While we were having breakfast on the fast and shaky train, my cup of tea was spilling all over the place.

An elderly lady at our table said, "Young man, you will find that if you leave the teaspoon in your cup, the tea will not spill."

It works! I have passed that tip on to countless people down the years.

In the entered doghound class, our Drummer from Ampleforth was placed first. I do not think I have ever seen a better-looking hound before or since—he was nearly perfect. When the championship came up, for some strange reason, Drummer lost interest and sulked. We were in despair. The judges were about to put up another dog when suddenly Drummer transformed. Alert and on his toes, with his stern erect, straightaway, he was declared the undisputed champion. The crowd applauded explosively, I was in tears (as I am now writing this), and dear old Jack was ecstatic.

The following year we took the championship with Ringwood, an outstanding lemon and white dog. Many years later I was invited to judge the beagle bitches at Peterborough.

Ampleforth College Drummer 1936 was Peterborough Champion in 1938. As second whipper-in I was there and, with Jack Welch, ecstatic!

I said to my co-judge (who was a son of Robert Pawle, secretary of the Masters of Beagles Association), "The Ampleforth are the only beagles I have known. Please do not let me be biased."

Given that he liked the same type, Ampleforth swept the board. Fr Walter (who succeeded Fr Gerard) and Jack were over the moon—I was never invited again! Fr Walter was housemaster of St Cuthberts for many years, and probably the most popular housemaster ever. A knowledgeable hound and hunting man, he would follow the neighbouring foxhound packs whenever possible: we became lifelong friends.

Fortunately he had already gone to heaven when the school had to part with the pack. It would have broken his heart, but he had known it was to be. Happily the pack, now known as the "Old Ampleforth Beagles", is still going strong. Now kennelled with the Middleton foxhounds by kind arrangement with the Master, the pack is upholding a great tradition.

In my last couple of years in college, I was appointed Master of the ACB. What a thrill! Dad, proud of me, gave me a beautiful, small, lightweight hunting crop.

Always shy by nature, I remember well my nervousness at the opening meet. I was in charge of the large field of boys of the school and many local enthusiasts. Yet once hounds found, all butterflies left and I enjoyed my job.

Beagling is a great and necessary introduction to foxhunting. I reckon that everyone who intends to hunt should start with beagles. One learns to appreciate hound work, the lore of pure hunting, and the companionship of hounds. Moreover, one gets twice the enjoyment out of the sport.

A big wooden plaque is in the Long Passage in the college with the names of all the Masters; it was a title of honour. It was the Master's privilege to award hunt colours—an elegant and warm long-sleeved white jersey with dark and pale green trim—to those worthy of them. I awarded hunt colours to Owen Hare. It had become a tradition for the Master to win the point-to-point, a long

Thady, Master of Beagles, with Jack Welch, our brilliant kennel huntsman. A meet at Ampleforth Abbey, 1940.

cross-country race. I could run forever, but I had a limited top speed. In my turn I gave my all and Owen beat me by about fifty yards. I never forgave him!

In our hallway now hangs the mask of a hare killed on 20 February 1939 at Rudland Chapel, away out on the moors. It is a treasured memento awarded to me at the end of an epic run by John Smythe. Master of hounds in my earlier years, he was my idol in the school. It was he who awarded me my hunt colours. Sadly John was killed on active service when encouraging his troops in a charge with his hunting horn; he was known in the army as "Hunting Horn Smythe". His younger brother Julian was later my best man.

Ampleforth will always hold a special place in my heart. I have visited there several times over the years, and I hope to do so again. A treasured memory is the abundance of beautiful, heavy oak furniture throughout the old buildings. Notably the school library contains an immense long table with an adzed finish, as well as a multitude of handsome chairs backed and seated with leather. This fine furniture was handcrafted by the Thompson firm in Kilburn, a village not far from Ampleforth. Every piece has the trademark—a mouse—carved on it.

The magnificent Abbey Church has been completed, the old central building has been replaced, there are many more houses and a huge student roll. Even though all my masters (teachers) and many of my contemporaries have passed on, I still look on Ampleforth as my other home. The Benedictine ethos is as strong as ever and Thompson's mouse is still evident everywhere!

THREE

INITIATION TO MASTERSHIP IN THE 1940S

FIFTEEN

BACK TO THE SOIL

In retrospect I sometimes feel a twinge of guilt that I did not go into military service straight from college. As Ireland was a neutral country it was not compulsory for me to join up. Yet hundreds of Irish men and women did, including many of my friends from Ampleforth, a number of whom gave their lives. Like them, I had to make a decision. Dad's health was failing and he needed help, so I decided that my duty was to come home.

Because a couple of honours in my leaving certificate were no great help for farming (or hunting!), I felt I needed to attend an agricultural college even for a year at least. I put my name down for Glasnevin Agricultural College near Dublin. There were four hundred applicants for the forty vacancies that year. Irish was a compulsory subject in the entrance exam. I had not studied Irish since Killashee days so I was in trouble.

For several weeks in the evenings after work, I went to the Christian Brothers in the village of Hospital for a "grind". After a couple of weeks Br Isidore said I did not have a hope; the stumbling block would be the essay in Irish. But he had an inspiration. He got one of his top students to write an essay and took a guess at a title, "A Cycling Holiday". I learned the essay by heart. In the exam paper I spotted the Irish word for a bicycle. I closed my eyes, wrote out the essay—and passed in Irish. But I think I failed in maths. Maybe I should include this incident among my mortal sins (in chapter 27)! Anyway it did me no good.

Dad had a staff of about five men. Jim Finn, the head man, lived in Finn's Yard in a small, old cottage with mud walls and thatch covered with corrugated iron. Most of the old small farmhouses around the country were built in this style. The thick mud walls and thatch roof acted as first-class insulation, making the houses warm and comfortable. The thatch had to be maintained by adding more sea reed or hand-threshed wheaten straw. If it was allowed to deteriorate and leak, the mud walls would crumble.

In our hunting country we had two or three such houses. These were no longer occupied by people, but foxes lived under the corrugated sheeting in the thatch, an ideal shelter for them. One simply lobbed some stones on to the roof and the fox would bolt!

Bob Martin lived in a similar cottage in Grange—an adjoining twenty acres that Dad bought to give him a way out to the main road and Knocklong Station for loading cattle by rail. The other men lived in the area and cycled to work. Jim rang the bell in the yard at 9 A.M. to start the working day, at 1 P.M. for dinner hour and at 6 P.M. for the Angelus. Wages were 15 shillings per week for the men, while Jim got £1. Dad said that if all the wages reached £1, he would have to give up farming!

Limerick land, being heavy clay, all the dividing fences were double banks with a ditch each side. Into the ditches, field drains and ancient sod drains took the water. This entire system had been made by hand hundreds of years ago. At least one man was permanently employed keeping the ditches clean using spade, shovel, and a drag—mechanical diggers had not been invented.

Dad was a dry stock farmer. Quality shorthorn bullocks aged one-and-a-half to two years, known as "stirks", were brought in for the autumn, outwintered on high ground, "finished" on the spring grass, and sold in May or June. While the best were sold for beef, the majority were forward stores for the English market. They went by rail and ship to Birkenhead, where they were bought by big farmers and stall fed to slaughter condition. Dad liked to buy in Co. Clare. The Clare farmers bought most of their calves from the dairy herds in Co. Limerick and reared them on their sound limestone land for a year or more. The result was good cattle with great bone.

Traditionally, cattle were sold "by hand" in the cattle fairs held in the streets of local towns. There were also several good horse fairs around the country, the best known being Cahirmee in Co. Cork and Ballinasloe in Co. Galway. Many a famous showjumper or eventer was picked up at the horse fairs. They usually had a good selection of long-tails, that is, two- or three-year-olds very much in the rough, never handled, with just a rope halter tying them to the paling. The country was full of quality hunter-type mares that did the light work on the farm, took the milk to the creamery, the family to Mass on Sundays, and once or twice a week would carry their owner to hounds. These were bred to good thoroughbred sires and produced the world-renowned Irish hunter. They were the backbone of the sporthorse breeding industry.

Horse fair in Main Street, Tipperary. Many a famous show jumper or eventer was discovered at the horse fairs.

Nowadays the pool of breeding stock is greatly reduced and the average quality of stock coming to the fairs is low. If you see a good horse in the fair, in hand, or under saddle, you automatically ask yourself, "I wonder what is wrong with that one?"

Ballinasloe and Cahirmee remain the great annual gatherings of the travelling people (who do not like to be called "tinkers").

Our best local cattle fair was in Tipperary town on the second Tuesday of every month. On Monday we would select one or two wagons (nine or eighteen head) of evenly matched cattle, then at 2 A.M. on Tuesday I would help our two men to put them on the road. They took about four hours to walk the eleven miles to Tipperary Fair, which started at 6 A.M. I would tackle up our good driving cob and tub trap, drive with Dad to town and put the cob in Donovan's yard at the top of Henry Street. With luck we would be in time to get a good stand for the cattle on the pavement, near the one and only street lamp at the main crossroads, from where one street leads past the Royal Hotel to the station.

Picture the scene at 6 A.M. The main street of Tipperary was chock-a-block with cattle. Most of them had walked long distances and were happy to stand in their groups. The dealers would move through the fair, working fast because of competition. Among the great characters, Denny Gould from Charleville was one of the best known and had a sense of humour. Whenever he started a deal, a crowd would gather, partly to find out what the current value of the cattle was and partly for entertainment. The deal would go something like this:

Denny: "What do you want for your cattle?"

Farmer: "I won't take less than £30 a head."

Denny: "They are not worth half that. They haven't seen a decent bit of grub since the day they were born. I'll give you £20."

Farmer: "No, I won't take it."

Denny writes a docket with the price and tries to force it into the seller's hands.

Farmer: "No, I tell you, I won't."

Then a bystander comes into the fray. "Divide the tenner, Mr Gould. That'll be the price."

Both men say, "No."

Denny tears up the ticket and struts away in apparent disgust, but gives the odd look back to see if there is any change of mind.

Bystander: "Come back, Mr Gould, he will take it."

So back comes Denny and writes another ticket for £30.

Farmer: "No."

After a bit more haggling (the farmer is desperate to sell and Denny wants those cattle), the asking price is lowered to £25. Still no move from Denny.

"Come on Mr Gould, do as I say and divide", says the bystander and he takes Denny's right hand and the farmer's right hand and tries to get them to shake hands. "Don't break my word, the two of you."

They both agree finally and the deal is done to cheers from the onlookers.

Then there's the luck penny. It is an old Irish custom on these occasions for the seller to give some silver money to the buyer to "make the cattle lucky". Sometimes there's another deal to decide how much!

After the buyer puts a scissors mark on each beast, they are driven through the mass of cattle, causing bedlam accompanied by shouts, sticks, and choice language. Down at the station the buyer's agent loads them into the wagons. And so the fair progresses until most stock are sold.

Dad and I would have breakfast at The Royal, which was owned by Jerry McCormack (he comes into the story again: see chapter 25). By arrangement the dealers would meet the sellers at the bank at 10 A.M. and pay in cash. I can still see Denny on the steps of the bank, his pockets bulging with rolls of £100 notes. No security men needed, God be with the days!

The last beasts to be sold were the bulls. When I started a dairy herd later, I needed a bull for some late calvers. There was a fine two- or three-year old red shorthorn on the pavement. The rope from his ring led into Kiely's Bar. I followed the rope and found my man having a pint. With the help of his friends, we made the deal and Tom Downey led him home to Scarteen. Tom, a regular drover, must have walked thousands of miles in his long life. He died recently, just short of his 101st birthday—what a recipe for long living!

About midday the council workmen would hose down the streets, shopkeepers would wash their section of the pavement and take down the specially made wooden frames that protected their windows, and the "party" was over for another month. Primitive? Maybe, but fairs stood the test of time. A drawback was that one had to get out to several fairs for a week before selling to find out what one's cattle were worth. On the other hand, a bonus for the dealers and farmers was that their day's work was done by 11 A.M. Nowadays cattle markets go on all day, albeit in a little more comfort.

There was great excitement in Tipperary Fair one morning. The first Hereford-cross cattle to be seen in the country were for sale outside the Bank of Ireland at the top of the town. Everybody had to go and see "the cattle with the white faces". But the old men were saying, "Ah, they'll never take the place of the shorthorn." How wrong they were. Shorthorn cattle in Ireland now are as scarce as hens' teeth.

But cattle marts had to come. In due course, a group of farmers got together and decided to organise a cooperative mart in Kilmallock. With a site purchased alongside the station, a number of us travelled the country soliciting shares in the venture. I worked with a neighbour, Captain Bourke (he had served in the Free State Army), and we were successful. When we approached one big landowner, he declined, stating, "Thady, you are wasting your time; you will never get the fairs off the streets." He was proved wrong; in a few short years the Golden Vale Co-op Mart was flourishing and is now one of the biggest in the south of Ireland.

With petrol severely rationed during the war, only the clergy, doctors, and taxi drivers could get an allowance. Travelling as a group helped spread the cost of a taxi. I needed a bunch of heifers for my small dairy herd, so I joined Jack Finnan (a dairy farmer near Mooresfort and a sound judge of cattle), his friend and big Jim Carroll of Kilross. We crammed into John Cogan's Ford Prefect taxi and set off for Ennistymon in the heart of Co. Clare for the fair the following day.

The well-known Falls Hotel was booked out. Jack knew someone who had a pub and some spare rooms in Lisdoonvarna. Entering by the back door we stumbled over two chaps drunk and fast asleep. I said, "Jack, I'm not staying here", so we drove on to Lahinch, a picturesque seaside town that has one of the top golf links in Ireland. We were in luck. I shared a room with big Jim, but I got little sleep—you could hear him snoring from here!

The old West Clare Railway—immortalised in one of Percy French's songs—was operating, but it had one big drawback. The gauge was narrower than that of the other companies, so one had to take out the cattle in Ennis and reload them into the regular trains. A wild bullock escaped off down the track one time and I had a helluva job to get him back.

The story is told of an American tourist travelling in the west of Ireland. The train stopped out in the country for no obvious reason.

When the ticket checker was passing through, the American asked him, "Why are we stopped away out here?"

"Oh, there's a cow on the line, sir."

The train carried on. Half an hour later it stopped again. The American asked the checker again, "Say, what are we stopped for this time?"

"Oh, there's a cow on the line."

"What, another damn cow?"

"No sir, 'tis the same cow!"

The one job on the farm that I hated was dehorning. Bullocks destined as forward stores for the English market were worth far more if they were without horns so that they would not damage themselves in the fattening years. Correctly speaking, they should have been dehorned as young calves using a special caustic stick—this is the practice nowadays for the nonpolled breeds—but inevitably the majority had not been done. The standard procedure was to catch the bullock in the pen, rope his legs and throw him, tying all four legs tight together. One man would sit on his head while another cut off the horns with a sharp tenon saw. If bleeding was severe, a handful of cobwebs was clamped on the cut surface; if this was insufficient, the vein had to be constricted. I did the sawing because I would do it fast to reduce the pain. Then the beast was released. No anaesthetic was used, although I believe that the beast was less sensitive to the pain because he was so traumatised by the restriction of the ropes. However I relate the story against myself. It was cruel and I look back on it with disgust.

Some years later I leased a winterage on the Burren in Co. Clare. The Burren is unique—the whole area is almost completely limestone rock. Because the rock maintains the heat of the summer and is close to the sea and the Gulf Stream, it escapes any frost, and snow does not lie. For this reason a multitude of rare flowers flourish in the clefts, attracting botanists from all over the world. Over the centuries the rock has eroded vertically, yielding deep crevasses, and horizontally, creating huge flat slabs that rock as you walk on them. With its density of hazel bushes the Burren was also famous for woodcock—dangerous shooting on the rough rocks. Do visit the Burren in the spring—you will be amazed.

Areas of this strange landscape are left undergrazed through the summer, so the grass will be plentiful through the winter. Jerry McMahon, the auctioneer in Ennis, introduced me to Francie Caher. Francie owned a big portion of the Burren, and used to lease most of it to the Brutons, big farmers in Co. Meath. A bachelor, he lived alone in a little isolated cottage away among the rocks. Standing about six feet six inches, he had to stoop to come through the door. Dark and severe-looking with a big scar over one eye from fighting, he was an imposing sight. Every year he would take a week's holiday at Lisdoonvarna—a great place to find a spouse, but he never succeeded! We soon made a deal for leasing the winterage and became firm friends.

Claude Thompson, my brother-in-law, came with me. We bought eighty big three-year-old bullocks at about ten hundredweight (the winterage suited aged cattle only) in Loughrea, Ballinasloe and other fairs, as well as a number direct off the farms. Coras Iompair Eireann (the railway company), which had a monopoly on road transport, delivered the cattle. I was scared that these big bullocks would break their legs in the crevasses in the rock, but we never had any worries. They needed no forage and came off the winterage almost fat. Tim Murphy of Cork, who was a big cattle dealer, and later his son Noel bought a lot of cattle from us. Unfortunately the cost of transport eroded any profit, so I gave up the venture after a couple of years, but I still love the Burren.

DAIRY FARMING

As money was coming in too slowly, I decided to try milking. We had the long, old cowshed in the farmyard, which I refitted with wooden "bails" and neck chains so that it held thirty cows. I bought good-quality shorthorn in-calf heifers in the monthly dairy auctions in Tipperary and elsewhere. It was a spring calving herd. We milked in the shed until the grass was ready in April, then we milked in the corner of a field; this had been the custom in the area for years.

My cowman Tom Carroll milked ten of the cows. Tom was a real old-time milker and never without a quid of tobacco in his mouth. He had some wonderful expressions.

Each cow had the name of a flower—no ear tags then. Dad asked Tom one day at milking time, "What is that cow's name?"

Tom replied, "Oh, I don't know, sir, you'd want to be a bloody gardener to know all their names."

Another time I said, "Tom, Buttercup is down in her yield today. What do you think is wrong?"

"Och, nothing serious, sir, I think she has only swallowed a shnail."

If a cow or calf was sick and on the way out, Tom would say, "If she die she'll die and if she don't she won't!"

Mrs Fogarty and Mrs O'Dea milked the other twenty cows, ten each. Mary Fogarty was a tall, powerful Amazon of a woman. She and her husband, JJ, had fourteen children in a small cottage by Castlejane bridge; I think two drowned in the small river.

I asked Tom one morning "Where is Mary, she is not in?"

"Oh, she's having a baby, she'll be back tomorrow" and she was! I never twigged it!

In the cowshed Mary Fogarty was an overstrong milker. She used to strip the teats too forcefully with the result that we had endless trouble with spindles—damage to the teat canals. By contrast, Mrs O'Dea from the Cross of the Tree was a quiet, gentle person and a soft milker. She used to sing "The Boston Burglar" endlessly to keep the cows happy.

I stood in and milked for the others when necessary, but my fingers would get cramped! Peony, a beautiful red-roan with a perfect udder, was one of my favourites of the herd. I bought her from one of the best-known heifer dealers, Jimmy Starr of Nenagh.

I had one bad spell. Brucellosis, every dairy farmer's nightmare, was spreading through the country and the vaccine was not dependable. I dreaded coming down to the cowshed every morning to see how many cows had aborted. I used to implore my vet William Baker to stop the epidemic, but of course there was no cure. It was agonising.

While the milking went on, Denis, the white pony, stood close by. He was tackled to the cart with the heavy twenty-gallon tankards on board. After milking and a cup of tea, Tom would drive him the mile-and-a-half to Knockcarron Creamery, one of seven branches of Knocklong. There the milk was separated, and the cream was taken to Knocklong for butter making. Tom would bring home the skim for calves and pigs.

To weed out the poorer cows, I joined the Cow Testing Association. Michael Donovan called once a month, morning and evening, to take milk samples from all individual cows and test them for butterfat. He told me about a problem that had faced one of his clients, a small farmer of ten cows who took his milk to the creamery with a donkey and cart. The average test from Michael's calculation was away above the test that the farmer got from the creamery. He used to stand the milk churns with the night's milk in a small stream that ran through his yard, to keep the milk cool. Michael turned up one morning to find that the donkey, who was free in the yard, was putting his nose into each churn and drinking the cream off. With that discovery, the problem was solved!

Paddy Callaghan near Kilfrush had a few cows. He trained his donkey to deliver the milk on his own. After Paddy put him on the road, the donkey travelled along the left verge about one-and-a-half miles to Knocklong Creamery. The lads there would empty the fifteen-gallon churns into the tank and put the donkey on his road home again.

At the creamery the Downes sisters had the job of weighing out the individual one-pound lots of butter, wrapping them in butter paper, and packing them in boxes—all by hand. Knocklong Butter won prizes all over the country. Old Ned Dwyer, closely involved in all parish functions and extremely popular, was a senior member of the staff and a real gentleman. In his early years in the creamery, when it was owned by the Cleeves Dairy Company, they made buttons from casein. He was proud of the one he still had as a souvenir.

The creamery held an important place in Irish country life. As well as being a valuable source of employment, it provided a precious social occasion for neighbours to meet each other, enjoy a pipe and a chat, and share all their news. It dictated the easygoing pace of life in our part of the country. Time-consuming? Maybe, but it was time well spent. As the old saying has it, "All work and no joy makes Jack a dull boy."

The creamery company with its seven branches also generously sponsored many activities in the area including Knocklong Gymkhana. I started the gymkhana, the first in the area, in Ned's time. As the gymkhana became famous, horses came to it from all over Ireland. We made some good-quality jumps. One was a solid and imposing red brick wall in timber; it had two rows of wooden "bricks" on top.

Dundrum, just about 14.3 hands, was a famous Connemara cob at the time. He represented Ireland to win the Aga Khan Team Trophy in Dublin several times. In the puissance at Wembley, his owner-rider Tommy Wade first rode him under the seven-feet, two-inch fence, then came back and jumped it clear. Tommy always supported Knocklong Gymkhana, but Dundrum knew that those bricks were light and he invariably knocked one for four faults. Poor Tommy never won a competition and would come away furious. All the same the pair were extremely popular and always drew a crowd.

We always had side shows and fun-and-games (an essential part of a true gymkhana to entertain the crowd; pure showjumping on its own can be boring). One year I arranged a mock battle. Two armies of about eight riders wore tall conical paper hats and, as swords, carried rolls of newspaper. At a signal they galloped forward in line abreast and charged through the enemy line, knocking off their opponents' hats, if possible. The battle was repeated until one soldier survived with his hat on. "By arrangement", I was the second-last man to fight, and my adversary knocked me off my horse. I fell to the ground "dead". The Red Cross rushed out with a stretcher (the young assistants thought it was real). In the deathly hush an old man ran out from the crowd shouting, "Oh, Master Thady, Master Thady, are you hurt?" I jumped off the stretcher and ran away!

We had an obstacle race at one sports day. In one part of the race the competitors had to carry a lighted candle: one chap held the candle under his shirt and the hair on his chest caught fire! The hunt ran a successful gymkhana in Tipperary Showgrounds. When we advertised a pig-sticking competition, there was consternation. But the two contestants were armed with household mops, one with blue paint and the other with red. The first rider to mark the pig was the winner of that bout. Have you ever tried to ride close to a galloping, grunting pig? It was hilarious!

Eventually I enlarged my herd, installed a milking machine, and employed a super, young farmer who had been through Pallaskenry Agricultural College, near Limerick. Arthur Finnan was a nephew of Jack Finnan and we got on great.

We had one traumatic experience. It was winter and dark. On our way down to a farmer's meeting in Fermoy, we were approaching Mitchelstown on the last straight stretch of road. I could see there was trouble ahead, possibly a smash. A horse and hay cart galloped wildly past us. I dipped the lights and slowed down. We then saw a Volkswagen car with poor lights swerve across the road and land in the ditch. Stopping, we got out and ran forward. In complete darkness, we could only work by feel and found only a driver who was choking and fighting for breath, unconscious, with blood everywhere. Without really knowing what I was doing, I caught hold of the poor chap's tongue and pulled it forward. He started to breathe again.

A crowd gathered, a doctor and priest were summoned, but no ambulance was available. I offered to take him to Mallow Hospital about half an hour away. We pushed the passenger seat back and lifted him in carefully. His face looked badly smashed, but the doctor on the scene could do nothing for him. Arthur and I got him safely to the hospital, and we drove on to our meeting.

Many tragedies have a lighter side, including this one. The next morning the hospital phoned, asking by any chance, did I see the poor chap's dentures? They would be a help in rebuilding his broken mouth. I said I would ring them back. I pushed the car seat back and there they were.

The accident had occurred because the hay cart had no reflectors or lights, the car lights were poor, and the car crashed into the cart. The long extended shafts went through the windscreen and smashed the driver's face. However, the story had a happy ending. As Christmas approached I got a letter from the Casey family—please would I call in. They had a small shop in the main street. I called and found Mr Casey alive and well, if a bit disfigured. The family were overcome with gratitude and presented me with a beautiful turkey for Christmas.

TILLAGE

Flour, like many other essentials, was scarce during the war. None could be imported on account of the U-boats, so Ireland had to grow its own. With our wet climate the flour was poor quality, but better than none. The government made it compulsory for every farmer to till a portion of his land.

County Limerick, based in heavy clay and traditionally outstanding grazing land, had never been broken. Pakie Neill in Emly had the only tractor in our area, an early Fordson, for which he got a good ration of tractor vaporising oil (TVO, similar to paraffin or kerosene). We got him to plough the bawn (old pasture) land, a tough sod with a density of grass roots. I bought a four-foot spring tooth harrow to which we tackled a pair of our hunters. I was forever making new swings, as the hunters had no patience and would lunge forward and break the timber swings.

Johnny Ryan (no relation) was one of the many casual labourers who worked at Scarteen. Known as "the Moocher" he drove the team. Although they walked fast and Johnny must have travelled hundreds of miles, he loved the job. The harrow would bounce off the tough sods with little effect. It took about five runs on the length and a couple across to create enough tilth to cover the seed. A bonus was that the horses were more than half fit for the following hunting season.

Before I got a corn drill, the seed was sown by hand with the fiddle and covered with the grass harrow. The land was naturally rich and did not need artificial fertiliser. I am reminded of the two farmers travelling in a bus. A gorgeous blonde gets in an' she, heavily powdered and painted, lipstick an' all, sits across from them.

Paddy says to his pal, "Eh!, what do you make of that one?"

Mick takes a good look and replies, "I don't know, but it must be mighty poor land that needs all that top-dressing!"

The corn was cut with the horses and Deering mower going one way only when the corn was lodged. It was then taken out by hand into sheaves, which were bound with the straw—back-breaking work. A busload of soldiers from Limerick Barracks came out to give some much-appreciated help. However, after big problems with thistles caused a "mutiny", that source of help dried up.

Dad said, "If they cannot face thistles, what will they do if they have to face bullets?"

The sheaves were stooked, then hand-stacked. After a few weeks to season, they were brought in to the farmyard and stacked in two large, long ricks that ran in parallel, leaving enough space for the threshing mill. Hales' big steam threshing outfit from Co. Cork had to be booked well in advance. In readiness a huge pile of timber was logged; old whitethorn bushes gave the best heat.

Eventually I got my first tractor, from McCarthy's in Charleville. It was a second-hand little TVO Ferguson 20, steel wheels behind and rubber tyres in front—a little gem. Harry Ferguson's hydraulic lift revolutionised farm machinery, but dealt a body-blow to the Irish hunter breeding. The Fergy took the place of the working-and-breeding mare on the farms; worse still, the young generation of farmers changed from being horse handlers to mechanics!

Soon most of our machinery was adapted to tractor power. Then one day I got a sobering lesson. I had replaced the pole on the mower with a tractor hitch. After a period of broken weather, Sunday turned out fine. I thought I had better cut the meadow, although my choice of day worried Dad. I had hardly opened the meadow (cut the first swath) when the shaft broke in pieces. Dad was right. Sunday was God's day. I abandoned the job in shame.

Then the big day arrived. The large steam traction engine lumbered and chuffed its way into the yard and was lined up with the mill, then away she went. The groaning and soughing of the big Ransomes Mill summoned help from all the neighbours. I think many came for the crack and the grub (and Guinness!). Mum was wonderful, feeding up to thirty men for the two or three days.

The oats were stored in the lofts above the stables, where it had to be turned by hand daily to keep it "sweet". The wheat went by lorry to Ranks Mills on Limerick's Docks. The mill workers were awesome. Small and muscular, they humped the twenty-stone bags from the lorry to the bin as if they were matchboxes!

The threshing was a great social occasion—hard work enjoyed by all. Tillage and harvesting were a pleasure (in fair weather!). Ploughing the stubble land with the little Fergy was my favourite task, always trying to turn the perfect sod; I worked late into the night when the moon was full.

Mick Hammersley, a dairy farmer near Lattin village, used to help Dad catch the wild deer. Loving his hunting, he must have "walked" a whole pack of hound puppies over the years—a practice his son James and his lovely wife have carried on.

When compulsory tillage was started, Mick held out against it for as long as he could: "Tis a sin to break this good grazing land." Eventually he had to give in. He said, "Well I'll redden it anyway for them." That was as far as he went!

His farm was crowded with horses—old thoroughbreds and retired hunters. I asked him one day why he kept so many. "Ah, just relics of old dacency" was his reply. He tried for years to get his son James keen on horses, and begged me to help. Instead I sold James my old army jeep and, being mechanically minded, he got it going great.

Well, Mick was fit to eat me: "What in the name of fortune did you think you were doing!"

The following winter was a rough one. When I met Mick after Christmas, he said, "That yoke you sold to James is the best thing that ever came into the place. I can drive it all over the farm and fodder the horses and cattle whatever the weather." We were friends again!

SIXTEEN

CUPID STRIKES A NEW TARGET

Cupid loosed off several arrows in my direction. Most were well off their mark, but he had one near miss. Trish Lambert was a delightful, attractive girl. I visited her several times in her beautiful home Dysertmore, not far from New Ross in Co. Wexford, and she visited Scarteen. After the flame of love burned brightly for a while, inexplicably it weakened and burned out. Later she married a Scandinavian, but they had no family. Tragically she became ill and died at a young age.

Lord Donoughmore was Master of the Tipperary hounds for several seasons. He kindly mounted Tony Villiers (my amateur whip at the time) and myself for a day with "the Tipps". We had a good run in the evening and hounds marked to ground at the back of the Furry Hills near Cashel. A tall lady—I recognised her as Miss Armitage but I did not know her personally—turned to ride home towards Killenaule. Accompanying her was a charming blonde girl who caught my eye; the memory haunted me for several days.

Hunt dance, Cappawhite, 1949. I score a bull! My first meeting with Anne. Front row: Pam Manning, Gwen Ryan, Irene Nowak (a friend from Austria), Doaty Ryan (South Africa), Anne Peter (New Zealand), Rosie Villiers. Back row: Tony Villiers (amateur whippper-in), me, Sir Morgan O'Connell, Arthur G. Ryan, John Ryan-Purcell, Grania Cazenove, unknown. Parkview photo

Shortly after, we had a Scarteen Hunt Dance in Cappawhite. My distant cousin Arthur Ryan of Inch (near Thurles) brought a party, with "my girl" as his partner. This was his big mistake; Cupid had scored a bull!

The Armitages of Noan were cousins of Anne Peter's family in New Zealand. The two unmarried sisters Doris and Nello lived with their father Fred Armitage on more than one thousand acres near Killenaule, and were passionate about horses and hunting. Nello bred some outstanding steeplechasers. They gave Anne a present of a season's hunting with the Co. Tipperary hounds. It was near the close of that season that we met. She decided to stay on for a second season: she has always insisted that it was the hunting that influenced her decision, but I like to think that I had just a small influence in it, too!

Anne was descended from the Petres, an old titled Catholic family in the south of England. The present Baron Petre still resides in the original family home. In the mid–eighteenth century one of the family moved to Scotland, where he was involved in a textile company. He became a staunch Anglican and changed his name to Peter.

In 1848 a son of his, William, emigrated to South Australia at the age of nineteen years and took up some land adjoining the Burra Burra Copper Mining company near Adelaide. He married Jane Seymour from Ballymore Castle in Co. Galway; yet when fire destroyed their home, Anama, all records were lost. With their six children, they moved to New Zealand, taking up land in the South Island province of Canterbury. The property was eventually divided among the family. In company with many other farming families, the Great Depression of the early 1930s hit them hard. One of the family, John Peter, was Anne's father.

My early courtship was not easy. Doris and Nello were allowed to have Anne to stay on condition that she would be returned to New Zealand whole and single. Now they were in deep trouble! On my early visits there I got a cold reception. The sisters made it quite clear to me that this was not on, I must break off my relationship with Anne. But of course their opposition made me all the more determined. To complicate matters, they had a delightful housekeeper, Winnie Grey, who had become a bosom friend of Anne's. With a mischievous twinkle in her eye, Winnie would corner me into embarrassing situations with Doris and Nello whenever possible just for pure mischief. Working in my favour was that I got on well with old Mr Armitage. Not only was he amused by the developments, he was also on my side.

A further complication was the question of religion. The Armitages were staunch and dedicated members of the Anglican church, as were Anne's family. For their faith and commitment I greatly admired them, but of course my family was Catholic. In those days there was still unfortunate bigotry on both sides—a factor which regrettably has been at the root of so much trouble in Ireland. I look back on it with a sense of shame. It was so un-Christian.

My Mum and Dad had not known the Armitages previously. To try to "help matters" they invited Doris and Nello to dinner.

"Now," the sisters thought, "this is our opportunity to persuade Thady's parents to get him to break off the whole affair."

Unexpectedly their defence was shattered. They were bowled over by Mum and Dad, became excellent friends, and warmly accepted me from then on!

After Anne came to stay at Scarteen and hunt with us, she rapidly became a favourite among my family.

One day I said to my father, "Dad, I am thinking of asking Anne to be my wife. How would you feel about it?"

I shall never forget his reply: "Lad, if I was in the running, you would not stand a chance!"

Kilfeacle Church beyond Tipperary holds a warm spot in my heart. On my various visits to Noan I used to call in there to pray for guidance to do God's Holy Will and ask Him to bless our union.

Anne returned home to New Zealand. She was faced with the tough challenge, all on her own, of reassuring her family. Fortunately there was a precedent. Anne's older cousin Sheila Howell had married an Irishman and popular veterinarian, Harry Langley, who had never visited his wife's home country. They had settled in Archerstown, near Thurles, where Harry's family had farmed for generations. Harry himself was a leading Hereford breeder. He and I became great friends.

He used to taunt me by saying, "You will never be accepted by the aunts!" Anne's mother had five sisters, almost all were six foot, and together they were a formidable band.

I would retort, "You did not have the courage to face them. At least I am going out to have a go!"

Letters took a painfully long time to travel. Two years slipped by slowly. I'm reminded of the story of Pat and Mary. Friends from school days, they had been 'walking out' for years and were now getting long in the tooth.

One day, Pat sez to Mary, "D'ye know, Mary", sez he, "they are sayin' we ought to get married."

"Arah Pat", sez she, "is it outer yer mind ye are. 'Shure who'd marry us?"

It is said that "Absence makes the heart grow fonder". Anne and I surely put that to the test. My favourite song in those days ran:

> Beloved be faithful, Beloved be true,
> Though I am away, Dear, I trust in you.
> I'll never forsake you though we are apart.
> Beloved be faithful to my faithful heart.

During those two long years of waiting, one meet was at Limerick Junction. We got away from Ballykisteen Covert in a great hurry. There was a barbed wire fence across Jim Stapleton's big field with a gate at the far end. I was riding Woodcock, who would jump anything. The field went for the gate, but I decided to chance the wire. We cleared it and raced on.

Ann Grubb, one of our regular followers spotted me. Not to be outdone, she followed me. We crossed the Ballygodoon road and swung sharp right and over a cut and laid fence into plough. I had not seen the wire in it; Woodcock and I took a helluva fall. Nothing broken, but shoulder ligaments badly torn. I lay in agony, screaming like a stuck pig. Ann Grubb rode on!

Betty Howell, Anne's first cousin, was staying at Noan. A trained physio, she kindly came to stay at Scarteen and gave me treatment. If I had not already met Anne, Betty might have become Mrs Ryan!

Finally I took the plunge. I left Scarteen laden with love and prayers from all the family. Claude Thompson would hunt hounds in my absence for the final few weeks of the season.

The first adventure was getting to New Zealand. Flying was financially way beyond my reach. Instead I boarded the small liner, the *M. V. Rangitane* of the New Zealand Shipping Line, in Tilbury Docks. We sailed down the Thames and out to sea on the most important journey of my life. We were to travel on the shortest route possible, through the Panama Canal. Even then it was to be five weeks completely cut off from the rest of the world. There was no turning back now.

Life on board was most enjoyable. I was allotted a seat at the table of the purser, Mr Maugham. With us too were a young couple, the Springfields, who were just married and emigrating to New Zealand. Although on occasions he could let his hair down, Mr Maugham was a strict disciplinarian. On St Patrick's Day one of the young dining room stewards was displaying some green shamrock decoration on the lapel of his uniform. Mr Maugham called him up and ordered him to "remove that stuff" at once. I bristled with rage! But he explained that no decorations (other than medals) are allowed to be worn on uniforms. The young lad blushed with embarrassment.

General Sir W. Madden and his wife were also on board. He was returning I believe to take command of the New Zealand Armed Forces. The couple were seated at the captain's table for dinner on an evening when the sea was a bit rough. The young steward was serving the soup, the ship lurched, and the poor lad spilt the soup down Lady Madden's neck. She was not amused, but the rest of us had difficulty in suppressing our laughter. The poor steward was just about court-martialled!

On a long voyage it is essential to take serious exercise, otherwise one would become gross from the excellent food. I pal'ed up with a nice Kiwi (as New Zealanders are sometimes called), Don Ross. He travelled a lot for his family firm of wool merchants, Ross and Glendenning, based in Dunedin. Every morning, we would have an energetic game of deck quoits, then a shower, a dip in the pool, and a beer before lunch.

It was a thrill to see our first albatross—what amazing birds. The Panama Canal is a wonderful engineering experience. Going through it one can almost touch the sides of the locks. When we anchored off Pitcairn Island for a few hours, the inhabitants rowed out to us in small boats. They came on board with their wares—beautifully carved wooden artifacts, along with fresh fruit: the small, true bananas straight off the tree were scrumptious.

Then Auckland, New Zealand. Could it be true?

There was still some travelling to do, however. I went down by train to Wellington at the bottom of the North Island. There my darling Anne was waiting for me—it was such ecstatic joy to be with her again. Together we travelled to the South Island on the ferry (what a difference from the *Rangitane*!).

Sure enough the "formidable" aunts met us on the wharf. Yet the ice (if there was any) was quickly broken and we got on great. I fell for Anne's dear mother in a big way. She was just wonderful, like my own mother. She asked me what I would be happy to call her. Without hesitation I said, "Mum". She was overjoyed!

Anne's dear father was pushing on in years and for a while he found it hard to accept me. He had one son from his previous marriage, Geoff, who, together with his wife Sybil, made me feel welcome. Anne was the only child of John Peter's second marriage, which took place after his first wife died and he retired from farming. John and Norah (née Hinds-Howell) settled happily in Orari Road, Geraldine, a small town in rural Canterbury. Anne took to hunting and competed successfully in point-to-points and horse shows around the country.

I soon felt happy in their family home in Orari Road. Anne and I got down to some serious hunting—hares, only because foxes have never been introduced to New Zealand. Anne used to look after Ian Ritchie's horses. Ian, who, along with his wife Annette, was like family, arranged for me to have a seasoned hunter and part Clyde called Ben. On my first hunt we jumped wire on to a road in front of all the car followers who had come out to see a "real live MFH". After I put Ben at the regular seven-strand barbed wire off the road, without any warning at the very last moment, he ducked down the road. Of course I went on, but did not quite clear the fence, and tore my brand new hunt coat in shreds. Cheers from the onlookers: "He is human after all. He'll do!"

Looking through the regular hunters (known as "hacks" in New Zealand), I was lonesome for our big, quality three-quarter bred Irish hunters that we had at home. I resolved that, if ever the occasion arose, I would do something about it. The only source of strength among New Zealand horses was the Clyde.

Hunting in New Zealand, although totally different from at home, is still good fun. The wire fences are taken at a gallop, and falls are frequent. Because of the pace and the hard ground, there are also more bones broken. It is very much a sociable sport. At the end of the day horses are tied to their floats (trailers) and boxes with a haynet handy, and all the riders and car followers pool their picnic lunches and enjoy a party, often in warm sunshine, against the most beautiful backdrop of snow-capped mountains.

On that first visit we did a brief tour of the North Island; later we did the South Island. Plans for the wedding also took shape. Anne's first cousin Betty Howell (the one who had tended me in Ireland in my hour of need) was to be her bridesmaid. By good fortune Julian Smythe from Ampleforth days (brother of Hunting Horn Smythe) had settled with his wife and family in New Zealand and he was delighted to be my best man.

After all preparations were made, on 15 June 1953 Anne and I were married in the beautiful Sacred Heart Basilica in Timaru by Fr Daly, parish priest of Geraldine. To our great delight outside the church after the ceremony, we were met by the South Canterbury hounds—a lovely surprise!

The next few weeks passed all too quickly. I was getting fond of this beautiful country and its charming people, but home was beckoning strongly with a pack of hounds to hunt.

Boarding that grand old liner, the *Dominion Monarch*, in Auckland, we set sail for home. As this was to be part of our honeymoon, we chose the longest route possible via South Africa. Little did we guess that about thirty years later we would be back in this great little country for keeps.

Wow—the Tasman Sea over to Australia was rough! On a couple of occasions Anne and the captain were the only ones down for breakfast (my hereditary tendency for seasickness would not see me among them). Melbourne was our first port of call. We were met on the wharf by the Ardlie sisters, two elderly cousins of mine who were overjoyed to meet someone from Scarteen. Ag was waving a fox's pad (that Dad had sent them years before as a souvenir) so that we would recognise them. They took us sightseeing, but the six hours were all too short. On the way back to the ship, we got lost. When we finally found it, the last gang plank was being raised and the loudspeaker was blaring, "Has anyone seen Mr and Mrs Ryan?"

A brief stop at Fremantle, then fourteen days on the Indian Ocean—little sun, wet weather, and choppy seas. We were glad to reach Cape Town and its spectacular Table Mountain. Here we were greeted by Cousin Gwen (Uncle Hugh's daughter). With her husband Bob Devenish she had come all the way from Knysna in the east to spend the two days with us. In that time they took us on some fabulous scenic trips. We were tempted to accept an invitation to visit my cousins in Kenya and fly home, but time and cash were too scarce.

On then through the heat of the tropics and into the northern hemisphere. We had a brief stop in Las Palmas, where we saw the sculpture of "our hounds" in the market place. And so to London, where Anne boarded the train with our baggage, while I went to make a phone call. When I came out from the phone, box the crowded train had left!

"Has anyone seen Thady?" Anne asked up and down the train.

One friend who had been with us on the ship said to her jokingly, "Don't you know an Irishman. As soon as he touched land he gave you the slip!"

I asked the station master to phone his opposite number in Paddington. There, to the great amusement of our shipboard friends, it was announced over the public address system that Thady Ryan was coming on the next train. In the milling crowd, we finally found each other, thank God!

We crossed from Fishguard to Cork, where a car awaited us. The plan was to drive to Charleville Station, board the train and arrive in Knocklong Station yard to a "state reception". But we had a puncture and missed the connection. The train pulled into Knocklong, alongside the huge crowd with the hounds wild with excitement. Then the train pulled out again—no bridal couple! Just as the crowd was about to disperse, we drove into the station yard with the carhorn blazing. A tumultuous reception! We climbed into the big old "dog-cart" bedecked with flowers and with Keith Reynolds' trusty black hunter Matt in the shafts. We drove home in state.

After three months' absence it was wonderful to be home with my beloved, and to catch up with all our family and friends. Dad and Mum were living in the front of the house, with the pantry as their kitchen. Anne and I took over the rear portion, complete with six bedrooms, cosy sitting room, other spare rooms, the large kitchen with an Aga cooker, and the small family oratory, where we had Mass occasionally when a priest was available.

And so my life started a new chapter. I was no longer on my own. My wife was at my side.

SEVENTEEN

INTO HARNESS I

Dear Dad had ongoing heart problems. On 16 December 1954 in his eighty-fourth year, they finally caught up with him.

How I missed Dad. He was a shy man and avoided publicity when he could, yet he was immensely popular throughout Scarteen Hunt country. I never heard him use bad language. Out hunting if someone barged into him on a bank he would call out, "We'll meet in heaven, please God!" Even during a hunt, if he had occasion to speak to a farmer when galloping through his yard, or maybe the farmer was upset because his cows were frightened or whatever, Dad would dismount to talk to him, rather than belittling him by talking down at him. He used to quote to me a piece of advice that he received from his Uncle Clem: "If a farmer is overagitated and cross, kill him with civility and he can say nothing."

During a hunt, too, if Dad spotted a landowner, he would ride over to him and say, "How is the missus?" (an Irish term for wife) or "Your cows are looking great," or "We are having a great hunt," or "Great to see you, thanks for your welcome," or some such chat. These gestures may seem insignificant but they are greatly appreciated and the best possible act to achieve good public relations. Members of the field should follow this custom too.

The country was much easier to cross in Dad's time and in my early seasons. With cheap labour, the ditches were cleared by hand. There was no barbed wire, and bushes were less plentiful, so one could take one's own line and live with hounds. How different from riding over land farmed using modern methods. The ditches, cleaned with mechanical excavators, are huge and electric fences make it almost impossible to cross the country.

It is extremely difficult now for a huntsman to be close to hounds at the crucial moment at a check to note where they actually stopped speaking, or if a fresh fox (or a hare!) gets up and the pack divides. The whipper-in has an equal disadvantage. His job is to get to the leading hounds to stop them. It is a waste of time calling them back from away behind them.

Patt Hogan (a keen foxhunter living in Kilfrush, who returns again in chapter 26) said to me one day, "We need better horses now than what our fathers had because they have to be able to jump far more challenging fences and also be able to gallop the long way around to catch up with hounds who are running straight."

I am not detracting in any way from Dad's ability to ride across country. Far from it, he was a genius. However my real joy was in watching Dad handling hounds. In particular he seemed to have a sensitive understanding of the unique character and mental attitude of his hounds. Noticeable characteristics of the Kerry beagle are that they are independent, highly strung, and will not take punishment lightly. On a cold scenting day when they are engrossed in their work, one has to treat them quietly; overdoing voice and horn will lift their heads and you are in trouble.

Dad's strong advice was, "Never lift hounds unless you have something better to offer them than what they have already". He would add, "Always allow hounds to finish their cast themselves and then pay them the compliment of going to them to lift them in the direction where you think the fox has gone. Don't just stand and call them from a distance. It is hard on them and harder still on your whip to turn them to you when they might not even have heard you."

With Dad gone, I must do my best to follow in his footsteps. Whenever I wanted to lift hounds after they had finished their efforts, I used to whistle to them and encourage them forward, preferably at a moment when they were already heading in the direction I wanted. If I wanted them to come in a hurry, for instance, if I had news of where the fox had gone, then I would call them with the horn and my whip would turn them to me.

Our hounds, as a breed, are noted for their singleminded fire and drive when they are on a fox, and to see them making their own figure-of-eight cast is something else. Sometimes at the moment of a check the pack would split; one half would cast to the left, the other half to the right. Technically this is incorrect, they should work together, but I would allow it because they were covering twice the ground. As soon as a hound owned the line, both packs would race to him. I remember one day when there was a hot scent and hounds were flying. At one point the fox had turned sharp and hounds flashed on—straight into a pond! They stopped abruptly, bewildered by the water.

At a check and when hounds have done all they can, a huntsman is faced with a host of options. He must choose one quickly because the fox is not waiting. Which way is the wind? (One should always cast, and draw a covert upwind.) Has he run through cattle or across fields freshly spread with fertiliser, or swum a river? In all these cases one has to cast well forward so that his coat has shaken off surplus water and his pads are cleaned. Has your fox been headed? Is he possibly making for another covert?

Dad's golden rule was, "Give your fox the credit for being a good fox, and cast forward."

Hunting a fox is such an enthralling experience. Many books have been written, and will be written on the subject but, as Dad used to say, "When you think you know all the answers, you are only just beginning to learn."

Writing about it now has my heart racing at the memory of it all. Dad seemed to know the mind of a fox and of his hounds whom he loved so dearly. From every point of view, he left me a hard act to follow.

After Dad's death, my dear mother moved out of Scarteen and spent some years with my sister Jean. Later she had several years with Gwen, my elder sister, before spending her final years at her old home, Burton Park, with my brother John and his family.

EIGHTEEN

THE FIRST GREAT LOVE OF MY LIFE—MY FAMILY

In due course Anne and I had our own family. Rachel Mary came first—the apple of our eye. Next came John, assuring Scarteen of a son-and-heir. As planned we put his name down for Ampleforth College to be sure of getting him in.

In hindsight we made one big error. We should have insured against having twins because neither family had a known history of multiple births—we could have made a fortune! To our great delight and surprise, Hugh and Chris arrived and captured everyone's attention. Fortunately (?!), they were not identical; Hugh was a big bouncing boy with a great appetite, Chris short and slight, a shy feeder but equally boss with his twin brother: I could, and still do, see in Chris a similarity with Anne's father. The arrival of the twins upset all domestic calculation; from now on everything had to be multiplied by two.

Anne with Rachel, twins Hugh and Chris, and John, the eldest boy. Ambrose O'Mullane photo

Mark's happy arrival next put us thinking seriously about education. We decided that there was no way that we would be able to afford to send all four sons to Ampleforth with the high fees and the cost of travel, so we reluctantly took John's name off the college list.

Later Anne and I walked up and down the walkway by Glenstal Abbey, home of the Belgian Benedictines, discussing the situation with Fr (later Abbot) Celestine, the Headmaster. I argued that for our lads to come to Glenstal, this would not be "going to school" as I understood it. I could see Glenstal from the top floor of Scarteen; they should go right away for their education to broaden their minds. On the contrary Fr Celestine insisted that school and home should be as close as possible so as not to damage the close family bond between parents and their children.

He won us around, but, and I shall never forget his unbiased generosity, he said that if we found that we could afford it and still wanted to send all four to Ampleforth, we were welcome to do so, and he would not be upset (though he would be disappointed!). And so the four names were entered for Glenstal. I was happy because I could feel already that Glenstal possessed the same Benedictine ethos that I had enjoyed so much during my time at Ampleforth.

With five extra in the household, Anne was busy; she did a wonderful job rearing them all and she was a shining example for young mothers. Occasionally she got some help, but in true Kiwi tradition she preferred to do the work herself. We did have a governess for a couple of years, Miss Murphy from Rosscarberry, who gave the children a good start, maybe with a slight Cork accent!

Rachel did a year at the convent in the village of Hospital, then four years in Our Lady's School in Rathnew, Co. Wicklow, before finishing with a year at Mayfield in Sussex. She then got her qualifications for secretarial work in the School of Commerce in Limerick and secured a well-paid job with a leading public relations firm in Dublin.

After some months she said to me, "Dad, I am not happy. I sit at a desk all day with not enough to do and earning too much money, but no satisfaction."

She always loved children and was impressed by the Children's House, the first pure Montessori school in Ireland, started by my first cousin Veronica in Stillorgan. Sion Hill College was booked out, so Rachel qualified at the AMI Montessori College in London. A new and exciting career opened up before her.

The boys went to St Gerard's Preparatory School in Co. Wicklow, and from there to Glenstal. Mark attended Knocklong National School for a while and enjoyed it. I collected him after his first day there and he was in tears.

"What is wrong, old man?" I said.

"Daddy, I can't read." He thought he was going to be able to read instantly.

A short time later we were together in the car and there was the most beautiful view of the sunset with glorious autumn colours. I pulled up and said, "Mark just look at that, isn't it wonderful?"

"Yes Dad, but please don't interrupt. I'm reading my book!"

We used to fetch them home on the occasional Sunday, but not too frequently as there were usually matches and they enjoyed games and athletics. Anne's mother used to save up her pension and come to stay with us for six months every two years, preferring to travel by cargo-passenger vessels. She adored her grandchildren and so enjoyed visiting Glenstal to see them. One day, when years were catching up on her, she and I had an argument.

She said: "Thady, I am going to take a single ticket back to New Zealand this time. I find the journey too tiring."

I said, "Mum you will take a return ticket or no ticket at all."

We settled for the latter and she spent her final twelve years with us surrounded by her grandchildren and blissfully happy. They all loved her. In a happy home grandparents play an important part in a child's upbringing, and certainly Mum demonstrated this.

In the long summer holidays we used to go camping or borrow a friend's house. One year we rented "Bunnow"—a charming cottage on the Kerry coast built like a swallow's nest and actually on the rocks. It was a dream location for children to paddle, collect shells, fish for crabs, and just potter about. The house belonged to Bertie and Marjorie Waller; even though she was almost completely blind, Marjorie had the most beautiful rock garden, which she tended lovingly.

On another occasion the boys and I took a tent to Connemara. We pitched it by a lake in the lee of a mountain, an idyllic site, but for the midges—they are ravenous up in the turf bogs—and went fishing. On our return we cooked our meal on an open fire hoping the smoke would deter the insect invaders, but they won the battle. The boys turned in, Chris with his pet kestrel Kit in the tent. I drove down to the local post office to phone Anne and report on our doings.

When I got back a strong storm was brewing. The wind changed direction and came roaring up the valley. The first thing it struck was our tent. I awakened the lads. Each one of us clung on to a pole to stop the tent taking off. Soon we could stick it no longer. We struck the tent and, in pitch dark and driving rain, we gathered all the belongings we could into our old minibus and drove a few miles to the home of John and Liz Marks (my cousin). Cold and perished, we begged a bed. They welcomed us with open arms.

I shared a room with Mark who said, "Dad, Isn't it wonderful to have friends?"

Next morning not a breath of wind, the lake as smooth as glass—just a trail of clothes, pots and pans, and belongings right down to the lakeshore. In hindsight it was a great and worthwhile experience of fighting for our very survival!

After college John came home to help run the farm. After Hugh did a year at an agricultural college in Northern Ireland (all the ones down south being full), he joined John at home. Both of them were determined to get Scarteen "back in the blue" after the farm had been neglected by their father, grandfather, and great-grand-uncle, each of whom had spent too much time hunting and not enough time farming. I am endlessly indebted to them for all their hard work.

Our family, September, 1973: Claire, Mark, Chris, Hugh, John, Rachel, Anne, Thady

Chris went to work at Bruree Stud. Then he moved on to Newmarket for three years with one of the leading trainers, Tom Thompson-Jones, and reached the onerous position of assistant head lad. Then back in Ireland he had a season each with two successful trainers. He travelled out to Japan in charge of the outstanding filly Stanerra, who was placed in the Japan Cup. The following year they went out again and she won the cup. He was obviously cut out for a career with horses.

Mark did a couple of terms at Trinity College University studying economics.

One day he said, "Dad, I don't think I am on the right road for what I want to do."

I said, "Have a talk with your tutor for advice."

His tutor recommended that he get out into the world for a year and discover what career to follow, then return to university if appropriate. Mark hit off for the United States.

NINETEEN

OUR GREATEST SORROW

Within a couple of years, to our unbounded joy and delight, Claire Bernadette was born—we had completed our half dozen! Our gem of gems she was equally adored by her sister and brothers. She grew up fast in the company of her elders and added a new dimension to the happiness of our home.

Of the six children, Claire, Rachel, and Chris seemed to have the greatest attraction to ponies. I contacted Mrs Bland in Co. Leix to see if she could help us find a reliable pony. She said that by chance she had just bought a small one from a travelling family that seemed ideal and in the habit of young children all around it. Delighted, I went up and fetched it right away. On arrival home, the family were elated and rushed out to stroke it.

Claire, our youngest child, was adored by her sister and brothers and added a new dimension to the happiness of our home.

Next morning the children went into the stable to see the new arrival again. To their horror the pony had its ears back and chased them out. They came running in to tell Anne and myself. It turned out that the little mare was permanently "in season" and had been doped. Mrs Bland, terribly upset, removed her immediately.

We soon had a replacement, when Doris and Nello Armitage loaned us a beautiful white pony, Shadow, by the Arab stallion Nazeel. One morning Rachel started cantering on her in the side lawn and Shadow broke into gallop. Rachel got frightened and fell off, which put her off riding for some time.

After a few months Rachel said to me, "Daddy, could I have a pony?"

I said, "There is a perfectly good pony out in the field doing nothing."

"Oh no, not Shadow, Daddy", she replied.

"Well I cannot afford to buy another one", I replied cruelly.

A few days later while shaving I spotted Rachel riding Shadow out of the yard, her confidence restored. Maureen Hogan (the only child of the Gubbins of Kilfrush: see chapter 10) found her a good hunting pony for the Christmas holidays. I heard her shouting at Rachel in the middle of a hunt, "Don't gallop at your banks!"

Claire was proving to be a great little rider. When we found an excellent hunting pony for her, she was thrilled. She won a competition in Limerick Show on Mickey Mouse and was soon hunting him. I shall never forget the joy on her face having jumped a double bank below Knockderk Hill.

Claire, a great little rider, hunting at Knockderk.

Then one day Claire complained of a small lump on the inside of her thigh. The doctor thought at first that it was just a strained muscle. However the lump was getting larger. We brought her to Croom Hospital and the surgeon confirmed our worst suspicions—our little treasure had cancer.

Mr Meehan was most helpful and understanding. He told us that there was a 500 to 1 chance that amputation could prevent the disease from spreading. This was a terrible decision that we had to take. Before giving a final verdict, I decided to bring Claire to Lourdes to ask Our Lady for a cure. My cousin Betty came with us. Claire was on crutches, but was a tower of strength throughout the trip. However a cure was not God's wish. She was admitted to Croom Hospital and the operation was performed. She awoke from the anaesthetic to find that she only had one leg: what a shock for our little one.

But a miracle had occurred, if not the one we had hoped for. Claire had been gifted with a serene acceptance of God's decision and became the soul of courage and prayerful resignation to her sufferings and disappointment. She was *such* a living example to all of fortitude and bravery. Never complaining, instead she exuded love and happiness. We sometimes find it hard to understand God's will in allowing such a perfect, innocent, and beautiful little child to go through such an ordeal, but we must just accept it. I believe that all who saw her were rewarded by her selfless concern for their feelings, including their mental anguish over her condition.

Claire returned rapidly to normal life. She loved to be back with her friends at convent school in Hospital, where she had always been a great favourite. To her great joy she was one of a group who received the Sacrament of Confirmation. She had chosen the name Theresa for her Confirmation.

By sheer determination she also managed to ride her pony by balance alone.

She asked, "Dad, can I try a jump?"

I said, "Don't be silly—you can't jump with one leg!"

"I think I can, Dad." And she jumped a small log on the ground. "Make it a bit higher Dad", she said and she cleared it with glee!

We decided to get her measured for an artificial limb. Before going to Dublin for this, Anne took her to the hospital for a final check-up with the surgeon—she hesitated to tell me the verdict. On the way to Dublin, I said that I was going to call to our solicitor to change my will to cater for six children.

Anne said, "There will only be five."

The deadly disease had spread. God was asking us for a further proof of our faith in Him. He wanted Claire even more that we did, and we could not refuse Him. And so we changed our prayers and asked Him to take her quickly.

Her cough was becoming more troublesome. One morning I called in to see her early. Fr Ryan our curate was due to come and say Mass in the house.

Claire said, "Dad, this is the last day of term and we all have to be present. Will I get there in time?"

I assured her that she would be in time. She turned over on her tummy with her face on the pillow.

I said, "Sweetheart, don't lie like that. You cannot breathe."

Our darling little Claire had already gone to Heaven.

This has been a difficult chapter to write. I don't mind admitting that my eyes have been moist. I deliberated for some time over whether to publish it or not. Finally I decided to go ahead on the chance that sometime some parents in similar circumstances may derive some strength and consolation out of sharing our experiences and our grief.

It has always been the salutary custom in Ireland that children, on receiving the Sacrament of Confirmation, take a pledge to refrain from alcoholic drink until the age of twenty-one. Darling Claire had been happy to take the pledge, but her years were cut short. I thought she would wish me to finish the pledge for her, which I did. When the time was up I decided to extend it for the rest of my life in thanksgiving to God for the gift of Claire's life. I joined the Pioneer Total Abstinence Association, which means abstaining for life from alcoholic drink in atonement to God for the sins of intemperance throughout the world. There is nothing wrong with alcohol as such; its abuse is where the trouble lies.

A wholesome thought is that our children are not entirely ours. They belong to God and we have them only on loan from Him.

"A friend in need is a friend indeed." Never was a truer word spoken. On hearing of our great loss, a good hunting friend from the United States, Pam Stokes, generously gave Anne and myself the use of their beautiful house in the Bahamas for three weeks, to take our minds off our tragedy. We flew to Eleuthera and went by launch to the tiny Harbour Island. It is about two miles long by an average of half a mile wide, with warm sandy beaches, waving palms, and unbroken sunshine. The delightful housekeeper, an islander, could not do enough for us and we had every comfort.

Out game fishing one day with a young American chap and two "crew", we caught a variety of fish, including king mackerel—delicious. Our surplus was shared among the local people. I hooked one huge fish that I never saw. My reel screeched as he tore away; unfortunately one of the crew tightened my brake too soon and the steel trace snapped.

I also tried my hand catching bone fish, the greatest fighting fish of all. They come in to the miles of shallow water ("Bahamas" translated means "shallow seas") but are extremely wary. Anne and I have travelled a lot but this was one of the few times when we were on a pure holiday with no commitments—bliss!

APOLOGIA II

My readers, at the start of the book I promised that I would not bore you with my hounds and horses and hunting. I have done my best to keep off the subject, but my patience has finally run out! However, even if you are not a hunting person, I beg you, do not put the book down. I am certain that you will find further interest and entertainment in the ensuing chapters. Give them a try—you'll see what I mean.

FOUR

THE SECOND LOVE OF MY LIFE

TWENTY

DARK AS HELL AND SMELLS OF CHEESE

> Mr Jorrocks and his faithful huntsman Mr Pig had had a heavy night. Early next morning Mr Jorrocks asked Mr Pig to put his head out the window and find out what sort of a hunting day it would be. Mr Pig mistook the cupboard door for the window and gave the above report!

It is time, my readers, for us to share some of a huntsman's thoughts and feelings. Imagine that dawn is breaking late in February on a hunting morn. It is the closing day of the season, earlier than normal because there has been a false spring, a let-up from the frost and snow, and the precious grass is growing. Winter feed is almost finished and some herds are already out by night, so it has been decided to cease hunting in the farmers' interests.

The huntsman, we'll call him Jack, has been roused before cockcrow by hounds in kennel. They had only a light feed early yesterday, which means today is a hunting day; they are excited and sing constantly. Jack scans the sky. Clouds are high, as is his barometer, and they are in a dead straight line, just below the mountaintops—a good sign. No frost, just a suspicion of a breeze from the east. (A frost followed by a hot sun is disastrous for scent and one has to wait for the frost to return in the evening, then you can get a flyer—a short, sharp, fast run on a good fox with a strong scent. There is an old true saying, "When the drop is on the thorn, the huntsman may put up his horn". It refers to the drop on the whitethorn bushes caused by condensation after a touch of fog, as distinct from raindrops.)

Jack lets the pack into the big grass yard to relieve themselves. They rush out noisily engaging in mock battles with each other, alert and on their toes, while he hoses down the lodges and yards (the most important kennel chore; hounds cannot be healthy on anything less than a spotless floor with a good slope for it to dry quickly). Jack feels that all the signs are there for a good scent, so he will draw a big mixed pack, dogs and bitches (no need to spare hounds for the next day); sixteen-and-a-half couple should suffice. He will not take any old hounds because the pace will be hot. There is just one exception, old Stormer, who will have his last day's hunting after seven hard seasons.

Jack calls each hound by name; some of the older hounds try to hide among the crowd, hoping that he will not notice them as he draws the unwanted ones first. The first called are divided between the lodges. The hunting pack are left in the centre yard while Jack goes in to get on his hunting kit and have some breakfast. He is particular about turnout. Horn and buttons shining, boots gleaming—"dammit, the stock is too tight!"

In the big oak wood, the first covert of the day, the beautiful dawn chorus of all the song birds has been ringing out since daybreak, rabbits scurry here and there, and an old badger returns from the meadow, snuffling and grunting from a night feed on roots and grubs. (Although lovely animals, sadly, they do spread tuberculosis and brucellosis by feeding on infected afterbirth of cows. Occasionally they kill a weak lamb and woe betide poultry if they can get into the hen houses—they kill for the fun of killing, a habit shared with the fox.)

As it is the mating season, a big dog fox has travelled many miles to find a vixen. He has been successful and goes to rest in an earth in the middle of the wood—but it is closed against him; the earthstopper (who closes all known fox-holes to stop a fox going to ground) has done a thorough job earlier in the night. So he lies up in some thick scrub. We'll call this fox Charles, a big handsome chap, lean and rangy, fit as an athlete, with a white chest and a big white tag to his brush, easy to recognise. A blackbird has spotted him and is annoying him with his staccato warning notes.

Jack mounts his seasoned ten-year-old hunter. The moment the kennel door is opened, hounds rush out and are all around him baying happily. Jack's horse lowers his head and enjoys their company too. The meet is twelve miles away, just over two hours to hack. They walk for half a mile to settle down, then travel at a hound jog of about six miles per hour.

For Jack this is a real pleasure. He chooses secondary roads to avoid traffic, and he can afford to let hounds spread out and run on ahead while he studies their every movement. They are alert and interested in every little scent, maybe of a rat, a mouse, or a rabbit. They pass puddles of water without stopping for a lap. (Conversely on bad scenting days hounds are forever thirsty.) If a car is coming, they quickly obey their huntsman's command to "get over". Every hound sneezes rapidly from the exhaust fumes, which seem to irritate their scenting organs, extra sensitive on a good scenting day. (Conversely again on a poor scenting day hounds can be enveloped in fumes or smoke and never sneeze.)

An occasional halt for a word with a farmer. Maybe there is news of an early litter of cubs or a family wedding. Hacking on is an ideal opportunity to keep in touch with the locality. Modern transport is expensive; horseboxes and vans have ruined all the joys we used to have in hacking through the country. Now the journey to the meet involves just another lorry, and hounds and horses are never seen.

Nearing the meet, Jack takes stock of the situation. The breeze has strengthened a bit, so he will draw upwind and place his whipper-in at the gate at the north end of the wood. Another piece of Jorrocks' advice was, "Never take your hounds out on a windy day"—so true.

Arriving at the meet, horses, hounds, and huntsman are relaxed. The Master greets Jack, as do the followers. "How many couple out?" "Hounds are looking great." "What do you think of scent today?" Everybody is in good humour.

Following a short call on Jack's horn, they move off. The whip gallops ahead to get to his point. At covertside, "Leu in my lads!" Hounds burst in through the fence. Another short call on the horn to rouse any sleeping fox, but Charles has already heard the horse gallop by. He has been through all this many times before and is not going to delay. A magpie gives several of his harsh "kekekek kek" warning calls as he passes. The whip hears it, then a hound speaks, and another and soon the whole pack own the line.

Jack doubles his horn. Then a flash of rich tan over the lane. It has to be a fox—count to ten—then a high-pitched holloa. Galloping to the spot, Jack blows the "gone away". Charles is fleet of foot and running free—this is his life, born to run, the wind rushing through his nostrils as he heads for home. Over the swollen river, laden with water as he mounts the bank on the far side, he shakes it off and gets back into his stride. Hounds are at fault on the landing side. Their cast is just a bit short, so Jack holds them on to the next field, where they can pick up the scent again. Mile after mile they race over the green turf and yawning ditches, a few riderless horses closing on them.

Charles jumps on to a wall and runs the top of it for about twenty yards, then on . . . on . . . on . . . Jack spots him away ahead. Crows are mobbing him, cawing crossly. Hounds check at the wall, but not for long. Then the railway—a train is approaching at speed whistling, the pack just makes it across in time, all except one hound. Stormer has got tailed off. Jack sees it coming, it is all over in an instant. A good friend gone, a sudden end to eight years of honest service. Jack feels the pang of grief. Mercifully it was quick.

The pace is telling. Charles' tongue is out and his brush is drooping, but he is still full of running. He jumps on to a road, turns sharp left, and runs the straight stretch of the road for three hundred or four hundred yards, then into the field, the far side and away. Hounds are racing and overrun the line where the fox had turned, all except Music, a fantastic road hunter, who turns sharp left on the fox's line. Scent is sketchy on a dry road, so she can only barely own it. The pack swings back over the road again, casts parallel with it for 100 yards or so, then over the road again, on 100 yards; they hit off the line where the fox has left the road and race on. Music has worked every inch of the line along the road in silence because the scent is not strong enough to speak to it. By the time she gets to the point where the fox has left the road, the pack has gone two fields.

(I witnessed this very incident some years ago exactly as I have described it, the loveliest piece of hound work I have ever seen. We were only walking down the road after Music and could enjoy it all. With pride in my hounds I said to some followers close by "*Did* you see that?" They said, "See what?" I was mad, "Oh go home!")

On they race with glorious cry, straight through a big field of dairy cows that scarcely lift their heads. (You can judge a man's character by the behaviour of his stock. If a man is quiet and happy, his cows are likewise; if he is highly strung and excitable, so are his stock.) Hounds are brought to their noses, but soon puzzle the line through the cows then on again at racing pace.

Charles heads for the small copse near the village, where new generation foxes are numerous—semi-domesticated and feeding off the rubbish bins, they do not know how to run. Hounds check in the copse, then hit off a line in a different direction.

After a couple of fields, Jack curses to himself. "Dammit, I should have recognised the change in the note to a higher pitch." The older hounds are not speaking.

The fat, fresh fox soon pays the penalty. Charles is able to take it easier for a while but Jack soon has hounds back on his line, so he pushes on, on the long climb up the hill through the thick heather with hounds closing on him and—oh bliss—into the deep, dark crevice in the rocks where, he is safe. Hounds mark keenly, but can not follow.

Jack blows to ground and says, "Good on ye, mate, you won this time. We'll meet again next year."

Hounds were cheated of their rightful quarry, but they had the satisfaction of a kill. What a run—ten miles as hounds ran with an eight-mile point. Then the long, doleful call on the horn for home. Another season is over.

Some followers ride up alongside Jack. "Thanks for a great run and a great season. Your hounds are a credit to you."

Back in kennel Jack goes to check the litter of eight beautiful puppies that were born a few days earlier, eyes not yet open, but their markings just like old Stormer, their sire.

Down by the stream beyond the oak wood, playing in the sunshine in and out of a big sandy earth while their mother looks on, are five lively cubs. They are already showing the looks of their father and they are handsome—Charles is their father.

Hunting, and especially hunting hounds, give a wonderful opportunity to learn and enjoy the marvels of nature, and to share the privilege with farmers and their families all through the country. Our Creator has done a splendid job in giving us this privilege. I pray that it may continue to be appreciated for generations to come.

TWENTY-ONE

SOME THOUGHTS ON HOUNDS AND THEIR ORIGIN

So we'll all go a-hunting today
All nature looks smiling and gay.
We will join the glad throng that goes laughing along
And we'll all go a-hunting today.
(Chorus from an ancient hunting song.)

Farming used to be a wonderful way of life. It still is, thank God, but alas it has also become a serious business, without the same time for leisure. However, every man and woman needs a break—we'd go mad if we did not get it. And this is where sport comes in. The most fulfilling and satisfying feeling of elation and relaxation, both mentally and physically, follows when your sport has demanded exhausting activity and achievement.

Furthermore, as a well-known philosopher once observed, "No sport is worth playing unless it contains an element of danger". All sportsmen and women can testify to this. And in my view hunting is the one sport that fits the bill to perfection.

Before I go any further, from the bottom of my heart I offer a huge and sincere thank-you to all landowners who so generously have welcomed my hounds, myself, my son Chris, and our followers through their farms over the years and who continue to do so to this day. It gladdens my heart to see so many of them and their families taking part in and enjoying what is equally their sport.

A level pack with Chris. Kerry beagles are independent, highly strung, do not take punishment lightly, and are distracted by excessive voice and horn on a cold scenting day. Yet they will perform a figure-of-eight cast themselves—a joy to watch—and scarcely need a huntsman. Catherine Power photo

THE KERRY BEAGLE

The history of the Kerry beagle has been well covered in Mike McEwan's *The Ryan Family and the Scarteen Hounds*. So here I give a general overview without going into great detail.

Daphne Moore is one of the great scholars and experts on hound breeding of our time. When she decided to write a book on famous fox hunters, she asked me for my curriculum vitae.

I declined, "I'm sorry, Daphne, I am privileged to be the huntsman of a famous pack of hounds, but I do not look on myself as a famous fox hunter."

Unwilling to take no for an answer, she instead asked a great sportsman and mutual friend, Bay de Courcy-Parry ("Dalesman" of *Horse & Hound* fame), to write it for me. The entry on "The Ryans of Scarteen" reads:

> Scarteen! Why it is a word with magic in it, for sure. When anyone has the necessary courage to enquire from anyone of the great family of Ryans how long the Black & Tan hounds have been at Scarteen, after a look of amazement at such a colossal degree of ignorance, the reply will come "Why for sure have they not always been here?"

However, those who have the good fortune to study the family chronicles will find at the very beginning these few words written in faded ink and in a spidery hand:

> When the land first appeared above the waters Noah himself was glad to be seeing it, for had he not been put to much bother by the Irish after the stout had run out, and what with the both of them singing and jigging the animals were forever being upset. So up gets Mr Noah and tells Mr and Mrs Ryan to have their bags packed and be off, and whilst they are at it they could be taking the two great red and black dogs with them, and he might then have a bit of peace at night when he was down off the ship and on the top of Knockmealdown Mountain. However no sooner was Mr Ryan on the ground than he turned to Mr Noah and said, "Ye know those two foxes that Mrs Noah is complaining of for the big powerful smell on them, we'll just tip the pair of them off before you draw up the anchor. Why for sure what could we be doing, after the water had lowered a trifle, without them?" "You may call the place Tipperary", said Mr Noah and his son, dropping out the two foxes and glad to be well ridden of them.

This unofficial version adds a touch of humour to Daphne's otherwise serious and excellent book!

The Kerry beagle is a unique breed. Lacking any connection with the foxhound, it is a harrier breed and the hare was its quarry for centuries. While all hounds originate from France, it is believed that the Kerry beagle came through Spain into Ireland in about the sixteenth century, when there was a strong trade between Ireland and Spain. The Spaniards used to land along the

Kerry coast—some Spanish place names still survive—for example, Valentia Island—and it is believed that the Spanish merchants were not satisfied with the hunting dogs that they found here, so they brought in their own.

These historical facts are corroborated by two "recent" events. First, in the 1930s, after some lads from Kerry joined Franco's Army in the Spanish Civil War, they wrote home to say that they had seen black and tan hounds just like the hounds in Kerry. Later, when my wife and I were returning to Ireland after our wedding in New Zealand, the *Dominion Monarch* called in to Las Palmas in the Canary Isles, a Spanish protectorate. In the cathedral square was an effigy of hounds so like ours that I could put names on them.

Two fine young entries stand proudly at the Puppy Show. Catherine Power photo

The breed spread throughout Kerry and West Cork, and through some parts of Co. Cavan. In due course there were three privately owned kennelled packs belonging to Daniel O'Connell's family, the Chutes of Chute Hall, and the Ryans; ours is the only one to survive. Obviously the three families used to exchange hounds. In the archives of Scarteen is a letter from Daniel O'Connell, the Liberator, to my great-great-grandfather, Oul Tha':

> Dear Tha, thank you for the hound, I have called him 'Shchamer' after yourself [then a blotch of ink] cursed bad pen. Yours Dan.

Many trencher-fed packs are kept by farmers and cottiers. However these hounds are kept by their owners in their homes in ones and twos, as distinct from the Scarteen hounds, which are the only kennelled pack of the breed in the world. On Sundays the trencher-fed hounds are brought to the church and tied to the railings. After Mass they are brought up the mountains and are sure to find a hare in the heather.

Trencher-fed hounds have a big advantage over kennelled hounds; they have a lot of freedom and are always breathing fresh air. Hounds cooped up in kennel are constantly breathing polluted air; I believe that this must affect their scenting organs. It is a wonderful experience to watch and hear these hounds hunting. Their cry and scenting ability and stamina are legendary—the envy of many foxhound packs.

The sheer volume of their hunting cry was brought home to me forcibly on the property of my strong supporters in the hunting scene, Patt and

The face of a Prime Minister, with a great deal more honesty!

Maureen Hogan. At Kilfrush, Maureen's former family home (see chapter 10), the Hogans had planted a half acre of covert in the demesne, mostly with that fast-growing thornless evergreen shrub, lonescera. The lonescara had grown matted, like an eiderdown, leaving a vacancy of about three feet at ground level. Hounds were hunting in covert one day and I thought I heard them marking to ground. I crept in on hands and knees to find the earth, but I was wrong. Instead the fox passed close to me and hounds were gaining on him. The roar of their rich music was deafening—of immeasurable decibels and intensified by the low ceiling of scrub. I thought if I was that fox, I would not hang about for long; he thought the same and he broke covert mighty quick!

As Dad did before me and my son Chris does now, I have used a dog or bitch from these trencher-fed packs as an outcross. One has to check up carefully on their breeding. I went to see one bitch who had a great hunting reputation. Her owner said she had not come home after the previous day's hunting. It was dusk and we could hear her beautiful note away on the mountain. I enquired about her breeding.

The owner told me, "She is out of Jack O'Donnell's brindled bitch by Mick McGrath's good black-and-tan dog. Now his dam was by a red setter, you can't beat the setter for nose!" But with care you can still find a good true-bred dog or bitch and see them hunting.

Most of them are black and tan. Acceptable colours are also a brindle or "brecked", a blue mottle or almost white, and tricolour but they are totally different from the foxhound tricolour. The Kerry beagle is more sensitive than the foxhound and will be easily upset by the use of a whip. They are lighter boned, fast, and move with great freedom; they have a kind nature to the point of being affectionate. Notably too, they have a "hare foot"—like the foot of a hare with the full pad on the ground and a long centre toe, as distinct from the foxhound's rounded "catfoot".

A lady who was about to write a book on hunting breeds of hounds called in to me. She seemed genuinely interested, so I spent a bit of time with her in kennel. She sent me a preliminary article in which she said, "I had an interesting visit to the Scarteen hounds. The Master mentioned that unlike foxhounds, the Kerry beagle has hair on his feet." I don't think the book was ever published!

Incidentally the name "Kerry beagle" is something of a misnomer. They have no connection with the foot beagle; in fact the name is pronounced "bagle". Some old men through Co. Kerry and West Cork will call any hound that hunts by scent a "bagle" (not to be confused with the American scone!).

County Kerry is a wild and beautiful part of the country, ideally suited to foot hunting. It is the Mecca for tourists from all over the world, with tourism boosting the economy in the south west of Ireland beyond belief in recent years. The Kerry folk are great people also: friendly, welcoming and with a sense of humour. A large proportion of them speak their native Gaelic language. When travelling down there I have enjoyed listening to conversations in Gaelic, but with a feeling of guilt and embarrassment at being unable to understand my own native tongue.

Back in the years when Eamonn de Valera was leading the country he made, to my mind, a big mistake. The Irish language was forced on the people. In the schools all subjects had to be taught through the medium of Irish, turning young people against it. Anyone seeking a job in the public service had to be a fluent Irish speaker. Now thankfully the language is undergoing a revival and people are learning to love it as part of our heritage. Old Irish music and songs are heard in the pubs all through the country—a great attraction for visitors from overseas who love to stay at farm guesthouses and meet the local people.

There is plenty of entertainment too. An American visitor walking along the road stopped to watch two men working for the council. One man was opening a trench by the side of the road with a spade, and his mate was following him, filling in the trench with a shovel.

The visitor was puzzled: "Say, will you explain to me what you are trying to do: one of you opening the trench, the other closing it, with a shovel?"

The two lads stopped working and leaned on their tools. "Well you see, sir, there's usually three of us at this job."

"But I still don't understand what you are doing."

"Well you see, sir, the third fella is away sick today."

"But", says the visitor, "what difference does that make?"

"Well don't you see, sir, he is the chap who lays the pipes!"

This puppy shows the high dome and long, low-slung ears of the true Kerry head. Catherine Power photo

But back to the Kerry beagle. A couple of seasons before I handed the horn over to Chris, my brother-in-law Claude heard of an outstanding hound in Kerry and we went to see him. Hyder was a handsome blue-mottled dog of about twnty-three inches (average for a dog; bitches are usually smaller). A true Kerry beagle type, he had the high dome and long low-slung ears, beautiful shoulder and conformation and the lithe freedom of a leopard. He belonged to a great sportsman, Paddy Corcoran of Ballinskellig by the shores of the Atlantic. I fell in love with the hound straight away.

"Could I borrow him for a few weeks to breed a couple of bitches?" I asked.

"Hyder won't leave my yard" said Paddy. (I said I thought all the more of himself and Hyder for that!) "But you can send down as many bitches to me as you like."

I think we bred a couple and a half. One litter was outstanding. When Chris took them on, they were first season hounds. Highlight was the champion of that litter, proving the best stud dog over several years.

Some years earlier I bred an outstanding litter of Jupiter, Jutland, Jury, and a helluva hound called Juggler. During their first season we were cub hunting along the foot of the Galty Mountains, only Tommy and myself mounted. Hounds took their fox away up the mountain, too steep to ride. A blinding rainstorm blotted out everything. When hounds could resume their work, up jumped a little horny mountainy sheep that raced down the hill with the whole pack after him in full cry, led by Juggler. By the time we got to them at the boundary fence, only four hooves and a couple of horns were left. On the way home, after giving hounds their due punishment, I called in to the owner of the sheep to confess our crime and offer compensation.

"You won't give me a penny, 'sure you could not help it and aren't there plenty of sheep up there", he said. What a sportsman!

According to "the book" I should have shot Juggler, but I could not do it. He never looked at a sheep again. If our hounds riot on hare or deer (but not sheep!), I forgive them because they have hunted both animals legitimately in their long history.

Which reminds me of the two Masters of hounds discussing sheep worry.

"I have one bad case and I cannot cure the brute", said one.

"Oh that is easily done", said the other. "Put your hound into a barrel with a cross old ram. That will sort him out."

A year later they were talking again: "Well, how did you get on with your sheep killer?"

"I don't know what about sheep", replied his friend, "but he will never go near another barrel!"

Chris and I still cannot agree which was the better hound: Juggler or Hyder. They are both long gone to Valhalla, so we'll never decide it.

THE DUMFRIESSHIRE EXPERIMENT

Some years ago, Anne and I were privileged to stay with the late Sir Jock Buchanan-Jardine. A most interesting man, he bred a rare breed of cattle, as well as breeding pigeons and old roses. He also founded the present Dumfriesshire foxhounds. I was keen to try an outcross with them.

What massive hounds they are—tall, strong-boned, deep-chested, and almost entirely black, just with pale tan spectacles and a dash of the same pale tan on the chest and beneath the stern. I remarked to Sir Jock that I thought their ribs could be more sprung to give them more lung room. He explained that well-sprung ribs interfered with the shoulder movement, and his hounds have ample lung room because of their depth of chest. They have a wonderful deep cry. If Sir Jock thought that the cry was getting a higher pitch, he would use a French staghound dog. The black and tan is so dominant that he could use a white French dog—he had imported one a few days before—without losing his black and tan.

Sir Jock's son Rupert showed us hounds. When he opened the door of the doghound lodge, the big, powerful hounds hit Rupert's knees and literally carried him the full length of the drawing yard on their backs. It might have been staged for out benefit, but it was for real!

Sir Jock kindly sent me over two fine stallion hounds to try the cross. Sadly one was too old to breed. The other, Nominal, was a big, handsome hound. He settled in with our lads and hunted with them well. One day hounds got away on a brace (two foxes) from Ballinacree Covert. Two-and-a-half couple stayed on one while the body of pack hunted the second one. The two-and-a-half couple stayed out hunting that night. Next morning two couple were back home, but Nominal was missing.

For more than a fortnight I traced him by his tracks and by local information from schools and creameries for surely eighteen miles or more away into the Doon Hills and finally lost him. The Dumfriesshire hounds are independent. At one point a farmer told me that Nominal had been sleeping in a hayshed close to where I was blowing my horn, but he had gone partly wild and would not pay any attention. I was mortified.

I had one more attempt at the Dumfriesshire outcross with the help of that great sportsman and authority on hound breeding, Ikey Bell. Sadly I knew him only in his latter years, when he was crippled, but he used to enjoy following our hounds in the car. I was embarrassed on a hunt in February, when foxes were scarce, but hares were plentiful and hounds were rioting real bad. At the end of the day I apologised to Ikey profusely.

He replied, "Don't worry. I have seen the best foxhounds do the same this time of year." I felt better!

Ikey got a beautiful bitch from Sir Jock for Tom and Elsie Morgan, Master of the West Waterford. Tally would have won in Peterborough, and she was a brilliant hunter. Unfortunately, she developed the awful crime of skirting, so Tom and Elsie lost patience with her. Disappointed, Ikey offered her to me.

"Tom and Elsie don't know a good hound when they see one", he said with a smile.

Well, Tally was one of the worst cases I have seen. She would draw well, and as soon as a hound spoke she would be out circling the covert. On hitting the line she would run mute for two or three fields and foil the line. This often happens with a good hound on changing packs; they are just jealous of the new competition. I gave up hunting her and bred her to one of my best doghounds. She produced seventeen matchbox-size puppies that failed to survive. In hindsight I believe I was wasting my time—there was too great a difference between the genes of both breeds for the cross to work. The only slim connection was the colour.

THE AMERICAN CONNECTION

The story was different with the American foxhound. Bob Crompton, Master of the Andrews Bridge Penn-Marydel hounds, sent Chris over a good-looking dog called "Minstrel". He was similar to our hounds, but with longer ears and the high dome. He had that loose skin around the larynx indicating a large larynx, which I believe is so important for good voice. The similarity to our hounds is to be expected. Many years ago two Kerry beagles, Mountain and Muse, were sent out from Kerry to the United States. They and others that followed had a big influence on the American hound-breeding scene. I believe that their similarity was particularly strong in the "July breed".

Minstrel hunted well, but seemed a bit nonplussed by the horrendous ditches, banks, and scrub of our country and he was happy to be a pack hound. His progeny are doing well and have great voice and nose.

Good voice and good nose, I believe, are more important that speed in a hound. The old adage holds true: "A hound is only as fast as his nose." This truth is particularly evident in the Scarteen hunt country nowadays. Because foxes are plentiful, they do not have to travel far to find a mate; therefore they twist and turn within a small area. If you do get on a straight-running fox it is difficult to stay with hounds because of the terrain. The solution would seem to be to breed a slower hound; but don't get me wrong. I am not advocating breeding a heavy-shouldered hound that cannot gallop; this would be heresy! There is a dilemma here because one automatically breeds for quality, which in turn brings speed, but I stand by the argument that nose and voice are far more important than speed.

Furthermore, foxes have changed their lifestyle. No longer wild animals, they are semi-domesticated and feed out of dustbins in built-up areas. Whereas formerly if a fox saw a man a field ahead he would give him a wide berth; nowadays he would leave between the man's legs!

I have a theory that because a wild animal loses his strong smell when domesticated, a "modern" fox has a weaker scent and is more difficult to hunt. Perhaps I am making excuses for my hounds not catching more foxes, but they have my sympathy.

"Running to view" with Thady. Frank H. Meads photo

THE FRENCH CONNECTION

The origin of our hounds has always intrigued me. And so, a few years ago Ian Hurst, one of my Joint-Masters, my wife, and myself set off for France. Ian drove us hundreds of miles in search of "our roots". In hindsight we should have done more research to locate the packs of likely hounds.

However, Jean Bocquillon helpfully directed us to several packs. A keen hound breeder and MSH himself, Jean hunts the Rallye Taillis-Tayaut hounds in the forest of Compiegne in the region of Oise. He is also one of his country's experts on the French hunting horn.

In *Hounds of the World* Sir Jock Buchanan-Jardine maintained that our hounds descended from the Gascon Saintongeois. In our travels, by sheer good fortune we came through a town where a hound show was in progress. We saw a multitude of different breeds, large and small. We thought the Gascon Saintongeois were a bit too light in body and limb. Another breed was the Bruneaux de Jura from the region of the Jural Mountains bordering Switzerland; they were black and tan, but too short and stocky.

Finally we found the Grand Bleu de Gasgogne and decided that they were most like ours, blue-mottled and about the right size. We then visited a pack of the breed in kennel and were even more convinced. They seemed to have the general appearance, movement, and nature of our lads, and they hunted hare. If I ever win Lotto, I will secure a doghound of this breed, and one from the Gascon Saintongeois, for Chris to try as an outcross. It would be exciting to see the results. However the Lotto win will have to come first as the exercise would be expensive; they would have to be fully quarantined due to rabies and foot-and-mouth in France.

Enough on hounds for the present!

Wattle and family, from the Irish Field, 1951. The Kerry beagle is an ancient harrier breed with no direct connection to either the foxhound or the foot beagle. Mary Tarry photo

TWENTY-TWO

A HUNTSMAN'S NIGHTMARE

Surely the greatest pain a huntsman has to suffer is to see someone else hunting his hounds. Dad had to endure this punishment for nine seasons. His uncle Sir Thomas Power had helped him financially for several years in the 1920s, but when the Depression struck in 1929 he refused to continue subsidising unless Dad gave up the hounds. The hounds had to leave Scarteen.

Dr Cecil McLoughlin and his nephew Sir Cecil Walker offered to take them on. "The Doctor" lived at Ballinamona, a delightful old house surrounded by beautiful trees and shrubs. When we were small we were taken there to tennis parties; my oldest memory is the homemade strawberry jam for tea. The home also has a lovely view of the Galty Mountains and always holds a fox. In the stag-hunting days one of the Doctor's two sisters, "Miss Edith", was riding home early (sidesaddle) when she looked back and saw the big red stag following her. Getting the fright of her life, she galloped home!

As the Doctor had no suitable accommodation for the hounds at his home, Ballinamona, Eileen Rea (who married Keith Reynolds: see chapter 10) agreed to kennel them in Kenmare. But a huge crisis arose. Because the floors of the sheds were cobblestones, the hounds got foot infection. Dad's ally and veterinary surgeon, Alan Baker, declared that the pack would die if they remained in Kenmare. After Sir Thomas passed on, the hounds came back to Scarteen, which angered the Doctor. He refused to carry on as Master and fell out with Dad. As the Doctor was a keen hunting man, this outcome hurt Dad deeply.

Dad worried greatly over the Doctor's "estrangement" and would frequently dream that they had made up. I am sure that the Doctor was still fond of Dad too, but could not get himself to change. In my time when I called to see him before hunting, his first question was always, "How is your father?"

Still under financial pressure, Dad's only option was to take on another Joint-Master. Occasionally he would follow the hunt himself on a young horse, but he would ride home before the end of the day and could hardly speak to us. To see a stranger hunting his beloved hounds was almost more than he could bear.

In answer to an advertisement in *Horse and Hound* for a Master, Joe Pickersgill (Pick) came over from England to carry the horn for the 1931 season. A dedicated fox-catcher, he killed every fox he could. Dad was anxious, having worked hard for years to introduce and preserve foxes in Scarteen Hunt country. However it is well known that the more foxes you kill, the more you will have.

Pick brought with him about five couple of English foxhounds. A few weeks after arriving, he said to Dad, "John, we'll have to shoot half your hounds. They are pure wild."

He did not understand the nature of the Kerry beagle. You can lead an Irishman, but he will not be driven; it is the same with his hounds. Pick, after hunting English foxhounds for some years, was accustomed to their tough character and instant obedience—they will accept punishment and come back for more. The sensitive Kerry beagle, on the other hand, has to be handled carefully. If you overdo discipline he gets upset. I have seen a good example of this temperament many times. When a Kerry beagle gets a shock from an electric fence—all too frequent nowadays—he will be cowed and will not hunt for the rest of the day.

Dad said to Pick, "You won't lay a finger on them. Wait until you get to know them and they you, and you will change your mind."

And so Pick did. He spent hours in kennel, grooming and rubbing in sulphur, yet hounds never had the healthy coat that they developed later when fed on raw flesh. Pick used to feed the best of oatmeal—the traditional hound feed—which I believe was too heating for them.

The Pickersgills rented Ballyscaddane for the season. Pick was tough on his daughter Rosemary. She had to school his hunters, turn them out superbly, and whip-in to her father three days a week. Although she was brilliant across country, I believe the pressure of the work for her father affected her. She gave up hunting soon after, instead taking to city life. Conversely, in those days, her brother Paddy was indifferent to hunting, yet a few years later, he became a dedicated Master and huntsman of the Co. Galway, the Blazers.

Clare Smith also deserves a mention. I think she was related to the Pickersgills; she was certainly like a mother to Rosemary and Paddy. In spite of having a physical disability, she was a trojan for work and was responsible for the Master's hunting kit and tack.

Dad and Pick got on well. As he was coming for only one season, Pick got Dad's permission to wear a pink coat. He had many of these coats, which he had fitted with a tan collar. This became an acceptable alternative to our regular hunting coat of black melton with tan collar, but members never adopted it. Pick moved on to take the Co. Limerick hounds for three seasons.

The next Master, from 1932 to 1934, was Captain George Barker. This was George's first experience as Master of Foxhounds and he was keen to learn the job from Dad. They rode on together with hounds to the first morning's cub hunting in Thomastown Wood beyond Kilfinane. On arrival at the gate, George asked Dad, "Now John, what do I do?"

George was kind but a strict disciplinarian. One to testify to this was Jimmy Corboy, a keen hunting farmer and great character from Old Pallas, who loved to ride a half-schooled, small thoroughbred. Hacking between coverts, he was having difficulty controlling his horse and got too close to hounds when the Master saw him. Jimmy pulled back quickly and said to Lady Dorothy Moore, "Keep away from him, let the sun shine on him. He threw an eye on me that would crack milk!"

Those were two happy seasons. The Barkers lived with us in Scarteen; their daughter Dawn became my first "flame"—we were just nine! After they returned to England, George took the Badsworth hounds for a few seasons, but sadly took a fatal fall while out hunting.

Then came David Price who stayed for four seasons from 1934 to 1938. Although he had hunted hounds in England (and so was accustomed to English foxhounds) he soon got to know our hounds. He showed good sport, but had one practice that angered Dad. On a poor scenting day he would lift hounds and cheer them on to the next covert at the gallop to "keep the tamboureen a'rolling" (to quote from Jorrocks). This may have pleased some followers, but it was totally against Dad's principles, making fools of his hounds.

Like Joe Pickersgill, David handled hounds as if they were foxhounds and did not allow them enough time to work out the line on their own before casting them. Yet one of the great characteristics of the Kerry beagle is that they will perform a figure-of-eight cast themselves—a joy to watch—so they scarcely need a huntsman. The first time David lifted hounds on (to keep up the pace), Dad was so disgusted that he left the hunt and rode home.

David was invited to bring hounds for a day's hunting in the Blazers' country in Co. Galway. The outing was disappointing in that hounds were not on their toes, weary from a hard hunt two days earlier and a four-hour journey in the van. Also they were unaccustomed to the stone walls that would crumble as they tried to change on them. Nevertheless a huge field enjoyed the event.

The Scarteen followers stayed overnight at the Old Ground Hotel in Ennis. As it was a Friday, the meat course was served at one half of the long table, the fish at the other. The waitress announced solemnly, "This is the pay (pea!)-soup end, this is the pay-soup end."

A visit to the United Hunt country was a different story. The meet was held at a small village called Killeendaniel (subsequently to be known as Killingdavid) in the heart of the tall, narrow, dry stonefaced banks. With a large field participating in a good day's sport, the banks took heavy punishment. It was said that a coach-and-four could be driven in the track of the hunt and they are still being repaired!

THE UNSUNG HERO

My Great Uncle Clem was skinning a jennet at the back of the kennels to feed to the hounds. A young lad turned up with a message for him.

"Hold that leg out, boy", Great Uncle Clem said.

The boy was Jack Dwyer and this direction was his first step into a long life devoted to hounds. His family had no previous connection with kennel or stable: his father had worked for the county council. Yet they lived in a cottage only about a mile from Scarteen. Perhaps the constant sound of hounds singing in kennel was the catalyst that kindled his love for them. No horseman, Jack's sole interest was hounds. With boundless energy he never let a day pass when he was not in kennel by 8 A.M.—a duty his son Tommy has faithfully continued.

Jack had a difficult task. Because each successive Master brought with him an English first whip and kennel huntsman, Jack was junior to them and had to take orders from them, but he never complained. His favourite time of the season was the cub hunting. He revelled in watching his young hounds enter with the pack, and of course we were on level terms, all on foot!

He loved foxes too. He and I went to repair the artificial earth in Cullen covert, which had been wrecked by badgers. Jack put in the terrier to be sure that the earth was empty, but there was a fox in it and the terrier started a fight. Although we soon got the terrier out, the fox had been damaged: Jack put penicillin ointment on his wounds before releasing him.

Jack was a shy man. At Mass he stood against the back wall of the church as he could not bear to have anyone behind him. He never wanted to travel far from home. When Dad took him down to Co. Kerry to see some hounds, Jack got his first-ever sight of the sea.

"Well Jack, what do you think of it?" Dad asked.

"Oh sir," he replied, "I never knew it was so big."

If hounds had had a good day's hunting, he would be as happy as could be. He would work late into the night checking any lame hound for blackthorns and stitching any serious wounds.

Jack and Nora kept their cottage and garden as neat as a new pin. He was proud of a topiary fox that he had shaped out of a whitethorn bush by the roadside. At exercise one day I saw a young hound stop and bay at the "bush fox"—it was that lifelike! It was also admired by many a passerby. To his delight Jack received a photo of it that one passerby later sent from the United States.

TWENTY-THREE

A FAMILY AFFAIR

Finally, in 1939 Claude Thompson came to Dad as Joint-Master. Arriving from England with his brother Geoffrey and their mother, he leased Ballyscaddane. Claude was quiet, shy, a perfectionist, and dangerously addicted to hounds, horses and hunting. He handled hounds with sympathy, patience, and firmness, just like Dad, and the hounds loved him. With Dad overjoyed to have such an instant friend and sportsman as his Joint-Master, there was happiness in the camp once more. With the help of a great sportsman, Chris McCarthy in Fethard, he assembled a number of excellent horses.

All too soon, however, World War II broke out and Claude and Geoffrey had to answer the call of duty. Sadly, like so many other brave sportsmen, Geoffrey was killed on active service. Claude remained on as Joint-Master during the war. On a couple of occasions while on leave, he managed to get a hunt with Dad. While he was away, unsurprisingly given his innate generosity, he gave Dad the use of his best horses and all his tack.

And so Dad was on his own once more hunting his precious hounds, with his two daughters whipping-in. Gwen and Jean were tough and rode through the country like swallows. They each had a fantastic high-pitched "holloa", the likes of which you have never heard (Gwen still has it!), and hounds would fly to it. With no motor transport the days were long and hard. Hacking home cold and wet on many occasions probably contributed to dear Jean's subsequent fatal illness.

Peg Watt was one of Dad's regular followers. She and husband Major Watt, former Master for many seasons of the United Hunt in Co. Cork, lived in Riversfield, an attractive small stud farm close to Kilmallock and just inside the Co. Limerick Hunt country. Short in stature, Peg had difficulty in gripping with her knees. She used curved short bars, which were hinged to the saddle and came over her thighs close to the knees. They gave her security, and in the event of a fall, they would fold away for safety.

One evening Peg Watt said to Gwen, "Will you tell your father to go home? I am exhausted." She would not leave on her own in case Dad found another fox!

With essential commodities and services short because of the war, times were difficult. Some critics might have thought that it was callous and morally wrong that hunting continued in Ireland while the horrors of war were experienced a short distance across the water. But there was another side to the story. In hundreds of families, sons and daughters were bravely playing their part in the war effort overseas and in constant danger of their lives. For those anxiously waiting for news back home, they needed some distraction to keep

Peg Watt was one of the great hunting characters. She used special hinged bars to clamp her to the saddle. Peg is photographed here with Mary and Willie O'Grady. Willie was an ex-jockey, trainer, and loads of fun in the hunting field.

sane. There was another bonus. Anyone in the Allied armed forces who had an uncle, aunt, or other close relative in Ireland could visit them when on leave.

Luke Lillingston, who lived in Mount Coote with his wife Sue, hunted regularly with Dad. Luke of course went to do his duty. He came home once on leave. Dad had a flyer from Knocktoran and hounds killed just short of Moorestown Plantation. He presented the brush to Luke who had it attached to the aerial of his tank! Tragically he was killed shortly afterwards.

Sue was a wonderfully generous and popular friend. She became a "universal aunt" to countless young officers on leave. A nearby small farmer and huntsman Tom Cotter owned a famous hunter mare, Nellie Cotter, whom he had bought for "a five pound note and a load of turnips". When Nellie was hired out to a young officer one day, Sue invited Tom to follow the hunt with her in her car. At the time there was bitter feeling between Winston Churchill and Irish President Eamonn de Valera ("Dev"). Winston needed the use of ports on the west of Ireland so that the Royal Navy could protect the convoys coming from the United States from U-boat attack. Dev obstinately refused to allow it.

While driving, Sue and Tom struck up a heated argument over the ports. Tom spotted the speedometer, and related the story afterwards: "I was holding me own great over the ports when I spotted the needle moving up fifty to sixty miles per hour, but when it reached seventy, I gave her ports and all!"

Another to hire Nellie was showjumper Mary Whitehead, who took the United hounds for a season after Major Watt had resigned the Mastership. She was a tall, strong lady, possibly a bit too heavy for Nellie. Hounds left Knocktoran Bog in a hurry heading for Slievereagh. Because the Morning Star River was in flood, horses had to half swim. Riders were jumping off and on to the far bank on foot to help their horses out. Not so Mary. She asked Nellie to jump out, held on by the reins and pulled Nellie back on top of her into the river. Nobody stopped to pull her out! However everyone, including Mary, had a good laugh about it in the pub later.

Mikey Horgan, the universal odd-job man, deserves a special mention. Mikey lived at the Cross of the Tree and walked about a mile and a half to Scarteen every day. Mounted on Brown Bess, the working mare, and with a lunging rein over his shoulder, which he would use to help us over the banks, he would accompany us on our ponies out hunting. He knew all the shortcuts and "easy" jumping spots. Mum and Dad were quite happy for our safety when Mikey was with us. With Jack Dwyer, Mikey would walk out hounds together if Dad or I were not around.

Occasionally we would hear of a litter of cubs in an area where the vixen was killing fowl. Mikey would arrange to catch them and rear them in a shed in the garden, to be relocated later in an area where foxes were scarce. The terriers were his responsibility. Also our invaluable earthstopper in the Scarteen locality, he would go about the job after dark when the foxes were out feeding.

Mikey was ageless, never seeming to change over the years we knew him. He did all the house chores, bringing in firewood, pumping the water from the well in the yard up into the storage tank in the attic, polishing the boots and shoes, scuffling the gravel, weeding the garden, and so on. He loved all wildlife and we loved him.

TWENTY-FOUR

EVENTIDE

As the years caught up on dear Dad, his old heart got tired. Sensing that he and I would not have too much more time together with him hunting hounds, I did my best to absorb some of his knowledge and hunting lore. One of my greatest regrets is that I did not have a chance to hunt more seasons watching him hunt hounds. He seemed to know the mind of the fox as well as that of his hounds.

Malcolm Shaw, Master of the Limerick Harriers for many years and a great huntsman, used to hunt with Dad frequently. I admired how he was always up with hounds and would ride quietly to one side of the pack, yet never interfered. On one occasion hounds were at fault for some time and there were no obvious clues to assist a choice of cast. Dad made a quick decision and cast hounds in what appeared to be the completely wrong direction. Hounds hit off the line and accounted for their fox after a good run.

Baffled, Malcolm asked Dad, "What on earth prompted you to cast in that direction?"

Dad replied "I don't really know, it was just instinct."

If hounds accounted for their fox after a good run with either a kill or mark to ground (and nine times out of ten they did), Dad would come home as happy as could be. Conversely if they had lost their fox, he could hardly speak for disappointment. He had let his hounds down and would take all the blame himself. He used to say, "If I can get to Heaven, one of the things I am looking forward to is finding out what happened to the foxes I lost."

On the first of many subsequent occasions, he said, "Tha', I want you to hunt hounds for me today. I'm not feeling too good."

I was scared, just out of school and still wet about the ears. "Dad, I'm sure you will be all right by 11:00. I'll take hounds on to the meet for you."

But he could not make it, so Gwen, Jean, and myself set off. The "butterflies" had settled down by the time we got there. As it turned out, the challenge was not too great; Dad had a super pack of hounds that only had to be shown the covert—they did the rest!

I have always had butterflies on a hunting morning. Top actors in the theatre world have told me that they have the same experience; in fact if they go on stage without nervousness, their performance is disappointing. A comforting thought!

Hacking home with Dad after a good day was something special. We'd discuss every incident in detail at a slow hound jog, sometimes by moonlight—it would be impossible nowadays with the fast traffic on the roads. When we reached the Lodge gate at the top of the avenue, Dad would sound his horn.

The head groom McArdle, with Jimmy Keeffe and Jimmy McEniry, would light up the acetylene gas lamps in the stables and Jack Dwyer had his lantern in the kennels. Hounds were allowed to run on ahead. If we were cold and wet, we would dismount and jog home leading our horses.

Hounds were fed on a warming meal and would fight for their portion of raw flesh, while horses were rugged up and tucked into a bucket of steaming bran mash. Dad would come in and sit on the second step of the back stairs and McArdle, who worshipped his Master, had the honour of pulling off his boots. Facing away from Dad, he would grip the heel between his hands and knees, while Dad placed his other foot against McArdle's buttock and pushed hard. This was a tough job as Dad's boots were tight fitting, but he would not use a boot jack (which would pull off the heels); I was often the puller myself. Then a good soak in a deep hot bath, a bowl of bread and milk (maybe with a drop of whiskey in it) and so to bed.

I treasured every day of those last couple of seasons with Dad hunting hounds. We had some great sport. With anything less than eight miles as hounds ran, Dad would say, "When are we going to have a hunt?"

One particular run comes to mind. We were running into the Co. Limerick Hunt country with Bruff away to our right. At a check the pack divided, five couple went right handed.

Dad said, "Tha', get after them and bring them back to me", and he followed the pack.

An English visitor asked me, "Can I come and give you a hand?"

I gladly accepted. Yet try as we did, we could not stop them. They were old hounds glued to the line.

Next thing Dad appeared with the pack saying, "Where are your hounds? We were on a hare!" So hounds were reunited, and marked to ground after a right good run.

That evening Dad said, "Who was that stranger with you? Someone said his name was Williams. I liked the look of him, he is a real sportsman." And so a lifelong bond of friendship was forged with Evan Williams!

Many years later I related this incident to his wife Gill, which she found delightful. Evan was an outstanding all-round sportsman. With a Grand National and many other 'chasing victories under his belt, he turned his attention to breeding hounds and took on the Mastership of the Tipperary Hunt. Within a few short years he was winning championships in Peterborough with the GRs. This litter of outstanding hounds included Grimston and Grimsby (I cannot remember the remainder); their "line" was keenly sought after by many packs in the United Kingdom.

A sight never to be forgotten was the judging of the championship in Peterborough Hound Show. Davey McMinn, kennel huntsman of the Kilkenny, and Mickey Flanagan, Evan's first whip and kennel huntsman, were two supreme artists at the job. Each tried to outdo the other in capturing the judges' eyes for their hound, and both hounds were overly alert, playing with

Evan Williams, MFH, Tipperary discusses hounds with renowned hound breeder, Ikey Bell.

the biscuit and enjoying the game. The packed spectators were on the edge of their chairs, tense with excitement. When the champion was announced, a burst of applause shook the arena.

When Evan took on the Tipperary, a great ally, Charles Parker, came over from England. For many seasons Charles had been right-hand man to Captain Ronnie Wallace MFH with the Heythrop, in charge of earthstopping, fencing, and general management, and he took on the same job with the Tipperary. Shortly after his arrival Evan was showing him around the hunt country.

Pointing to a hill some distance away, Charles said, "There is a litter of cubs up there, Master."

Evan was incredulous. How could he know? He had only just arrived. They went to investigate and sure enough found Charles was right. Pure genius? He is a born naturalist; there is nothing he does not know about foxes and all wildlife.

Charles did a superb job earthstopping, yet sport was poor the following season. Hounds accounted for a lot of foxes, but had few good runs. Charles gave the following explanation for this apparent paradox. Poor-running foxes live mainly underground. When the country was carefully stopped, these inferior foxes outnumbered the good ones. This example of selective culling and survival of the fittest proves that hunting with hounds is the best way of controlling fox numbers, as well as enhancing the health of the fox population. After a couple of seasons, sport improved immeasurably.

During the war years, because of the lack of transport, the Co. Limerick Hunt kindly loaned to Dad some of their country furthest from kennels. This was greatly appreciated as foxes were still scarce in the Scarteen country. Many of the fine old family estates had passed out of the hands of the original owners and the houses were in ruins. However, they all had ample scrub and rough land to hold foxes.

One such estate was Ballinagarde, the home of the Croker family. Old Mr Courtney-Croker, who hunted a scratch pack in the early nineteenth century before the foundation of the Co. Limerick Hunt, loved his home dearly.

The story is told that when the parson visited him on his deathbed, Mr Croker said, "Sweet Ballinagarde, how can I leave you?"

The parson said, "Never mind, Mr Croker, you are going to a far better place".

"I doubt it," says Croker. This phrase can still be heard throughout the locality!

When, much to the relief of all, the war ended, Claude Thompson returned and Dad handed him the horn. True to form Claude set about learning his way around the country, spending a lot of time with hounds, and preparing for his first full season. He lived with us all in Scarteen. Inevitably a romance struck up; to our delight he and my sister Jean announced their engagement. Two like souls devoted to horses, hounds, and hunting, what more could one wish for!

Claude showed great sport. At the close of the season he resigned from Mastership and handed over to me a pack of disciplined, hard-hunting hounds. He and Jean were married from Scarteen and moved out into a fine farm, which he had bought near Fethard in the Tipperary Hunt country.

And so dear Dad and I were together at the helm with the horn firmly in my hand for the first of forty happy and eventful seasons. It was a momentous privilege, for which I felt all too unworthy.

Scarteen Joint-Master Claude Thompson returned from World War II to accept the horn from Dad, then marry my sister, Jean.

The Hunt Committee presents a silver tea service and salver to John J. Ryan on his retirement. (l–r) John Ryan-Purcell, Thady, Mum, Dad, Jean, and Jack (Emly).

TWENTY-FIVE

INTO HARNESS II

Without a doubt, having hounds in the family for almost four centuries was a huge built-in bonus for a young Master starting up. Of course I was nervous, but also excited. I was acutely aware that I could not just lean on the laurels of my forebears. I must do my best to follow in the footsteps of my immensely popular father.

Not everything in the garden was rosy. Some members of the Hunt Committee, prompted by a couple of newcomers from overseas, were trying to insist that I should go to another hunt country and learn how to hunt hounds before taking on the job myself. Dad and Uncle Willie were furious at the suggestion, convinced that of course I should hunt my own hounds. A stormy committee meeting was held in Harris Hotel in Knocklong. The majority of members stood by Dad. Tempers ran high. While I was waiting in an adjoining room, Jerome McCormack, a longstanding friend, was sent in to get me to change my mind. Certainly they had a case and were entitled to their opinion. However my answer was a firm *no*.

Eventually a compromise was reached. They would accept me as huntsman provided that I employed an experienced first whip and kennel huntsman, to which I agreed. There is a true saying, "A strong opposition is the life of Parliament." Among my critics, one of the most vociferous was Dad's determined and regular follower Peg Watt (chapter 23). Nonetheless she assured me that it was for my own good; I respected and valued her motives.

Through the grapevine I heard of a man who had just the experience that the committee was seeking. He had been in hunt service in England for several years and was highly recommended by Mike Wellesley-Wesley, former Master of the South Dorset. Since he had retired to Ireland, Mike had become well known as chief steward at the Clonmel Hound Show. He caused great amusement by speaking as if he had a hot potato in his mouth. He would announce in a high-pitched, husky voice, "Limmewick Wollahwallah", and look around to see if his audience understood!

As to the highly recommended first whip and kennel huntsman—yes, he was available, yes, he would come over for a trial for a couple of weeks. He was Irish, a big bonus, and had a wife and family. We did up the cottage in the yard, all arrangements were completed, and Mick McGrath arrived.

It would be hard to imagine a more suitable and instantly likeable chap—an absolute answer to all our prayers. As well as hitting it off with me from the word go, more importantly Mick became immediate friends with Jack Dwyer. I recognised that I could learn a lot from him. If there was a problem, he had the uncanny knack of telling me what I should do and making it appear as if it was actually my suggestion. More than a hunt servant, he was a close friend and ally. He was also popular while always knowing his place. As a result the "atmosphere in the camp" became peaceful again and we got down to some serious hunting.

I had one embarrassing drama early in my first season. After atrocious weather, the land was under water. I announced that in the interests of our farmers, hunting would be discontinued until further notice. After a week the meet was scheduled for Elton, a most popular fixture. Without telephones I could not remind people that there would be no hunting, but hounds were fed on this assumption. I drove to Elton to confirm that we would not be hunting. To my dismay the village was packed with riders, mostly from the Co. Limerick Hunt. When I said we were not going to hunt, they were furious, and many vowed that they would not hunt with me again. Rightly or wrongly, I stuck to my guns. The season went well, we had great sport, and after Christmas all my deserters trickled back.

On another occasion, we drew Oola Shore, usually the second draw after Ballykisteen. Oola (from the Irish "UBHLA"—the place of apples) is a small village on the Tipperary-Limerick road. (If you asked one of the elders in the area how to spell the name, he would answer "Big ooh, little ooh, el ah"!) Close by on Gerard Grace's farm were the ruins of Castle Lloyd (a small private castle) in which there was a long dry shore (a drain running from the castle ruins to a ditch some distance away) that was a natural haunt for foxes. Gerard always welcomed us and was very proud if he had a fox. Hounds were held well back outside the farmyard gate and the terrier was put in at one end of the shore. Bolting the fox could take anything from five minutes to half an hour and an explosion of hollering announced his departure. Hounds got to know this routine and were almost uncontrollable with pent-up excitement—not good because they would race off with heads up and take some time to settle on the line. I used to dread the operation because it made hounds almost wild! On one occasion in my first season I attempted to take a short cut at the back of the farmyard and my horse and I turned upside down in a manure pit. I remounted, covered in liquid manure, and caught up with hounds when they checked. Embarrassed, black, and stinking from head to foot, I arrived just in time to hear my critics asking, "Where is that young Master?"!

Once, on a later occasion, it was a bitterly cold day. We had hacked on from Ballykisteen, and on the way through Oola village, Peg Watt, Willie O'Grady, and some friends stopped off at the Pub to have a "jar" and warm themselves, believing that there would be the usual delay in bolting the fox. Surprisingly the fox left the shore the minute the terrier was put in. The "revelers" eventually turned up to find Gerard's yard and the shore deserted—hounds had got away on a really good scent and we had a super run. Our friends were furious, but they had learned their lesson and did not try that one again.

One day Dad decided to give Gwen and Jean a treat: a day's hunting with the Co. Limerick hounds. Our meet that day was at Ballintubber School—not a popular part of the country, so I looked forward to a quiet day with no pressure. Mick McGrath and I hacked on with hounds; we arrived at the meet to find a large number of foreign visitors with pink coats and top hats. I was horrified. By sheer good luck we found a good fox in some rough country under the Galty Mountains and had a great hunt. Meanwhile the Co. Limerick hounds had had a blank day! Mick and I rode home elated.

TWENTY-SIX

DEBITS AND CREDITS—SOME HIGHS AND LOWS OF MY EARLY SEASONS

Tell me a man's a fox-hunter, and I loves him at once.
Jorrocks

I am often puzzled how anyone can take on a Mastership without hunting hounds themselves. They have all the worry and responsibility and miss out on the real pleasure and reward. Mind you, if it was not for them, hunting would grind to a halt—they deserve a medal!

Hunting hounds is a full-time job—or if it is not, then it should be. Summertime is as important as wintertime. The Master should get to know all the landowners personally, calling to see them before the start of the season. Delegating this job to the area manager is the next best thing, but landowners like to meet the Master. After all, they are entitled to the compliment of a call, and where would we be without them?

Blessing of hounds and followers, Opening Meet, Knocklong, 1979. (l–r) Rev. Brian Snow, Church of Ireland; Rev. Fr. Ryan, Catholic Curate, Knocklong; Tommy Dwyer, whipper-in; Eamon Moloney; Thady Ryan, MFH on Jacko. Mary Tarry photo

The local cattle mart is an ideal meeting place. Dad met a nonhunting farmer in the cattle fair who said to him, "Master, I hope we have not had a falling out. It is over three weeks since you hunted through my farm."

If the hunt causes some damage, the harm is likewise healed more quickly by a visit from the Master. I must admit my share of blame for at times not being as diligent in this regard as I should have been. Yet although it can be difficult to find the time to make these calls, especially if one is farming oneself, the pleasure of a welcome through the country is worth all the effort.

We were hunting at Old Pallas on a really wet day. The land sodden, hounds ran fast off the hill; scent was good as it usually is in wet conditions. Without thinking, I led the large field over the Nicker road and downhill through a paddock of early spring grass, which the farmer was preserving for his few cows. The horses skidded and ripped the grass to pieces. Glancing back, I was horrified. The paddock looked as if it had been ploughed for potatoes! I called to see the farmer next morning. My heart went out to this elderly widower—he only had about ten acres.

"Mick, I have come to apologise for what we did to you yesterday, and I want to give you some compensation."

"You won't give me a penny", he replied. "You are always welcome, as your father was before you, and shure won't the land be there after us?"

One has to be prepared for some surprises. I called to see the wife of a small farmer who lived close to Knocktoran Bog, so their fowl were vulnerable. On this occasion "the fox" had killed more than twenty hens. The fowl were never shut in, as she said she had nowhere to shut them. I went over to a small outhouse in the yard.

"This is ideal", I said, starting to clear out a heap of old sacks.

To my horror I uncovered what at first I thought was a corpse but it turned out to be an old man asleep. "What *have* we got here?" I asked in astonishment.

"Oh, that is an old chap from the mental asylum. He is allowed out in the summertime to visit his friends who put him up and give him some good meals."

I gave her some generous compensation for her hens and did not pursue the question of shutting them up!

Another great opportunity to meet the farmers and have a cuppa and a chat was to do the rounds collecting casualties—horse, cow, sheep, or whatever—as a service to farmers. These would be used as the raw flesh to feed to hounds.

I thought we might miss phone calls if we were all out, so I decided to install an answering machine. The first message on it went like this.

"Helloah, is that you, Misther Riyan. Lookit here I've got this cow, she's not exactly dead yet, so you would want to bring the humane killer and . . ." Then a pause and receiver was put down.

He tried a second call. "Helloah, Mr Riyan, that cow I was telling you about, now she's not exactly dead yet so." Another pause. "I heeard him talkin' so he must be there." Down went the receiver.

He tried a third time: ". . . about this cow . . . och, it's the same blooody thing again", and slammed down the receiver. Modern technology has its drawbacks!

We hunted twice a week, sometimes three times during school holidays, horses and country permitting. In reality the affairs of the hunt often occupied six days: preparing the day before, the hunt itself, and repairing the following day. We also had the pleasure of anticipating beforehand and digesting the day's sport afterwards. One misses a lot of the pleasure if one hunts four days a week.

One of my biggest regrets is that I did not keep a hunting diary. I believe that my Dad and his generation "had the best of it." In those days one could ride one's own line through the country and stay with hounds. I had a taste of those good times, and then saw the introduction of barbed wire, scientific farming, and (finally) electric fencing coupled with increased fast traffic on road and rail—all of which has made it next to impossible to stay with hounds. However, Chris is making the best of it and enjoying what he has, having never known the good days. Recently I came across a hunt account from 1981, which gives an idea of what we used to have!

Thursday Jan 8th 1981

Meet, Kilross 11 A.M. The Master took hounds in the back bohereen to draw the twigyard in Mooresfort. Little did anyone guess what a fine day's hunting was to follow.

Hounds found almost immediately and a holloa from Tommy was the signal that a fox had left in the direction of "The Laurels" behind the house. Hounds were quickly on his line, and with their well known cry, pushed their fox out by the haybarn, viewed by young Charlie Moore, going for the screens of the Lattin Avenue. With no delay, hounds raced out of Mooresfort, through Messrs Breen's land, where we are always given a very sporting right of way. Without a check, hounds were hunting with great drive and precision, never deviating for one moment from the line. They ran up to the Tipperary-Emly road, through Mr Daly's farm, over a lovely line of country through Lissobehane, and parallel with the G.S.R. Dublin-Cork main line railway, almost to Emly station, half a mile short of which hounds checked for the first time.

Owing to the danger of an oncoming fast train, the Master had to collect his hounds in a hurry, to avoid any fatal casualties, and it is quite possible the fox went to ground under the railway. There were plenty of thrills in this twenty-minute hunt, a foretaste of what was to come.

Mr R. Coffey's covert at Ballinacree held a fox which soon left with hounds on his brush, and after a short quick dart, unfortunately got to ground in "The Wash."

Hounds found a brace of foxes in Mr Jim Burn's bog, which ajoins the land of Balinacree. From this an outstanding good hunt was to follow. The hunted fox came back towards Glenbane, but without crossing any road, he turned back in a right-handed circle, as if for Balinacree covert, over Mr Lance Ryan's land. He then swung right again, and hounds skirting Burn's bog, ran on fast through Larry Hogan's farm for the second time. What a sportsman to have his gates thrown open for us! Thank you, Larry! Hounds were now flying. They ran over Mr Condon's land and Mr Rafferty's, over the hill of Longstone, and over the Knockaunavoher road, up to the Church at Templebraden. Mr Dick O'Brien had a great view from the summit of Sarsfield's Rock, seeing fox and hounds cross his land, and the road beneath him. With no delay hounds ran on as if for Derk, but they turned right handed before reaching the badger earths on Mr Jack Cummins's land below Derk gate, and ran through Mr Breen's farm at Newtown. Crossing the bye-road close to the front gates, hounds hunted beautifully over the hill of Rahard and on to the back of Garryhakin, overlooking the village of Oola. But turning again right handed, hounds crossed the rocky road, just above Cullen Church. Without entering Cullen covert, hounds ran on again over Longstone, but turned left

> handed this time, racing for Balinacree. The fox by this time must have been very tired, as hounds had been pressing him all the time, and he got to ground in a badger set on Mr Lance Ryan's land, just in front of hounds. This was a very fine hound hunt of one hour and ten miles as hounds ran, over big testing country."

With no motorised transport, they were long days in the saddle. Mum would send me out with a sandwich in my pocket. The sandwich consisted of a couple of big, brown sodabread scones, freshly made and stodgy, with a slab of cheese in them.

Riding on to the next draw on one hunt, Peg Watt came up alongside. "Master, I have a bone to pick with you." She was agitated.

"Right Peg, let's have it—oh, would you like to have a sandwich?"

"Yes I will", and she took a savage bite at the scone. Her dentures sank into it and stuck. She was unable to utter a word. That was the end of the bone!

Caherconlish was one of our furthest meets—sixteen miles at a hound jog of six miles per hour, so over two and a half hours away. Drawing towards home, we would have a hack of about twelve miles. Living at Caherconlish was John Power, who was a great character and long-standing member of the Hunt Committee, his wife, who was the dispensary doctor, and their family. I was the go-between in an ongoing "argument" over their son Dickie's education: Dr Power insisted that Dickie must not miss school; John insisted that hunting was an equally important part of his education. I don't know who finally won the argument, maybe they compromised, but anyway Dickie has turned out absolutely tops! To protect our farmers, fields are limited to no more than fifty. Dickie Power and his charming wife, Catherine, have the most unenviable job of deciding who shall hunt on a given day—a task that demands the height of diplomacy.

At about 6 A.M. one morning, one of my earthstoppers in the Boscal Bog area, old Mick Ryan, called to John Power's house. He worked for the county council drawing stones with his horse and butt-cart with its heavy steel-shod wheels. John put his head out the window.

"What do you want Mick?" he asked.

"Sir, that vixen I was telling you about has moved her brood of cubs from Sean Hayes' double ditch into McCarthy's gullet."

John was furious. "What in the name of fortune do you mean by waking me up at this ungodly hour just to tell me about a fox's domestic arrangements?"

"I wonder will she send me to the hospital?" said Mick.

"Why, what ails you?"

Mick put his hand into his pocket and produced a finger, with another finger just hanging on by a piece of skin. "An' I tacklin' the oul mare to the cart this morning, didn't I trip up and fall, an' she pulled the cart right over me hand." Mick was more concerned about the vixen and her cubs!

The very Rev Dr Purdue, former Bishop of Cork, lived for a while near Killaloe. The Manse had a few acres of good land, so he decided to keep a few pedigree Guernsey heifers and a good bull. A tall, fine man with a good sense of humour, Dr Purdue tells this story. He was doing a job in the yard, wearing his old working clothes. A neighbour called to him.

"Do you work here?" the neighbour asked.

Dr Purdue hesitated, unsure of what to say. "Ye-es, yes, I suppose I do."

"Oh gor sur, would ye ever give me a hand to fill the hole in the bounds fence? That bull of yours is breaking out into my cows."

They went together to repair the damage. The hole was obviously man-made and well used. The following spring there was a crop of beautiful Guernsey-cross calves in several adjoining farms. As Dr Purdue pointed out, in this life you must be prepared to give and take!

The same advice is sound for an MFH. One morning the phone rang—it was the manager of Herbertstown Cooperative Society. A member of the committee had some stirks grazing on a rented farm at the Red Gate near Scarteen. Could I oblige him by allowing him to use my cattle pen where he could dehorn them? I did not know who the member was. My cattle pen was in use as a collecting yard for the cows before milking. I could picture the mess—horns and blood all over the place and the cows all upset.

"I'm sorry," I said, "I have to refuse, but I will send up some help with my new Taylor cattle-handling crate so that the cattle can be done where they are."

"Hold on a moment", said the manager. He was back in a few minutes. "No, 'tis alright, he says he will make other arrangements", and he put the phone down.

I was uneasy, suspecting trouble.

A couple of months later, John Power was on the phone. "What on earth have you done to Mick McCarthy? No more hunting is allowed all around Caherline and the surrounding area."

I was devastated. Poor Mick was done-up with rheumatics. He had a big farm and was highly respected among all his neighbours; he and I had always got on well. I was sore. If I had known it was him asking for somewhere to do the dehorning, I would have allowed him to do the job in my dining room. I arranged straight away to collect John, along with Tom Dalton of Caherline House, and call on Mick. We found him seated by the fire. I opened my soul to him, apologised profusely and put my hand out to shake hands. He turned away.

For two years I could not get Mick to forgive me. Deeply hurt and in desperation, I asked his brother Jack if he could intercede for me. He did, the wound was healed and we were the best of friends again.

Jack himself had a small puck goat. One day the puck jumped into the farm of his neighbour Tom Hickey, who was a hunting man, as was his brother Joe of Oola Hills. When Tom's thoroughbred mare with foal saw the goat, they galloped like mad. Without knowing who owned the goat, Tom went in, got his gun and shot him. Jack was furious. There was going to be no more hunting in the Dromkeen area. I was at my wit's end. This time I called to Mick to ask him to intercede for me. He did, and we were all the best of friends once more!

To cap it all, Jack's son Pat McCarthy is the keenest hunt follower on foot and hardly ever misses a day. Filling his car with neighbours, he tears around the country, always being first to view the fox and report to Chris. His enthusiasm is breathtaking and contagious. In addition, Pat is a good judge of a horse; he and Pat Gleeson of Dromkeen House are breeding some top show hunters with great success.

When Major Watt ("Watty") retired from hunting the United, he and Peg bought Riversfield. A kindhearted and generous sporting couple, they offered their house freely for hunt dances, charity functions of all sorts, poker evenings, and entertainment unlimited—it was the quintessence of hospitality. As a hobby, Watty had a band that was constantly in demand—especially for hunt dances. To see him with a cute smile on his face happily playing the drums hour after hour was unforgettable.

One season we had lost a few days hunting on account of bad weather, so I planned a bye-day (an unscheduled extra day's hunting arranged at short notice—no cap is taken) and spread the word by mouth. It turned out to be the funeral day of Peg's brother Eamon Rohan—as a great judge of a horse, his loss was felt throughout the hunting world. So I thought it would be inappropriate to send word about the bye-day to Peg. We happened to have a helluva run. Two days later I got a telegram from Peg, exceedingly hurt at not being informed.

She would not speak to me for years afterwards. Then at a party I was with a group of friends, Peg among them. Taking a chance, I asked her why she would not speak with me. I had caught her in a unguarded moment and she listened to my explanation. The hatchet was buried permanently.

Another to hunt regularly with us was Willie O'Grady, who had been a jockey and was then training. I enjoyed his company, he was fun and livened up a disappointing day. If we were delayed in covert, Willie would amuse the followers. Dismounting, he would put a rock on the pommel of someone's saddle. The rock had to be passed around and woe betide anyone who dropped it. He was the life and soul of any party—you could hear his wolf whistle a mile away.

Late one night when he and Peg were driving home from a party in Cork, a line of painted tar barrels ran down the centre of a road under repair. For fun Willie took a belt at each barrel. However, it so happened that a policeman was on duty there. Stopping them, he opened the car door and got the strong smell of whiskey.

"You will spend the night in the barracks", said the young officer. After much persuasion he took them in.

"If we are staying here, we'll have a deck of cards", says Peg.

"Madam, we don't keep cards in the barracks."

"I bet you do", says Peg and takes a pack out of the top drawer of the chest. The night was gambled away!

A couple of months later Peg saw in the paper that the young officer had been promoted to the rank of sergeant, and she sent him a telegram of congratulations.

My long-time ambition was to do something for our landowners to show our appreciation of their generosity. I hit on the idea of having hunt socials—a free party and dance at local halls around the country, advertised at the creameries. Hunt members supplied sandwiches, cakes, and tea (no alcohol). We had a local band, singing, horn-blowing competitions, and the like. One venue was the Brook Hall at Dromkeen. I asked the owner about the conveniences.

"Oh yes", she said, "we have running water." And she showed me the "loo"—it was erected out over the brook!

From the socials we had one tragedy. A nice old chap who lived alone in a cottage on Wonder Hill went for a drink with friends after the party at Kilteely, one of the popular venues. As he had one too many, a friend drove him home and left him at his cottage gate. The poor chap put his hand through the stained glass panels of his front door and cut an artery. He was found dead the following day. I still feel a suspicion of guilt.

After a few years it appeared that the bulk of those coming to the socials were the working boys and girls, and we were no longer getting the people we wanted, so we gave up the venture.

We had one great success when we invited the local branch of *Macra na Feirme* (Young Farmers Club) to hold their field evening at Scarteen. Clubs take it in turns to invite others from all over the country for the occasion, which involves such events as stock judging, quiz competitions, and craft work. Getting a hundredweight of gams (pigs' hocks and crubeens or trotters) from the bacon factory, we par-cooked them in the kennel steamer (after it had been well scrubbed), then our Field Master Charlie Warren, with other helpers, barbecued them. With boiled spuds and carrots, followed by fruit salad and cream, everyone enjoyed a superb meal. For this beautiful warm summer evening, a huge marquee was erected on the tennis lawn and they danced until the early hours.

Some weeks later I was driving our little Renault home from Dublin when, just outside Abbeyleix at about 1 A.M., I got a puncture. The spare was almost flat. I came up the town carrying the spare to try to get it pumped up.

A voice behind me said, "Can I help you, Mr Ryan?"

Dumbfounded, I replied, "How do you know me?"

"Oh, you gave us a party of a lifetime a few weeks ago."

His sister had just bought a new Renault like ours, which was parked in the main street outside the drycleaning shop she ran. Prying open the boot with a screwdriver, my new friend gave me the spare wheel. I was elated. Next time coming through Abbeyleix, I gave his sister a big box of chocolates with her new wheel. One good turn deserves another!

After moving from England many years earlier, Charlie Warren ("Sir Charles Warren Baronet" to be correct) lived near Cahir in Co. Tipperary. He then moved to an old house in Castle Oliver farmyard, which needed extensive repair; however, he was a genius at such work and revelled in it. He also bought a couple of old thatched cottages in the charming fishing town Dunmore East in Co. Waterford. In the hunting off-season, he did some successful sea fishing including lobster catching. On several occasions our family rented the cottages and had a great time with him.

But hunting was Charlie's first love. A tall, powerful man with a large heart to match, he was a fearless rider across country. I persuaded him to be Field Master. He proved a model example for the task. He knew the country well, rode hard, and held the field close to hounds but without interference (a difficult task). He had a commanding manner, as well as being respected and loved by all—a real diplomat. I am deeply indebted to him for a job well done.

Sir Charles Warren was my best Field Master. Catherine Power photo

Another great sportsman not to be forgotten is Tom Nugent, a small farmer of Coolnadown near Emly. He was literally crazy about hunting. Following the hunt on his bicycle, whenever possible he would cadge a lift, throwing his bike into the boot of a car or just into the ditch.

Mooresfort, the big demesne and home of the Moore family (see chapter 10), had three or four big lime trees with a huge growth of twigs, making an ideal lie for a fox. After plastering some mud on the bark of the trees the evening before a hunt, Pat Barry (the steward) could tell if a fox was at home. He would produce a ladder and Tom would climb into the thicket with the terrier. I would hold hounds well away from the tree; the followers also at a distance could see the action. The fox would jump down and away, while poor Tom would be abandoned. On one occasion Tom jumped down on to his bike; on his way out the avenue, he heard cries for help. Napper Webb, our treasurer at the time, had fallen into the big ditch with his horse on top of him. Tom raised the alarm; but for him, Napper would have been a dead man.

On one hunt we were at Sheehan's Cross, not too far from Fedamore, where the Co. Limerick hounds also had a meet on the same day. It may seem strange, but having two nearby meets is quite popular among farmers and bloodstock owners, as there is only one stockwarning in the area instead of two. Some bloodstock owners and dairy farmers like to be advised when hounds are going to be in their area, which customarily comes in a card from the hunt honorary secretary. My sister Gwen Pearson sends such cards most conscientiously. It so happened that the Limerick hounds ran into the country we had just left. A charming English lady, Cynthia O'Kelly, whose late husband had been a leading member of the Co. Limerick Hunt, had been following the Limerick hounds in her automobile, but had lost touch with them.

She asked a fellow on a bicycle, "I say, have you seen the haans?"

"Yes, mam", said Tom Nugent, throwing his bike into the ditch and jumping into the car alongside her. "Turn right here, mam, straight on, now turn left. Here they are."

"Oh!" she said. "These are not the haans I was following."

"Gob, mam, these are the only hounds I know", says Tom.

I visited Tom in the Limerick Regional Hospital shortly before he died. His face lit up and we talked of all the fun we had had together. If there is hunting in Heaven and you see a chap cycling furiously after hounds, that will be Tom!

Grenane House near Tipperary town was the home of Gregor and Marjorie Mansergh. This handsome Georgian building was an ideal venue for a lawn meet, which they held every season. It had a large area of clipped laurels with a maze of walks. Hounds found a fox there and were in hot pursuit with wonderful cry. I was overexcited. A tall lad was in the thick of it, obviously a "townie," judging by his dress.

"Did you see the fox?" I half shouted to him.

"I did", he replied.

"Which way did he go?"

"That's your job to find out", he said. How right he was!

We were hunting in Grenane while the family were away on holiday. Hounds marked to ground in a hole in the base of a tall beech tree, which was obviously hollow from decay. I noticed another hole about ten feet up from the ground, but no terrier was available. I took hounds well away, and got a chap to light a small wisp of dried grass in the lower hole. Immediately no less than three foxes jumped out of the top hole, and away with us!

But that was not the end of the story. The hollow tree was a perfect chimney with a good draught. It caught fire, and that night it crashed to the ground. All the neighbours had firewood galore for Christmas. However, the Master had some explaining to do when the owners returned.

Another couple whose company I enjoyed over a cuppa was Arthur Morrissey and his wife, who lived on the hill of Kilfeacle on the main road to Dublin. Their son Mossey, who loved his hunting, was a zealous area manager. If Arthur got talking to a farmer who did not like the hunt coming through, Arthur would say to him, "You will die young". And it is true—people who are highly strung and worry a lot get ulcers and do not live long!

Across the main Dublin road, Johnny and Nina Marshall farmed some sound land—large rolling fields ideal for working young stock. With an eye for a good horse, Johnny was always in demand as a judge at horse shows around the country. He just beat me one year in the Hunt Cup at our point-to-point in Tipperary hills. I was riding a good hunter belonging to Claude Thompson, but Johnny's horse was close to thoroughbred. I got my own back a few years on riding Tom Tallow (see chapter 32).

Johnny was Master and huntsman of the Kilfeacle beagles (sadly, now disbanded) and showed great sport. His son John is carrying on ably in his father's footsteps and, as area manager, is the greatest help to my son Chris.

Old Mrs Finnan was the last woman that I remember to wear a shawl. She lived with her son Paddy (my earthstopper) on the side of Glenefy Hill.

When I called in one day for a cuppa and a chat, she said to me firmly, "You're no good".

"Oh, what have I done?" I was perplexed.

"I tell you, you are no good. You could have been the richest man in County Limerick and you let her slip through your fingers, and she has gone and married PP."

She had it all planned in her own mind that I should marry Maureen Gubbins and take on Kilfrush. I don't think she ever forgave me!

PP was Patt Hogan, already a successful amateur rider over fences and a fearless and dedicated fox hunter. When Maureen and Patt moved in to Kilfrush, Patt quickly realised his dream of setting up probably the best stable of point-to-pointers and likely 'chasers in the country. They built forty new loose boxes in the inner yard, which were soon occupied. Their generosity was also boundless; if a neighbour was in want of anything—the loan of machinery, some firewood or a helping hand—they never refused.

Camouflage! Hounds draw a wooded covert with Thady in Kilfrush. M. A. Keating photo

Maureen Hogan of Kilfrush, a lifetime hunt member, with two great sportsmen, Paddy McCann (left) and Alan Lillingston.

Patt's training success was phenomenal. He and Maureen shared the ability to spot top class young horses. As four-year-olds they had their "heads hunted off them" and were never known to refuse. Patt was one of the leading National Hunt (steeplechase) trainers for many years. He was a firm believer in giving his horses ample hunting experience followed by a full point-to-point season. This regimen made them courageous and foot sure. The sideboards in the dining room in Kilfrush were burdened down with the beautiful solid silver cups and trophies from most of the prestigious steeplechases in Punchestown, Fairyhouse, and throughout the country.

In the hunting field Patt's enthusiasm, jealousy, and exuberance were contagious. He would set people alight and frequently drove me to distraction overriding hounds—he could not help it. Eventually I thought of a solution. I appointed him Field Master, a job he performed brilliantly for years. If anyone crossed his path, woe betide them!

It would be invidious for me to name the numerous sporting friends who stayed at Kilfrush during the hunting season. However one person has to have a mention. While Paddy McCann broke stock on Tuesdays (the only day that the Limericks or Scarteens did not hunt), for the rest of the time he was in residence. A more popular figure would be hard to imagine.

He said to me once, "Your hounds are frequently in my way." That reflects his zeal aptly!

There was nothing I enjoyed more than to call in to Kilfrush after a good day's hunting. Sitting by the fire in the library with Patt, Maureen, and their three daughters, I would chat with them over a cup of tea, discussing the problems and joys of the day.

Sadly the pace could not last. Expenditure was never curbed, and Kilfrush had to be put on the market. The countryside was close to being in mourning—I certainly was—at the break-up of such a wonderful institution. Patt and Maureen were true and loyal friends to me down the years. Now Rathcannon is my first call on my visits home and I am sure of a big welcome from Patt and his loving daughter Susan.

My apologies! I have been rioting on too many fresh foxes. I must pick up my original line.

P. P. Hogan—steeplechase rider, trainer, and sportsman—drove me to distraction over-riding hounds in his enthusiasm. The solution? I appointed him Field Master! Frank H. Meads photo

TWENTY-SEVEN

(SOME OF) MY MORTAL SINS!

They say that confession is good for the soul. Several of the following anecdotes sit on the borderline for inclusion, but I said I would be honest so in they come! Some of them stretched my conscience almost to breaking point at the time, but even in hindsight I think I was justified in my decisions.

Alcohol was never a problem for me. I think I could count on the fingers of one hand the number of times I remember being drunk. One of those was when I had three farmers to see before a day's hunting. Being a bit of a coward, I decided to call on the two easy ones first. True to the traditionally hospitable custom, my first host brought me into the parlour. It was 10 A.M. Out came the bottle of whiskey and the glass was filled, leaving no room for water or soda. All was well. The story was the same in the second house. At the gate of my third call, I opened the car door and fell out on to the road. I crept home in disgrace!

Another incident was even more embarrassing. We were entertained for a lawn meet at Ballyscaddane, just across the road from Scarteen, by David and Doreen Gale. True to tradition, David brought me a chunk of rich fruit cake and a large glass or port (seriously laced), which I could not empty on the other side of my horse as he stood there talking. We moved off to draw. My hounds were a moving sea of colour. I did not dare speak to them, I could not blow my horn, I could barely stay in my saddle—I was in trouble. I think hounds found and my horse kept me close to them.

Other sins have involved an occasional flare of anger. For many years we held our hunt ball in a hotel in Limerick. City folk looked on it as the best party of the year. I was criticised for not having it in the centre of our hunting country, but my argument was that the ball was run to make money, and I did not wish to bleed our own followers, who all came anyway. The "Hunt Ball Meet" was at Longford Bridge on the main Limerick road the following day, and a big crowd turned up, including many visitors. Hounds and horsemen were spread all over the road (wrongly). A car came at speed from the Cork direction and zigzagged through the horses and hounds.

In a lack of judgement I lost my temper. I hit the roof of the car with my crop, shouting, "Where the hell are you going?"

The car screeched to a halt. Out jumped two of the most cross men in Ireland. They were taking greyhounds to the track in Limerick and were running late. One came at me and, along with language that is unprintable here, he shouted for all to hear, "You will never again hunt across my land or my neighbours' land." And he drove away at speed.

I recognised him: Patsy Hogan, a friend who had a lovely farm near Derk in the heart of our best hunting country. Knowing I was completely in the wrong, I felt miserable all day. The next morning I called to Patsy with my sister Gwen—he couldn't kill me in front of her! Patsy, down the farm cleaning a drain with a shovel, saw us coming and went on with his work. I did not know what to expect.

"Patsy, I have come to apologise sincerely for what I did to you yesterday."

"Oh Master will you stop. I was that ashamed of myself for the foul language I used in front of all them gentry." Our friendship was instantly restored.

There have been other hunting incidents for which I must confess my sins. J. P. Ryan of Mitchelstowndown, known to his myriad of friends as the Jap, was an all-round sportsman. Chairman of the regional branch of the Gaelic Athletic Association, he coached and fostered the local team, the Garry Bouncers, in Gaelic Games. At other times he travelled the country racing his super-class greyhounds. Tragically he was killed in a car crash. I have never ever attended a funeral larger than his.

The Jap was also crazy on hunting. Every year he and his friend Denis Carroll of Ballinahinch walked a couple of super hound puppies, following the hunt in their cars and never missing a day. Foxes had been scarce this season in the Knocktoran area and we were due to have a big meet at Elton, the most popular meet on the card. Having heard rumours that even if Knocktoran Bog was blank, we would find a fox, I was suspicious, but could say nothing.

Sure enough the bog was blank. We were hacking on to draw around Ballinahinch when there was a "holloa" a couple of fields in from the road. I took hounds to the holloa and found Denis with a sack over his arm. We looked at each other in silence knowing each other's thoughts. In theory, I should have gone right away at once with hounds, but had to make a quick decision. They had done it with the best intentions so that Knocktoran would not be labelled a blank, so—mea culpa—I relented and let hounds pick up the line. They ran barely a mile and marked to ground in Denis's farm. As we were coming out his driveway, Denis was coming in.

We stopped and I started to say to him, "He did not go very far . . ." when suddenly the pack rushed to the boot of his little Morris Minor. I jogged off briskly!

We left the Glen covert on Glenefy, close to the village of Galbally one evening in a hurry. Scent was strong, the light was failing and hounds were flying. We came to a farm that I knew was out of bounds as the result of an old wound many years before my time. Against my conscience, but fearful of losing hounds, I jumped in over the single bank only to take a nasty fall over the barbed wire fence on the landing side, breaking several paling posts—served me right! My whipper-in Denis Turner took on the fence away to my right and jumped into the arms of the farmer who was out cutting bushes. In fury he hit Denis's horse over the nose, cutting him badly.

That night at home we discussed what I should do. I decided to write a letter as follows:

> Dear Mr Smith,
> I am writing to apologise for what happened yesterday. I was the one who broke the paling, and I will come and repair it. You will be glad to hear that I think the black horse will be all right. I got my vet to stitch his nose that evening and he looks well today.
> Yours sincerely

I knew I had done wrong and Mr Smith knew he had done wrong, so I suppose we were quits. We have been welcome through his farm ever since.

Another time we were hacking on to draw Kilfrush from the opening meet at Knocklong. Patt Hogan, Field Master at the time, rode up alongside me.

"Master, the lads tell me that they see a dog fox regularly coming out of the laurels by the front gate. I suggest you draw there first before going to the main covert", he said.

I smelt a rat. "No, Patt. If we do that we might disturb a good fox in the covert. I think it would be safer to draw the cover first."

"All right, all right, have it your own way", and he dropped back to the field.

Fortunately we found in the covert and had a good run. During the day my sister Jean overheard two lads talking. "Ah, it was a shame they didn't hunt that big fox. He shot out of the bag with his tail over his back—he was a flyer!"

Tom Ryan of Kilfinane had a daughter whose French husband was a keen stag hunter. When the couple were home on a holiday, Tom asked me if the Frenchman could come out on foot to see hounds cub hunting. I said I would be delighted. We were due to have our first morning's cubbing on foot in Maguire's Glen on Slievereagh not far from Kilfinane at 7 A.M. the following morning.

I greeted the visitor in my best pidgin French; his English was equally poor. I put hounds into covert. The young entry hung around me for a while, then they heard a hound speak away up the glen and off with them. Unfortunately a beautiful shorthorn heifer heavy in calf was down in the stream for a drink. She took fright and away with her, followed by young 'uns in full cry. She jumped three double banks as good as any hunter and ended up unscathed, but stuck in the hen run at the back of the cowshed.

The farmer came out to see what the noise was about. Tommy Dwyer and I were giving hounds a hiding for their crime when our French friend turned up. I tried to explain as best I could that normally we hunt only foxes, but when we had a keen stag hunter out, I wanted to lay on something special to please him! However, another time we did find something to impress.

A GENUINE STAG HUNT

The following is not really a mortal sin—just a bit of unorthodox fun. A fallow stag was reported to be in the Newtown area on the hills between

Caherconlish and Inch St Lawrence, which had a lot of natural gorse covert. I arranged a meet at Inch St Lawrence in the hope of coming across him. I had arranged with my sister Jean that if the stag was spotted. she would give one of her exciting "holloas", and if we were on a fox, I would wait for a check, then lift hounds on to the stag.

Hounds found in the gorse gave us a nice half hour and marked to ground. We found again quickly and, as expected, I heard Jean's "holloa". When hounds checked, I lifted them as planned. An English visitor galloped up to tell me he had just viewed a brace ahead of hounds. I told him I did not want to know anything about foxes; he must have thought I was mad (and he was probably right). I galloped with hounds to where the stag had been seen in some scrub. The steady old hounds sniffed the stag's scent, puzzled. The young hounds spoke to it excitedly and I encouraged them. Then when the stag showed himself, some hounds were frightened. But they soon settled on the line.

Then all hell broke out—everyone was hollering like mad and galloped madly in pursuit. It was like a scene from *Alice in Wonderland*. The order of running was first the stag away ahead at full tilt, next Fr Sweeney, parish priest of Kilteely on his Thoroughbred, then the field, then hounds, and finally the Master.

Soon we got back into the correct order. Hounds were flying. They crossed the Limerick road by John Power's house near Caherconlish. I took a corner too fast on the tarmac and hit it hard, but nothing broken. Short of the Tipperary-Limerick road, we lost contact with hounds.

I shouted to a lad on the roadside, "Have you seen the hounds?"

"Yes sir, they were running the roadside towards Tipperary an' they flying—but there was a class of a goat in front of them!"

We soon made contact. The stag swam the Mulcair River heading for Glenstal Woods from where I thought he must have strayed. However he brought hounds back over the river and into the boggy lands near Dromkeen, where they checked. When a fox got up in front of them, I decided we would abandon our frivolity and get back into line. We had a lovely hunt of over eight miles and an experience of a lifetime.

Enough confessing! Such anecdotes could go on ad infinitum. But we have a lot of fresh country yet to cover. However I wish to hold you for just a little while longer in the hunting vein.

TWENTY-EIGHT

A SAD PARTING—BUT COMPENSATION FOLLOWS

During the three happy seasons that Mick McGrath was guiding me in my early experience as MFH, he taught me a lot. However, his English wife was not happy and wanted to return to her homeland. Unselfish as always, Mick agreed to her wishes and shortly after Christmas he gave me his notice. It felt like a body blow.

By good fortune, some months previously I had advertised for some responsible help on the farm and appointed a young English chap who applied. When I met him off the train at Knocklong Station, to my horror he was wearing plus-fours with a thumbstick and a black and white collie! However, I had no need to fear. He was soon in working clothes and doing all the farm chores.

Tony Villiers was accepted as one of the family. Clever with his hands, he did a great job repairing some buildings, including the puppy kennels. I could soon see that his attention was given more and more to the hounds, so when Mick left, Tony was the obvious person to take his place—everybody was happy! Soon after, Rosie Bell from Fota Island in Co. Cork came into the picture. They were soon married and we were to enjoy a couple of happy seasons together.

As Tony had done a stint in the army in one of the guards' regiments, punctuality and immaculate grooming and turnout were second nature to him. He taught me how to shine my hunting boots with spit-and-polish. This practice was soon forgotten when we took to using the French Bottes Deblon, leather-lined boots with rubber coating that dispensed with the need for trees to maintain their shape (in contrast to traditional leather boots). Waterproof and thornproof, they would last about four seasons.

Tony and I took a busman's holiday when Victor McCalmont invited us down to Mount Juliet for a day's hunting, mounted on his own horses. Some weeks earlier the Kilkennys had had an epic run from Mullinavat West so for this meet, in the same area, the whole hunting country turned up hopefully to hunt the same fox. No such luck! However, we had an enjoyable day, and all congregated back in Mount Juliet for a sumptuous hunt tea—scrambled eggs and bacon and all the trimmings. What a feast!

Victor's father, Major Dermot McCalmont, was seated at the head of the long dining room table, his wife June was at the other end and I was privileged to be on her right. June, a charming lady from a great hunting family in England, was shy so conversation was a bit difficult. Little did I guess then that she was to become my Joint-Master a few years later.

Toward the end of the meal, Victor asked Tony and myself if we would like to come out to the kennels and see hounds fed. We jumped at the opportunity. Davey McMinn was the famous kennel huntsman with the Kilkenny for many years; the kennels were his pride and joy. The hot-boiled meat and soup were bucketed out of the boilers into the long wooden trough. Davey, his short legs astride the trough, would handle every bit of meat—a job he would entrust to no one else—to remove any chips of bone that might be in it. Then the cooked oatmeal, like porridge, was added and well mixed. Finally some minced raw meat was scattered along the top. Quite a feast—you could eat it yourself!

Meanwhile in the sleeping lodges the benches were banked up with crisp oaten straw, in which hounds tumbled and rolled to dry themselves. When dinner was ready they rushed in to devour it—front legs spread apart and hungrily scooping and swallowing it with zest. While they were feeding, the soiled straw was removed from the benches, discarded, and replaced with fresh straw. Hounds were taken out from the feeding yard while some hot soup and minced raw meat were added to the trough. Hounds were let back in to lick up the last scraps, then they were full. I thought of my lads after a hard day, tearing at a raw carcass and sleeping on bare boards as I could not afford straw.

In due course a vacancy for a huntsman occurred with the United Hunt. Watty had retired and Mary Whitehead had taken over as Master. Tony seized the opportunity of a lifetime to do what was his life's ambition. He parted with my best wishes for a great future.

After Tony Villiers' departure, I advertised again for an amateur whip. In this way Denis Turner joined the family, along with his wife Lynn and young twins Tony and Bea. Denis's father, who had been personal physician to the Duke of Gloucester, had wanted his son to be a doctor and his wishes had prevailed against Denis's hopes of being a vet.

Denis said, "If I must doctor, then I will go and doctor where I can enjoy myself", and hit off with his family for Central Africa.

A true naturalist, he enjoyed studying the African wildlife for a few years. His stories and experiences were spellbinding, told through a large bushy moustache that was still not big enough to hide his infectious smile and sense of humour.

After a couple of enjoyable seasons, Denis retired from the job, and he and Lynn went their separate ways. Lynn married Walter Trench, who was home in Castle Oliver from a life farming in Kenya. Although Castle Oliver had been empty for many years and Walter tried unsuccessfully to sell it, he got fond of the old place and made it habitable. He and Lynn did some serious and successful pig rearing and fattening, growing all the feed on the farm. Tragically Walter died within a few short years. Lynn and her son Tony changed to dairy farming, and eventually sold out.

Meantime Denis had bought a portion of Aughinish Island in the Shannon Estuary, where he enjoyed life among the myriad of native and migratory waterfowl of all kinds. With encouragement and tax incentives from the Irish

Government, the giant Alcan Alumina Company from Canada set about establishing an aluminium smelting plant on Aughinish Island, with the raw material, bauxite, coming from Africa. After long and friendly negotiations for Denis's portion of the island, a deal was struck strongly in Denis's favour. As a result, he could assist his children financially: Tony bought a farm in New Zealand and Bea bought a farm of good land near the village of Elton in our hunting country. The newly born Aughinish Alumina Company was soon to play a big part in nonthoroughbred horse breeding in Ireland (see chapter 33).

By now Tommy Dwyer, younger son of our long-time kennel huntsman Jack Dwyer, was in full charge of the Scarteen hounds. After Tommy had finished school he joined Jimmy Keeffe, my head groom, and Jimmy McEniry in the stables. Unlike his father, Tommy was a natural horseman. A fearless rider, he took to hunting like a duck to water. Gradually as his father aged, Tommy had stepped into his shoes. No Master could wish for a more dedicated first whip and kennel huntsman.

Next to hunting, Tommy's love was for Gaelic Games. As well as being a long-time member of the local branch of the Gaelic Athletic Association, the Garry Bouncers, he was an outstanding hurler. Hurling is the Irish national game, second fastest-team game in the world (after ice hockey). His close friendship with J. P. Ryan ("the Jap", see chapter 27) and his brilliance on the hurling field endeared him to a large circle of sportsmen and admirers in the hunting country, an invaluable asset in his hunting career.

As in his hunting, so in his hurling, Tommy's courage, bravery, dedication, and sheer guts were phenomenal. His mother used to tell me that she was far more scared about his risk of injury when hurling than in hunting.

Like his father, Tommy never missed his attendance at 8 A.M. in the kennels, and no day was too long for him. My son Chris is blessed to have Tommy continuing in service with him.

A few years back towards the end of the season, Tommy said to Chris, "Master, don't buy me a horse for next season. I think I am going to hang up my boots."

There was gloom in Scarteen. Then the next day they had a terrific hunt; Tommy was glowing with pride in his hounds.

He said to Chris that evening, "Master, I have changed my mind. I won't retire."

This shows the spirit of the man. The ties between his family and mine, deep-rooted in our love for hounds and hunting, have been growing ever stronger as the years go by.

Tommy Dwyer receives presentation from Nora Russell celebrating his forty years as first whipper-in and kennel huntsman, St Stevens day, 1992. He's still going strong!

TWENTY-NINE

A HAPPY UNION

Mount Juliet in Co. Kilkenny must be one of the finest estates in Ireland. A large, handsome house, it is set in beautiful park land overlooking the River Nore, famous for its salmon fishing. For years it was the home of the McCalmont family. Since it has changed hands, like so many of the great houses in Ireland, it has become a luxurious hotel with a superb golf course.

When Major Dermot McCalmont took over the Kilkenny hounds, he moved them into the magnificent new kennels that he had built in Mount Juliet. His predecessor was the foxhound breeder Isaac ("Ikey") Bell, who bred an outstanding pack of hounds. Dermot, and later his son Victor, continued the tradition. Kilkenny hounds won countless championships in Clonmel and Peterborough Hound Shows. Dermot was looked up to as the father of foxhunting in Ireland.

For many years Dermot was chairman of the Irish Masters of Foxhounds Association (IMFHA). I also had the honour of serving as a committee member for a long period, as well as having a spell as chairman. Another long-time IMFHA member was Dick Russell, who served as honorary secretary. A great sportsman and Master of the Waterford hounds, Dick was quiet with a soft and slightly nasal voice. Committee meetings were usually held at the Club House in Kilkenny.

At one meeting Lord Daresbury ("Toby") and myself were seated together. Toby had a thorn in his side in the person of a poacher, who, unknown to Toby, would occasionally produce a bagman (a bagged fox) for the Limerick hounds. The chairman turned to the honorary secretary.

"Any correspondence, Dick?"

Dick's face flushed with embarrassment. "Ye-es, Chairman, there is one letter . . . eh . . . shall I read it out?"

"Of course, man, get on with it. We have not got all day."

Hesitantly, with the occasional glance at Toby and myself, Dick read the letter. From an anti-bloodsport enthusiast, it went something like this:

> My wife and I heard that a fox had been caught and was being kept in a silage tower, and was to be released the following day for the County Limerick hounds to hunt. We went there by night and released the fortunate creature. This practice is going on also in the Scarteen country.

Toby and I must have looked like two naughty schoolboys. The furious chairman exclaimed, "What the hell is going on in County Limerick?"

Victor was Dermot's son from his first marriage. On the death of his first wife, Dermot married June, the charming lady whom I first met during a hunt tea (chapter 28), and they had three sons. Upon Dermot's death, Victor and his wife Bunny took over Mount Juliet and the hounds. They continued the tradition of excellence in hound breeding and in the thoroughbred bloodstock world.

June then bought a fine farm of land between Elton and Kilmallock in the Scarteen Hunt country. She built a magnificent Georgian-style house with stables to match, which became Martinstown Stud. Of course she hunted regularly with us, and inevitably I invited her to become Joint-Master. She accepted eagerly and we had eleven happy seasons together.

June was a kind, generous, and popular person who involved herself in all sorts of charitable works. She was also a chain smoker. Crossing a river on a hunt, her horse stumbled and they both went under water. Followers near her swear that when she surfaced the cigarette was still alight in her lips! Her late husband had been a connoisseur of good cigars, of which June had a store. After dinner with her I could not refuse her offer of one of these cigars, although the occasional one had gone off with the damp.

Alas, when June was hunting with the Co. Limerick hounds near Kilmallock, her black cob failed to clear a wide trench and came back on top of her. In his efforts to get out he must have struck her head. She was knocked unconscious, half submerged. By good chance someone recognised her riderless cob, rushed back to the trench and rescued her. She spent a couple of weeks in hospital in Limerick. One day a friend called and left her some smoked salmon.

Her nurse was upset over her own efforts with the fish. "Madam, I have boiled and boiled it and I cannot get it tender." June was amused.

Unfortunately, and amid protests from the nurses, June discharged herself too early with the result that she frequently had blackouts. Eventually she became partially paralysed and lost her speech, but she bore it all with great

Two great sportsmen at the Scarteen Puppy Show, 1981: June McCalmont, MFH and Lord (Toby) Daresbury, MFH of County Limerick. Mary Tarry photo

June McCalmont, a charming lady from a great hunting family in England, became my Joint-MFH. We are photographed here with Michael Kennedy in 1979. Mary Tarry photo

courage. Her family moved her to England to be near them, but she did not survive long. Dear June—I miss her greatly. When she bought the farm, her dream had been that one of her sons would come and live there. For my part, I dreamed that he would continue the Joint-Mastership, but that was not to be. Fortunately J. P. McManus, a great sportsman and bookmaker, bought the farm, ensuring it is now lovingly cared for.

June's three sons presented a magnificent solid silver fox to the Scarteen Hunt in memory of their dear mother. It is treasured annually by the winner of the Scarteen Members Cross-Country Race.

My wife, Anne, presents the June McCalmont Memorial Trophy, donated by June's sons, to Jim Mulcahy on winning the Scarteen Hunt Cup, 1985. Mary Tarry photo

Thady negotiates the big double in Derk in the Scarteen Hunt Cup race, 1985. Mary Tarry photo

Tommy Dwyer is in trouble with Jacko in the Hunt Cup, 1981. Mary Tarry photo

THIRTY

THE FAMILY INCREASES

If you want to shoot a lion or an elephant, you go to Africa; if you want to bag a tiger, you go to India; if you want to shoot, grouse you go to Scotland; but if you want to hunt foxes, you come to Ireland. The popularity of foxhunting in Ireland has escalated dramatically in recent years. The excitement of hunting a wild animal in its natural environment, and of risking one's neck over hazardous and challenging obstacles, lures sportsmen and women from all over the globe.

It is incredible that today we can ride to hounds in the same manner as our forefathers did, albeit with greater difficulty due to modern farming practices. This experience is made possible because of the generosity and welcome that farmers accord to the sport. It is encouraging that each year more and more landowners and their families follow hounds and enjoy what is truly *their* sport.

But there is far more to hunting than chasing foxes. To my mind, its greatest asset is its function as a catalyst in bringing people together. Locals can meet visitors from all over the world whom they would never otherwise encounter. There are no political, ethnic, sectarian, or social boundaries—all are equal in the hunting field. Frequently members of families in the hunting country are invited by their new friends to visit them in their homeland. More than this, hunting can act as a fruitful marriage bureau. Countless romances have started in the hunting field, to which I can testify personally, thank God!

To help to keep the pot boiling, Anne and I decided to take in paying hunting guests. Only once did we ever advertise, putting a small advertisement in the *Chronicle of the Horse* (the United States equivalent of the *Horse & Hound*). Replies came thick and fast and soon we had a regular flow of great sporting folk, many of whom came back year after year.

With the loss of dear June McCalmont as Joint-Master, I could not afford to carry on by myself. In 1971 I invited three others to become Joint-Masters: all three were friends who had stayed with us many times and we had got to know each other well. As they accepted the invitation without hesitation, overnight, together with our son Chris, we became as close as a family of five.

One Joint-Master was Bill Hobby, Lieutenant Governor of Texas. For years, Bill and his family rented a friend's house in our hunting country and came with friends for a month each season.

Semon Wolf was another who agreed to be Joint-Master. He "broke stock" in New York but he and his wife Beverly could not resist buying Fedamore House, and moved in permanently. Fedamore, a beautifully modernised Georgian house on good land, is just inside the Co. Limerick Hunt country, but within easy range of Scarteen.

My third Joint-Master, Ian Hurst, is a South African who has spent most of his life in Switzerland. To our delight he married Bea Turner, daughter of my former amateur whip Denis (chapter 28). Bea sold her farm and they bought Kilshane House between Tipperary and Bansha, the former home of the Lowe family. Their large house stood in attractive grounds, wooded and dense with rhododendrons—and foxes! The Holy Ghost Fathers had owned it as their seminary for many years.

We had fifteen happy seasons together. I think that our "family" have been the envy of many hunts in Ireland and abroad.

It was the cause of intense happiness for me when, on our departure for New Zealand, all three Joint-Masters agreed to carry on with Chris as senior Master. God bless them.

Our family of five! (l-r) Scarteen Masters Thady, Semon Wolf, Ian Hurst, Bill Hobby, Chris, 1984.
Mary Tarry photo

THIRTY-ONE

CEÁD MÍILE FÁILTE

(A Hundred Thousand Welcomes)

Some of my MFH friends were critical of my actions to encourage visitors to come to hunt in Ireland. However, over the years, I think they have come to realise the benefits of the move. In addition to the social advantages, visitors bring considerable benefits to individual hunts. They are happy to pay the going rate for cap fees (subscription for the day's hunting) and for the hireling fee (for hiring a good horse from a farmer, helping him to pay for his own hunting expenses). In many cases visitors purchase hirelings after they have had a good trial of them.

There is ample accommodation at hotels and guest houses in the area. The Dunraven Arms in Adare, Co. Limerick is probably the best-known hunting hotel in Ireland. Their excellent service includes arranging bookings with local hunt secretaries, car hire, and valeting. Another excellent hunting establishment is Lismacue House close to Tipperary, where Jim and Kate Nicholson give a warm welcome and excellent service to their guests.

Kate Nicholson's father, William Baker, followed in his own father's footsteps as a noted veterinary expert in horse practice (see chapter 22). William was a mighty man to follow hounds. Yet I defeated him one day! I was riding a high class horse that I had bought for a song because he had a stop in him (for no apparent reason, he would just stop dead unexpectedly on the flat). Following a tip I had been given, I put some pebbles in a shoe-polish tin; when the horse stopped, I would shake the tin between his ears and he would race ahead like an arrow. William was in trouble at a fence, as his horse would not jump out through a real bullfinch of a place (I don't blame him!). I was close behind him.

"Look out Willie!" I shouted, shaking my tin of pebbles. My horse and I were through the dense bushes like a flash!

Sadly the tin of pebbles was not a complete cure. Suspicious I got William to examine my horse's heart. He found it was "rotten"; I don't know how that horse lasted as long as he did.

Beyond the numerous excellent hotels and guest houses around the country that cater for hunting visitors, there are ancillary services (such as publicans and sports outfitters) that supply the best in food, drink, and hunting wear. One name stands out here: the late William Frazer in the village of Hospital. William was an expert in making hunting breeches, coats, and suits, of the best-quality material at an incredibly reasonable price. It was a real family business involving his wife, all the daughters, and sons-in-law. His clients came from all over the world. One had to allow an extra hour for a measuring or a fitting while he delighted in showing you his list of clients, with comments alongside (VPB was his abbreviation for Very Prominent Bust!). His son Michael is carrying on the tradition of excellence.

William enjoyed a bit of gossip. Denny Johnson called in to him to be measured for a pair of jodhpurs, at a time when she was married to her third husband. William, sitting cross-legged on the table, asked her, "What's the name now, missus?" Denny used to tell this story herself.

William Frazer, the world-renowned hunting tailor in the village of Hospital, delighted in showing clients the numerous order tickets from famous people worldwide awaiting custom breeches, coats, and suits from his shop. Mary Tarry photo

And not forgetting doctors and hospitals! The orthopaedic hospital in Croom, Co. Limerick serves us well and is kept busy during the hunting season. I suggested that they should pay a hunt subscription.

Some years ago the hospital sprang into action for my Joint-Master Semon Wolf, who took a nasty fall and smashed his elbow badly. The surgeon in Croom used five pins in the repair. After the season Semon called to his own surgeon in New York to check the break.

The surgeon asked Semon, "Who did the operation for you?"

Semon replied, "The orthopaedic surgeon in a small town in Ireland."

His surgeon was amazed. "I don't care where you go, be it Harley Street in London or wherever, you would not have got a better treatment."

His elbow is now perfect. Semon has the five pins framed and hanging in his office.

Other annual visitors were Dick Collins and his wife from Pebble Beach in California. For years they brought over two groups of fox hunters and stayed at the Dunraven Arms. In more recent times Randy Rouse, Master of the Fairfax, did likewise. Randy would invite neighbouring Masters and friends to their farewell dinner.

At the end of his speech after the dinner, Randy asked, "Is there anyone else who would like to say a word?"

"Yes, Master." A tall lawyer from the United States stood up. "When I agreed to come with you to Ireland, you promised that we would see the most beautiful scenic landscapes imaginable. I have been too frightened to open my eyes." And he sat down!

United States visitors especially are a pleasure to have hunting. They are courteous, considerate, and never any trouble. To my mind they are incredibly brave (or foolish?) to come hunting in Ireland on strange horses over the most formidable obstacles, so different from the straightforward post-and-rail fences and coops at home. There are other hazards too: driving a hired car along our narrow winding lanes on the "wrong" side of the road and with many of the place names on the signposts in Irish can be quite a challenge.

A visitor stopped at a crossroads for directions from an old man seated on the fence. "Can you tell me please which is the road to Tipperary?" he asked.

"Well now, that I don't know", the old man replied.

"Well then, which is the road to Limerick?"

"I'm afraid I can't tell you that either."

The frustrated visitor said, "You don't know much, do you?"

"No", said the old man, "maybe not, but I know one thing sir."

"And what's that?" asked the visitor.

The old boy replied, "I'm not lost!"

I was embarrassed on one hunt when scent was poor and we were just walking after hounds enjoying watching them working every inch of the line. In spite of the Field Master's plea, the followers kept coming too close to hounds. Twice I turned around, begging them to "Hold hard!" and give hounds a chance. A third time I lost my temper and used some strong language. In the middle of my tirade my false teeth fell out. I just caught them on the pommel of my saddle but I was speechless! We had to abandon that fox.

On the way to the next covert a visitor rode up to me, saying, "Gee Master, I searched the ground where you were standing. I could not find them dentures anywhere."

The moral of the story is: don't get cross!

Maguire's Mills was one of the oldest family businesses in Limerick City. Matty Maguire used to be one of our regular followers. At one meet in Emly, a group of French visitors were hunting with us. In the absence of public conveniences in the village, a couple of them were using a lamppost.

One of our foot followers said to Matty in astonishment, "Do you see what those Frenchmen are doing?"

Matty has a characteristic slight hesitation in his speech. He replied, "D-don't b-be s-surprised, w-w-wait till we join th-the EEC. . . . Th-that will b-be all the rage!"

Dave Russell is one name that will never be forgotten in the Scarteen Hunt. A veterinarian by profession, he was known affectionately all over the country as "the vet Russell" and had a multitude of friends abroad. He and his wife Norah were honorary treasurers of the hunt for many years. If ever I had a problem, wanted sound advice, or simply wanted to share some news, Dave—the soul of diplomacy and a real gentleman—was the first person I would call. He was invaluable to me in handling a difficult case of damage or compensation; his opinion and judgement were widely accepted. He always had a hearty welcome for hunting friends old and new, who reciprocated warmly—in spite of the fact that he had the little red bag handy for the cap fees!

A more conscientious man you could not imagine. While in practice in Northern Ireland, he took a break as a locum for a vet in a big, highly organised clinic in the south of England, which had several partners. Each morning

Dave and Nora Russell were pillars of the Hunt and long-serving Joint Honorary Treasurers.

the partners would come to the office and find a clean white coat and a list of the duties for the day. Dave was constantly worrying about how his pals back in Ireland were coping without him.

One morning he turned up to find a note on his white coat: "If a man thinks that he is indispensable, let him place his finger in a basin of water and upon withdrawing it, observe the hole that is left!"

Dave was great company and a fine raconteur. He will be remembered forever for his inimitable impersonation of Winston Churchill, "Some chicken, some neck" and for his rendering of Will R. Ogilvie's immortal ballad that ends, "Good men follow where good men are gone, but hounds are running, they're running on".

We had an English visitor out one day, a real "cut 'em down" from the Shires with silk topper, red swallow-tails, white buckskin breeches, champagne tops—the lot. He was going to show us how to go. He rode Jim Doherty's strong quality grey. The horse was a magnificent, brave jumper, but his mouth was as strong as his will: brakes and steering needed attention. We were hunting in big blind bushy country near Boher on the road between Tipperary and Limerick. Our friend was having a rough time being carted through dense bushes and briars.

At the end of the day when he dismounted stiffly, he asked Jim, "How much do I owe you?"

Jim took the horse and replied, "Five pounds, sir" (the going rate in those days).

He counted the crisp notes into Jim's hands, saying, "Money down the drain."

Jim was furious. The following week the same gentleman was out on a different hireling, and Jim was riding the grey. He waited until the visitor was only just making it to the top of a tall single bank, then Jim cannoned into him with the grey, knocking him and his horse back into the field.

"Money down the drain to you, sir", says Jim and gallops off. I doubt whether that gentleman ever returned to hunt again!

On a personal note, Anne and I have made a huge circle of friends down the years, not only those who stayed at Scarteen, but also the many who have bought property in the country or stayed in the area for short visits. In this circle too are the numerous great sportsmen from Cork and Kerry, as well as their counterparts from the border packs in the north of England, who come regularly to follow hounds on foot.

Paddy Callaghan and Tony Fitzpatrick are among my oldest friends. Tony hunts the Bride Valley otter (sorry, mink!) hounds. Paddy has a small private pack and frequently takes them down to Kerry to hunt with the lads there. He has been most helpful to our son Chris in locating the best Kerry out-crosses with great success.

It is invidious to mention individuals for fear of omitting and hurting the many who should be included. Although I would like to go through our visitor's book and talk about all the great characters we have had the privilege of entertaining, that would fill many volumes. I must mention just a few.

I had a letter out of the blue one day from Frank Bogart in California. Frank organised a riding holiday club, (*cabalgata*). Each year they would travel to a different country or state, where they spent a couple of weeks riding through the countryside. They wanted to visit Ireland, could I help? I replied that we would be delighted to do what we could for them. And so Frank and his friend Ray Corliss came to Scarteen, where we laid plans.

The group, Cabalgata Irlandese, numbered about twenty-five, of whom seventeen were riders. We accommodated the riders at Scarteen and two other private houses, while the nonriders stayed at the Dunraven Arms in Adare. With the landowners' consent, we spent four days riding through forests and farms, mostly on tracks and as little roadwork as possible. The nonriders came with us, where convenient, in a pony and trap. Some of our local hunting friends rode with us to give us a hand. Of necessity, we had to jump a few banks and ditches, which was a new experience for them.

One chap, a retired doctor and a big heavy fellow, insisted that he must have a western saddle. After many enquiries, we found one. Now, riding over banks is not comfortable for a bloke in a western saddle. So when we came to a big double, Doc would dismount and we would help him across, then get the horse across, and manoeuvre Doc up into his saddle again to everyone's amusement. The group was great fun and everyone enjoyed themselves, then went on down to Killarney for a couple of nights to recuperate!

Bill and Brady Bryson were our first-ever house guests. Replying to our advertisement in the *Chronicle*, they wrote asking for more details. I explained all the options, hunting with different packs in varying types of country—the banks and ditches of Limerick, the stone walls of Galway and so on. I also said that they would live with us as family and the food would be excellent because my wife was a top class cook. My handwriting is poor. Apparently they told their friends that they were going to hunt in Ireland and stay with the Master, and "It should be exciting because he says that his wife is a topless cook!"

One particular instance endeared Brady to me. At dinner, after a good day's hunting, he asked me, "Master, I am curious. You remember we came down off those (Pallas) hills and hounds crossed a road running hard and checked after about three fields. You cast them right-handed without success, then abandoned that fox and went on to the next draw. Why did you not cast forward?"

"Brady," I said, "you have caught me out. I tried to cover my tracks by making a futile right-handed cast. I did not think anyone would notice it. The reason was that the next farm ahead was out of bounds. My opinion of you as a huntsman has soared!"

We were privileged to have a charming sportsman from England come to stay. Air Vice Marshall Sir Charles Barraclough was a big man. He had never hunted over banks before, and I suggested that it would be a good idea if we went together for a school across our farm before he took on a day's hunting. I put him on Dr Mack, a rather plain but powerful 16-hand horse and a patent safety over any obstacle. I explained that we do not sit forward when jumping off banks (as one is accustomed to doing over fly fences). He got on well and we were both pleased.

"There is one fence we have not met yet and it is a normal one in our country—a steep drop into a river", I said.

We found a typical spot. Dr Mack cautiously dropped short into the river and put his head down to have a drink. Sir Charles landed around the horse's ears and for one awful moment I thought I was going to drown the Royal Air Force. Fortunately Dr Mack was strong, lifted his head and put Sir Charles back into his saddle!

Sir Charles came with his friend Chief Justice Lord Kenneth Diplock, both of them keen hunting men. Anne and I felt a big responsibility in having two such important personages to look after, but they could not have been more agreeable. Lord Diplock came over on his own in the following season but unfortunately hit two weeks of freak weather. Hunting was cancelled all over the country by snow.

On the road from Tipperary to Cashel and just inside the Tipperary Hunt country, nestling among beautiful trees and shrubs, with a gorse fox covert behind it, is Cahervillehow. This small attractive house was formerly the home of John Harris, and later of his son George, manager of Ballykisteen Stud for many years. It was purchased as a hunting lodge by Myles and Joy Valentine from Pennsylvania.

Anne and I first met Myles and Joy at the Rome Olympics when we were staying with Count "Pippo" Cigala Fulgosi MFH whom they also knew well (and of whom stories abound in chapter 35). They had leased a big house from a family who had moved out of Rome to avoid the crowds and hassle of the occasion. However, with the owners' Labradors left behind, Myles could not sleep for their constant lonesome howling. After shouting "Silenzio!" without effect, he got some grapefruit from the dining room to peg at them. That had the desired result!

One evening we were joined for dinner by Howard and Jean Fair, other mutual friends from the United States. We were seated at a table in a tiny courtyard amongst the tall ancient terra cotta buildings near the Forum. The

Two popular hostesses: Joy Valentine from Pennsylvania and my wife, Anne Ryan. Mary Tarry photo

night was warm and the moon was full. Soon we were serenaded by two musicians in colourful costume. Howard, a talented violinist, borrowed the violin from one of the men and played the most heavenly rendering of "O Sole Mio"—a magical night that we shall never forget.

Cahervillehow was constantly occupied by the family and friends. On one occasion almost the entire United States International Three-Day Event team were there for some hunting. I had arranged specially to have a meet for them at Elton in the heart of our best hunting country. The plan was to have them all back after the hunt to Scarteen, where they could have hot baths and a good dinner.

The day was appalling—stormy and cold with horizontal heavy rain without a break. We had a short run and to ground from Knocktoran bog and then blank. No self-respecting fox would be out on a day like that. I was bitterly disappointed and everybody was drenched and perished. As I rode into the yard with hounds, Anne came rushing out to tell me that one of the big heavy slates on the roof of the house was flapping in the storm. If it fell it would cause fearful damage. I took our son Hugh, then aged about twelve, and with a torch and some wire and the step ladder got up into the attic through the manhole in the top bathroom.

Meanwhile everyone was warming up with some "central heating" by the open fire in the drawing room and Anne was directing them to the various baths. She brought Jimmy Wofford's delightful wife Gail to the top bathroom, and while there removed our ladder leading up to the attic.

Once Hugh and I had tied down the slate, I said, "You go ahead first. I know my way around up here."

He attempted to climb down and suddenly shouted "Dad, the ladder is gone and there is a lady in the bath."

Gail saw a strange man coming at her through the ceiling, grabbed a towel and screamed! Soon the storm was forgotten and we had a hilarious night. Anne and I have enjoyed warm hospitality and many wonderful dinners at Cahervillehow down the years.

Ballykisteen was a model small stud farm alongside what is now Tipperary Racecourse. George Harris's policy was to make available to small Thoroughbred breeders a couple of well-bred sires at reasonable service fees. Being an intensely keen hunting man, he planted three fox coverts on the property, and erected gates and hunt jumps between all the paddocks. We could hunt there as often as we liked. On a hunt day all mares, foals and yearlings were stabled, and the staff were all out watching the sport. The only hazard was the main line railway close by. All is changed now. The stud has been disbanded, stable yards are gone, and the place is a high-class golf course.

The Scarteen Hunt Ball has always been one of the highlights of the hunting season. Visitors from the United States would try to plan their trip to include it. The Oyster Ballroom in Dromkeen was the venue for some years. We decorated the hall with fine trophies from big game safaris in Africa loaned from Mooresfort, along with foxes' masks and masses of greenery. It looked splendid and had a great atmosphere.

However, nothing can beat a private house for a true hunt ball atmosphere. We held it in Scarteen one year. We danced in a huge marquee on the lawn and used the conveniences in the house. With the rain pouring all right, a flood developed between the dance area and the bar but could not dampen people's spirits. It was a night of nights!

Castle Oliver was the venue on two memorable occasions. While Walter Trench and his family were living out in Kenya and the gaunt old castle was empty, I asked him if we could have our hunt ball in Castle Oliver. Of course he agreed. It had a big ballroom and a vast entrance hall with a beautiful timber stairway winding its way up to the numerous bedrooms. The large drawing room had ample space for sitting out. Another smaller room adjoining was the bar. Although the big dining room had only a small kitchen and pantry, they sufficed.

All the same, there were problems. The house was wired for electricity but the generator and batteries were long since defunct, so there was no power. And there was not a stick of furniture anywhere. The thick walls were damp, so after Walter's caretaker removed years of jackdaws' nests from the chimney, we lit a fire in the broad open fireplace in the entrance hall. The sight of logs piled high and burning merrily was unforgettable and the heat was welcome. However, soon there were streams of water from condensation on the cold walls flowing down the long tiled passageway!

Despite it all, we transformed the old house. A wonderful ladies' committee did Trojan work making long black and tan drapes in the big rooms. I collected a huge assortment of furniture from friends all around the country. I also borrowed a generator, powered by an ancient Morris-Cowley car engine, from a travelling show. All the light bulbs were replaced and we nervously turned on the power. Behold there was light! But we could have only half the lights on. Any more and the old engine packed up—it could not take the load.

Came the big night. Over two hundred guests turned up including tenor Joseph Locke who entertained us with his wonderful rendering of songs from "The White Horse Inn". The massive red sandstone walls and towers all floodlit outside and the stirring music from Mick Delahunty's dance orchestra echoing around the great house (who will ever forget Mick's saxophone and haunting signature tune "Cool Clear Water") . . . these are memories of the good old days.

The ladies had produced a magnificent buffet supper. During the night they came to me in distress. There was no more meat.

I said, "That is impossible. There were fourteen big turkeys and eight hams."

Looking into the waste bins I saw that they contained masses of untouched portions of turkey. I ordered everyone out of the kitchen, spread newspaper on the floor, tipped up the bins, arranged the meat on the big serving dishes and sent them back into the dining rooms. Everyone had their fill! The lesson was: hire small dinner plates in future. People would fill the large plates with more than they could eat. Nobody ever guessed the origin of the turkey that appeared in such sudden abundance.

THIRTY-TWO

A HORSE IS MAN'S BEST FRIEND

Right from my first season, I have been fortunate in having at least one good Master's horse in the stable. Some have been outstanding, deserving a mention in this book. Plush and Redwing (by Sandeman, a noted sire of hunters and show horses) started me off. My brother-in-law Claude Thompson had given them to Dad. Then after riding them for his one-season hunting hounds, Claude handed them on to me. Plush was a heavyweight with quality and a patent safety. His one fault was to swerve sharply in the middle of a field at a gallop to avoid a "ghost", which had Dad and myself on the floor many times.

A friend persuaded me to buy a big half-bred mare in the Thurles area. By Sir Rowland's son, she was great 'chasing blood and well-named as Amazon. Her claim to fame was to be the dam of the wonder horse Bandoola and his sister Bandoolina, both by Vince Hartigan's good thoroughbred sire Sadler's Wells (no relation to the current champion sire). It was a rare stroke of luck to breed a full brother and sister to carry the Master and first whip for several seasons. Bandoola was a striking gelding, jet black, 16.3 hands, with quality, pace, and a limitless jump. Not well broken, he had an insensitive mouth that matched his indomitable spirit—a great ride out in front, but reckless if he was overtaken.

After I loaned Bandoola to Patt Hogan for a hunt, this experienced horse trainer and enthusiastic fox hunter (see chapter 26) dismounted before the finish. Patt said to me, "I would not ride that horse again. He is pure dangerous."

I'm afraid I would not have the nerve to ride him myself now. Confound old age!

We had a flyer one evening after a long day's hunting, with only five of us left—Patt and Maureen Hogan, John Lawrence (Lord Oaksey), my whip Tommy, and myself. Hounds raced with a hot scent from Ballyscaddane to Glenefy. Bandoola was flying his banks. I circled a big field three times, trying to bring him to hand. But he seemed to have a fifth leg whenever necessary and I had complete confidence in him.

One summer day we had all the hunters in off grass to have their feet trimmed. Tom Morgan from West Waterford brought in a big German industrialist who wanted a strong horse. As we went through the lot, I pointed out the ones who were not for sale, starting with Bandoola.

He said to Tom, "I will rhide ze big, black horse."

I repeated that he was not for sale.

Tom said, "Don't be a fool. This chap will give you any price you like."

So I agreed, but warned him that Bandoola was a difficult ride. "Oh that is no trouble. I am in ze habit of ze big horses."

Bandoola behaved like a gentleman in all paces until the big man faced him at a schooling wall. The horse charged it like a bull and the rider nearly went out the back door.

Pulling up breathless, the German said, "I see what you mean. This horse is dangerous."

So no deal, thankfully. I hunted him for many seasons after that!

Dad used to favour horses from Co. Wexford, particularly from the Killinick Hunt country, because that area is one of the blindest and most difficult in the whole of Ireland. One has to gallop on at a huge bunch of gorse and briars that conceal anything from a single bank to a double bank (with two ditches) to a wide trench. Yet the local horses rarely fall, seeming to have an uncanny instinct of knowing where to put their feet.

Dad bought many a good horse from John Codd of Mayglass in Co. Wexford. A big man and a great judge of a horse, John had an infectious sense of humour, with a laugh that could be heard in the next county. Dad, Cousin Jack (the great snipe shot) of Emly, and I had been travelling all day with John Codd seeing horses. If there was one fault in a horse's conformation that Jack hated most of all, it was the condition of "back of the knee", meaning the canon bone is tilted back from the vertical and the knee is bending the wrong way, a source of great weakness. Now John knew Jack's feelings on horses' knees. It was late in the evening and John took us miles in the opposite direction from home to see "just one more horse". Into a farmer's yard and the owner led a grand-looking horse out of the stable, but he was the worst case of back of the knee imaginable. John exploded with laughter. Jack was furious.

John owned a big area of the South Slob—low, flat grazing land close to the sea, a haven for wild geese and great land to keep horses. Once when Dad, Cousin Jack, and I called by and walked out on to the Slob with him, there was not an animal in sight. With a soft rope halter on his arm, John gave the odd whistle in between yarns. Soon there was a stampede of hooves and more than twenty horses came milling around us. John quietly put the halter on a pale chestnut and took him out on to the passageway. He was a straight mover with sound limbs, a hard-looking sort with a small alert eye.

"I've had him only a couple of weeks and I know little about him. He is supposed to be a good hunter", said John.

We had a deal there and then. We got veterinarian Barty Hicky to examine him—sound as a bell—and we got him home. Buck! He had a wicked one before, during, or after a hunt or at exercise. But I forgave him all because he was a brave and brilliant performer. We named the horse "Vinegar Hill", the site of a fierce battle near Enniscorthy away back in the time of the Troubles.

The following August I met John at the Dublin Horse Show.

Rather nervously he asked, "How did that chestnut horse go on?"

"Absolutely brilliant. One of the best horses I have had", I said.

John broke into uncontrollable laughter.

"What's the joke John?" I asked.

He said, "Shortly after you took the horse, I met a neighbour of the man I bought him from. He asked me what became of the chestnut horse that I bought down near him. I said I sold him to a Master of hounds up in Co. Limerick. 'You what?' he said. 'Sure that horse was unrideable.' I was scared to ask you earlier how he was going on."

George and Didi Earle from England bought a property near Murroe in Co. Limerick, in our hunting country, quickly transforming the big house and gardens into an attractive home. Both were avid fox hunters for many years. Didi's other love had been motor rallying, which, she told me, she used to get an even greater "buzz" from than hunting. Her reasoning was that in hunting she shared the danger with her horse, whereas in a car she was solely responsible for her fate. She was not fully satisfied until she was going so fast that one mile per hour more would be fatal. A remarkable lady.

George was about to buy a good hunter called "Waterford" (county of origin) from my Joint-Master June McCalmont. In the meantime she loaned Waterford to a friend who took a nasty fall off him, so, lucky for me, George did not buy. I took the opportunity to swap him for another horse that suited June better. I hunted Waterford, an honest and reliable performer, for years. I have never known another horse to get so excited as soon as hounds found.

Another source of good horses for hunting and showjumping was James Breen, a keen hunting farmer. He tried to sell me Kennedy, a big strong bay three-year-old with a white face and big feet—obvious Clydesdale connections. He came to hand quickly and turned into a super hunter, and was in great demand as a hireling for heavy riders. I resisted for some time, not wanting to touch Clyde blood on principle. I suppose I am biased in favour of the Irish Draught breed, the only indigenous horse in Ireland. Although the word "draught" conjures up the idea of a heavy work horse, the Irish Draught will do only light farm work; instead, it is a great cross-country performer, acquiring its jumping and eventing skills from long years of survival among the difficult natural obstacles on the farm lands of Ireland.

In the scale of horse breeds, the Thoroughbred would be at the top of the scale (*saing pûre* in French) while at the bottom of the scale would be the Shire and Clyde, the heavy draught breeds known as cold bloods. Now don't get me wrong. I am not condemning the breeds, as they are brilliant for the jobs they were bred for, such as shunting heavy wagons in the railyards in England (or pulling the big drays loaded with barrels of Guinness uphill from the brewery by the Liffey in Dublin!). A Clyde crossed with a Thoroughbred will produce a useful pleasure-riding horse that can be broken as a two- or three-year-old. It is a good horse dealer's animal that can be sold on in a short time.

In contrast, the Irish Draught X Thoroughbred cross will take a year longer to bring to the same stage, but because of his innate ability and courage, he is the best cross with the thoroughbred to produce outstanding all-round sport horses. He has that fighting spirit to get him out of trouble. I have always said that if during a hunt a Clyde cross fails to get to the top of a big bank and falls back into the ditch on top of his rider, he will happily lie still and eat grass from the bank. In contrast, in the same situation an Irish Draught will fight to get free. If he could talk, he would call out, "Get me the hell out of this." Of course there are exceptions, and my Kennedy was one. Yes, I gave in! And there's a story behind how it happened.

We had a good hunt—the longest in my years as huntsman, eighteen miles away into the Limerick country. Kennedy, with a big visitor, was one of the few to finish, weakening my resolution. Finally James persuaded me to ride Kennedy in the East Galway fifteen-stone race in their point-to-point and I won it. So of course I bought Kennedy.

No fence was too big or too challenging for him. Sadly he developed foot trouble after a few short years. X-rays showed severe damage to both front pedal bones. They were badly deformed from the heavy work as a hireling when he was still immature.

Talking of hirelings, one horse must be mentioned—Billy Gleeson's Puddleduck. She was the copybook patent safety hunter. Her name was a household word among hunting visitors from America. On arrival in Shannon their first request was, "Can I have Puddleduck?" Billy was in England one time and the members hunt race in the point-to-point was coming up. A delightful American lass, Betsy Maher, who was a regular hunting guest with Billy and Helen Gleeson, was persuaded by the local lads to ride the Crow—another good horse in Billy's stable. Betsy was extremely popular and all the lads were trying to help her mount. She was a featherweight and had to carry about three stone of lead to make up the required weight. Without thinking, all the lead was inserted in one side of the weight cloth. Betsy cantered down to the start but did not get there; the saddle slipped right round the horse's belly and poor Betsy hit the dust!

Two old faithfuls, Spencer and Lombardy, carried my whip Tommy and me bravely for over ten seasons. Willie O'Grady told me to go and buy a horse from his neighbour George Spencer that was outstanding with the Tipperary hounds. I called during the summer to find a stout-legged horse about 16 hands, round, fat, and, I thought, a bit short of quality. How wrong I was! A more honest and super-safe performer you could not imagine. Spencer came close to winning the Member's Race in the point-to-point a year later.

Lombardy came originally from Dan Coleman, well known for his quality, genuinely proven hunters, in the Duhallow country. I bought Lombardy from his second owner. He proved a patent safety, but with great courage and ability. Our daughter Rachel enjoyed many a good day on him.

Villain was a high-class performer. Quality and power written all over him, he had pace to burn, with the character and heart of a true champion and was never known to refuse. I bought him from Vivi and Alan Lillingston, providing one inspiration for the name I gave him. (There was another reason—a villain being full of mischief, but not of vice.) When back among the followers, he was an extremely difficult ride, but out in front he was a dream.

Jenny Wardell from New Zealand did a great job of looking after my horses for many years. She persuaded me to enter Villain in the Gowran Grange National Competition at the Punchestown Three-Day Event. As a result of her excellent schooling, Villain surprised everybody—myself most of all—with an outstanding dressage score. I then took him for a pipe-opener on the airfield, where he bolted with me completely. We decided on a pelham for the second day, but I thought the curb chain was unnecessarily severe, so I ran it through a rubber tube. I might just as well have taken it right off! Phase B was a gift. We set off on the steeplechase with great expectations.

The Kildare Hunt point-to-point had been run over the same course earlier in the year. With the rough ground and desperately heavy going, sand was spread at the take-off of some fences. After we cleared the first, I let Villain go on a bit on the longer approach to the second. He bolted, taking off from the edge of the sand, so it had to be an impossible jump. Although Villain did his best, he could not clear. He hit the rough landing at one hundred miles an hour and turned over three times. We both got up. I shouted to some onlookers to help me, but the saddle was broken, so were my ribs and collarbone; poor Villain was lame, and I passed out. When I came to later in the Red Cross tent, the girl who was on Phase C ahead of me told me that she had felt quite sick—she had never seen a man being killed before! That was my eventing swansong but Villain carried me hunting hounds for many more seasons.

A horse I must mention, though I did not own him, was the thoroughbred stallion Ballinamona Boy. He belonged to that great sportsman Sir Hugh Walker, who lives at Ballinamona with Norna and their two sons. Hugh is one of the pillars of the hunt. If there is work to be done planting fox coverts, repairing damage, pulling cars out of boggy car parks, or helping anyone in a fix, Hugh is always first to volunteer. Hugh could also never be separated from his pipe. I do not know what brand of plug he uses, but it is powerfully strong. On more than one occasion at a check on a slow scenting day, I have had to ask Hugh to go down wind of hounds to enable them to work out the line of the fox!

Like his owner, Ballinamona Boy was an outstanding and versatile character, and he carried Hugh at twenty-one opening meets. Hugh would never refuse a service to a farmer, and too late in life, the old horse proved that he could produce some high-class show jumpers.

My cousin Jim Ryan of Ballytrent bought me Tom Tallow from a former Joint-Master of the Island hounds. A magnificent horse, almost thoroughbred, Tom Tallow was a true middleweight of about 16.3 hands. In the hunting field occasionally he was short of the fifth leg and we took the occasional toss, but he was a thrilling ride. I entered him for the Members Race in our point-to-point. Three days before the race I took him at a strong pace over some big banks, contravening Dad's advice of "Never go schooling on your own". When his hind legs missed on one bank, he landed in the bottom of a big ditch on his back on the landing side. Fortunately I escaped but stood helplessly watching my valuable horse smashing his head against a bush stump. By sheer strength

Chris and Sir Hugh Walker at Opening Meet, 1989, on two famous horses, Jacko and Sir Hugh's Thoroughbred stallion, Ballinamona Boy. There was no task, monumental or menial, that Sir Hugh wouldn't perform for the Hunt. Mary Tarry photo

and determination and to my intense relief he struggled free. We went on to win the Hunt Cup, a large, beautiful, old silver rose bowl, which has pride of place in our sitting room.

When Lady Dorothy Mack, one of the great ladies to hounds in Leicestershire in her young days, came to see our horses, she checked with a friend who was with her, "Do you think Thady would be offended if I offered to produce (school and prepare for a show) his big bay horse for Dublin Horse Show? He is sure to win the Hunter Championship."

Needless to say, with neither the time nor the expertise to do Tom Tallow justice, I accepted her offer in a flash. Her belief in the horse soon began to pay off; we won the Hunter Championship in Longford Show. Thereafter Dorothy and her husband moved to Cappaghmore, Clondalkin close to Dublin. I went up to ride the big horse as often as I could.

At Dublin Horse Show the Duke of Beaufort ("Master", see chapter 32) and Jack Castle were judging the middleweights. In those days the weight cups were judged in their respective rings, not in the jumping enclosure as they are today. Glen Browne, a keen hunting enthusiast in the United Hunt in Co. Cork, had a pretty chestnut Sandara (by Sandeman) in our class. Jack Castle wanted Sandara while Master wanted my horse. Being junior judge (his first time in Dublin Horse Show) Master let Jack Castle have his way. Sandara gave a well-schooled show, but without brilliance. Tom Tallow lacked the space in the small ring to show his extravagant stride.

Sandara was sold to the United States, and Glen said he was pleased to part with him. I sold Tom Tallow to Bob Hanson in Leicestershire, where he distinguished himself for many seasons. Master offered Bob a blank cheque for him, but Bob would not part with the horse.

The story has an ironic twist. A couple of years earlier on a visit to Wexford, John Codd said he had heard that there was a good sort of horse near Old Ross on our road home, and maybe we should see him. We spotted the horse about three fields in from the road in boggy land.

Dad said, "Thady, I am tired. You go and have a look at him and if you think it worthwhile, Jack and I will come in."

It was near dusk. I have never seen such a sick, hungry-looking horse, thin with a stary coat (a dry coat with the hair on end, as distinct from the sleek coat of a well-conditioned horse). He looked rotten with redworm. We left him there. Two years later he beat me for the Hunter Championship in Dublin—he was Sandara!

But the story had far greater importance. It was the catalyst for a major upheaval in the organisation of the Dublin Horse Show. More anon!

"Master, I have your horse", said James Breen to me one day.

"Thank you, James," I replied, "but I don't need another horse at present."

"Ah Master, come and try him. He is just your handwriting." (If only he knew, that was no great compliment to the horse because my handwriting is appalling!)

James persisted. I weakened, went over, and rode the horse. It was love at first sight, I bought him at once. This was Jacko.

Brown, about 16.2 hands, with a kind, intelligent eye, powerful limbs and stature, and a great rein (long sloping shoulder), Jacko was "the goods". James said he was rising five, and by one of two excellent sires, either Six O'Clock (whom I believe he looked more like) or Carnival Night. He was bred near Millstreet in Co. Cork and bought as a yearling by "Noel C." Duggan of Millstreet Show fame. Two years later Noel thought he was going to be too small, so he sent him to Tallow Horse Fair, where James Breen bought him.

Jacko had a most powerful spring. Coupled with his correct technique, courage, and equable personality, it singled him out for a showjumping career. At Millstreet International Annual Show, Noel C. included a class known as the Young Irelander; the purpose was to assemble the best four- and five-year-old likely show jumpers. Qualifying rounds were held at shows throughout the country. Noel C. reserved the right to nominate a handful of horses who had not qualified, but showed exceptional ability; by this means, he invited Jacko. The class was judged on ability and aptitude over a vertical and an oxer (spread) under saddle, and on conformation and paces. The international showjumpers Harvey Smith and David Barker were always the judges, Harvey doing the ride.

After Jacko (with Jenny Wardell riding), reached the final nine horses, Harvey mounted him. Jacko jumped superbly. Harvey told the stewards to raise the oxer to five foot square, just for Jacko, and he again cleared it with feet to spare.

After the competition, David Barker said to me, “I would like to have a word with you.” We went to have a cup of tea. “What are you going to do with your young horse?” he asked.

“You keep your hands off Jacko. He is going to be my number one hunter”, I replied.

“You must be a bloody millionaire to be hunting that horse”, he said and I heard that he had a blank cheque from Harvey in his pocket for me!

Maybe I was a fool to turn down the offer. Yet I could not put a value on the twelve consecutive seasons of loyal service that Jacko gave me, carrying me with brilliance and safety hunting hounds.

Jacko had unlimited scope. At one of the hunter trials, the final obstacle was a regulation steeplechase fence. Jacko reached for the sky and I ascended further still. When I came down he was no longer there, I saw stars! Of course we had the occasional fall, but it was never his fault. Once when, with a huge leap, he cleared a ditch filled with briars, I had not spotted a stiff overhanging branch. I hit it with all his force, broke my hunting cap, cracked a vertebra in my neck and broke the tree of my saddle. Fortunately he was unhurt.

Also a show-off, Jacko obviously enjoyed parading hounds with myself and later with my son Chris. But his real love was hounds. No day was too long nor too arduous for him. I am privileged to have Peter Curlings’ brilliant painting of Tommy Dwyer, Jacko, hounds, and myself at Knocktoran Bog, which was a presentation from members of the Scarteen Hunt. Three hundred prints were taken from it and are hanging in sporting homes worldwide, making Jacko world famous! He spent his retirement years with Mike and Irene Snow at Moore Abbey near the Galty Mountains, to whom I am endlessly grateful for the love and care they lavished on him. With tears in my eyes I learned recently that his health suddenly deteriorated and he went to his happy hunting ground at the ripe old age of thirty years. A friend of a lifetime, he is buried in Scarteen.

There is a true saying that women, land, and horses get the best and the worst out of a man. Certainly horse breeding and horse dealing are endemic in the Irish character. When striking a deal for a horse, both buyer and vendor seem to put up their guard like two boxers entering the ring. The story is told of an Englishman who came into a farmer’s yard to buy a horse. After much haggling, a deal was struck and the buyer wrote out the cheque.

Then he said to the farmer, “The horse is now mine and you have my cheque. Is there anything you would like to tell me about the horse that maybe you were too shy to mention before we made the deal?”

“Well no sir, no, not exactly.”

“Are you sure?” said the buyer, getting suspicious.

“Well sir, perhaps I should tell you, he can be hard to catch in the field.”

“Oh, my good man that is no trouble, my paddocks are well fenced and I have good grooms. Is there anything else?”

“Well sir, when you have him caught, he is no bloody good!”

On another occasion a foreigner was buying a horse. The farmer could see that the longer the visitor looked at the horse, the better he liked him.

Eventually the visitor said to the owner, "How much do you want for your horse?"

"I want four thousand pounds", he replied.

"Eh, what did you say?" said the buyer.

"I want five thousand pounds", said the farmer.

"Oh, I thought you said four thousand."

"I did sir," he replied, "but I didn't think you heard me!"

Thady and hounds arrive at Opening Meet in Knocklong, 1985. Mary Tarry photo

THIRTY-THREE

SPORTHORSE OR HUNTER?

For generations Ireland has had a name as one of the leading countries in the world for producing top-class horses, both Thoroughbred and non-Thoroughbred. The Irish hunter was recognised worldwide for its quality, durability, versatility, natural jumping ability, courage, and equable character. The hunting field was, and still is, the greatest possible testing ground for a horse to prove its mettle.

However among a growing number of riders who compete in equestrian sports, the term "hunter" does not describe adequately a horse's versatility and suitability for the popular competition sports of three-day eventing and show jumping. This is partly because the vast majority of competitors probably have never ridden to hounds, and partly because in many parts of the world a hunter is a person who goes after game with a gun. And so "sporthorse" has come to be accepted worldwide as a replacement term. I am treading on dangerous ground here because many of my older friends doggedly refuse to recognise the word, maintaining that "hunter" has sufficed down the years. But one must move with the times.

It is all too true that top-class eventers and show jumpers have become too valuable to risk hunting them, certainly in Ireland—perish the thought! At one time Major Joe Lynch was trainer for the Irish Three-Day Event team for the European Championships. He stayed at Scarteen, where he ran a clinic to try out some likely horses for selection.

He said to me, "I would prefer to train a team of horses that had not been well hunted in County Limerick."

I replied, "You must be out of your mind. A horse *must* hunt in order to learn to look after himself."

But Joe made the point that hunting over the big banks and ditches can make a horse overcautious. I saw his point, but insisted that just a small bit of hunting remained essential.

Down the years generations of natural and knowledgeable horsemen and women in Ireland have bred high-class horses, relying on their innate instinct and experience, and without any assistance, financial or otherwise, from government sources. The country was full of quality halfbred mares and suitable thoroughbred stallions.

For example, Dad went down to Co. Cork to see a horse that he had heard of. The horse was tackled with another to a spring harrow as the farmer was preparing a field for corn. Untackling the good horse, Dad gave him a trot down the road. The horse's action was not great, so he left the horse to his harrow—one could afford to be particular, as good horses were plentiful and Dad believed in the old saying, "The day you buy is the day you sell." Three years later the same horse won the Aintree Grand National; his name was Workman!

The light-working mare on the farm was the backbone of the hunter breeding industry. She did all the farm work (except the ploughing), took the milk to the creamery, took the family to Mass on Sunday in the tub trap, and produced a foal every year. With a steady trade in England for hunters, show horses, and latterly showjumpers and eventers, the horses paid their way.

Harry Ferguson dealt a mortal blow to the horse-breeding industry when he invented the hydraulic lift, a small tractor so versatile that it could do all the farm chores. So the tractor came in the front gate and the mare went out the back. Worse still the farmer's son became mechanically minded and had no time for the horse. Coupled with the collapse of the hunter trade during and immediately after World War II, these trends resulted in the wholesale disposal of breeding stock to the continent both on the hoof and in carcass form for meat; horse factories were set up around the country. Ireland has never recovered from this loss of the cream of our good mares.

The Royal Dublin (RDS) Society was the first official body to spot this serious problem. In response it organised the RDS Premium Scheme. A panel of experienced judges was appointed to select suitable young nonthoroughbred mares at shows around the country. The number of premiums varied according to the density and quality of mares in each district. Chosen mares were awarded a grant of £16 payable on the production of a foal by an approved thoroughbred stallion. With the kudos of winning an RDS premium meaning more to a farmer than the £16 cheque, the scheme was highly successful.

Adamstown Show in Co. Wexford, in the centre of the best horse-breeding area in the country, was allotted the highest number of premiums. At one show there I was judging the class, with over thirty mares contesting for twenty-five premiums. I have never seen such a selection of beautiful mares—mostly bay with black points, good flat bone and overall quality. The standard was so high that I decided to award thirty premiums, and the RDS backed my decision. Two years later I was back at the same show. This time about fifteen mares were in the class but premiums had been reduced to ten. I could award only five; I was almost in tears. Lack of trade and farm modernisation, as mentioned, were the prime causes of this calamity.

BORD NA GCAPALL

In 1972, on the advice of leading breeders and judges, the then Minister of Agriculture appointed twelve members, including myself to form a voluntary body, *Bord na gCapall* (the Irish Horse Board). Our brief was to promote and assist financially the horse-breeding industry, but not to dictate. The indigenous dedication and judgement of the multitude of successful breeders all through the country must not be jeopardised.

The Bord na gCapall *(Irish Horse Board) was formed to promote and assist the horse breeding industry. The Minister of Agriculture appointed the twelve founding board members: (front row, l–r) Thady Ryan; Declan Fitzgerald; Jim Gibbons, Minister of Agriculture; Noel Tanner, Chairman; Colonel Bill Rea; Frank Costello; (back row) Tom Duggan; William Kearns; Alan Lillingston; Frank O'Reilly; Sean O'Cathain; Pat Britton.*

The Bord initiated several breeding incentive schemes, a successful Farrier Apprenticeship Scheme and a progressive marketing operation. We had a stand at two major continental shows, the Salon de Cheval in Paris and Essen Equitana. The various activities were financed by the government, augmented by grants from the European Community Fund.

As chairman of the Marketing Division in 1972, I visited the Verona Horse Show in Northern Italy to see if it would be worthwhile mounting a stand there in the future. It so happened that an Italian dealer had just imported a number of Irish horses, which he offered to display on our behalf. It sounded a good idea and he set up a display. However, when I saw the horses, I was disgusted. They looked thin and the worse for wear from the long journey, and anyhow lacked quality. I was in the process of telling the dealer as diplomatically as possible that we would rather he did not display the horses when another Bord member turned up, saw the horses under an Irish banner, and exploded with rage.

The young lady interpreter came to me in trouble: "Please Mr Ryan, can you help me. I cannot understand what that gentleman is saying."

I replied, "It is just as well that you cannot understand what he is saying. It is unprintable!"

I was also puzzled. There was a huge number of horses in the show, almost all were big, fat, heavy horses being judged on conformation.

I asked someone, "What are these horses used for—is it farmwork or forestry or what?"

"Oh no," he replied, "they are for meat." I came home sickened.

There were other lighter moments during my time on the Bord. Dad used to tell me that down the years Co. Galway was famous for family feuds and factions, so it was no great surprise to learn that there was disagreement between some organisations up there. After they appealed to Bord na gCapall to help, I was detailed to go up and chair the meeting. It went off well and we sorted out the problem amicably. A room had been booked for me in the Ardilawn House Hotel, where the meeting was held. We had had a long day's hunting, and after a two-hour drive and a late meeting, I was glad to turn in.

I had to meet a hunting visitor at Shannon at 7 A.M. next morning, so I asked the hall porter to call me early with a cuppa. It so happened that the circuit of Ireland motor rally was based in Galway that night and—any excuse for a party—the city was in full swing until the early hours. I was thankful to turn my back on it and get some sleep. However, as it turned out, I forgot to lock my room door.

At 5 A.M. the phone rang, "Your tea is ready in the hall, sir."

My alarm went off, I turned on the light, and rubbed my eyes, to find that the twin bed alongside mine was occupied. I was puzzled. Definitely there had been no one there when I went to bed. Getting up, I dressed quietly so as not to wake him. Then I saw a skirt and handbag on the end of the bed, and the blonde turned over! I closed the door silently and on the way down the stairs I had to step over a bloke "out for the count".

I said to the hall porter "This is a great hotel—you provide everything, but why didn't you tell me in time?"

"What do you mean sir?"

"There was a blonde in the bed alongside mine, and I never knew it 'til you woke me!"

Unfortunately trouble was brewing. Bord na gCapall had become top heavy with staff and the bulk of the funding was being squandered on wages and running expenses. Travel and other privileges were being abused by some members. In the circumstances three of us felt we could no longer serve and handed in our resignations, the Minister of Agriculture disbanded the entire Bord then. As a member of the outgoing governing party, he appointed an entirely new Bord on the eve of the general election. Some of these new members, clearly the Minister's political supporters, had not even been consulted. At their first meeting they resigned en bloc, and Bord na gCapall was in abeyance for a couple of years. Now I am delighted that the Irish Horse Board set up in 1993 is running under new management and doing great work.

The old saying "Horsemen are not made, they are born" applies particularly to Ireland. Among the Irish people the love and understanding of horses have been part of the culture for centuries. Instinctively breeders have recognised the best traits of excellence in conformation, soundness, stamina, courage, and performance. They have concentrated on these bloodlines with the result that, more than any other nation of comparable size, Ireland has been the source of the best all-round sport horses and hunters in the world. This is our heritage, and the current Irish Horse Board has the heavy responsibility of preserving this source of excellence unadulterated by any foreign breed of horse.

THE IRISH HUNTER IMPROVEMENT SOCIETY

Shortly after World War II two great hunter breeding enthusiasts, Major "Jed" O'Dwyer and Kathleen Heffernan, formed the Irish Hunter Improvement Society. Worried that breeders were favouring quality too strongly at the expense of bone, they started a scheme to encourage farmers to breed from stronger mares.

While in the army, Jed was a member of the Irish International Showjumping team, together with Dan Corry, Fred Ahern, and Michael Tubridy. They represented Ireland with success in the United States, the Netherlands, Germany, and other countries. Popular everywhere they went, they were ideal ambassadors for Ireland.

When stationed at the Curragh in Co. Kildare, the officers had an opportunity to hunt occasionally with the Kildare hounds. The barracks had one exceptional hunter whom they would take turns to ride. When Jed's turn came, he vowed that nothing would interfere with his day's hunting. Hounds were running hard and Jed was enjoying the good horse. On landing over a fence he spotted a heavy man with a pink coat lying on the ground groaning, with his big plain horse alongside him. Jed looked the other way and rode on. After a couple of fields his conscience got the better of him. "The poor chap, could be mortally wounded." With mixed feelings he rode back.

The poor chap was groaning, "My back, my back."

Then Jed spotted that the big ugly horse was standing on the chap's coat tails. He could not get up, so thought that his back was broken! Jed rode back to barracks furious that he had missed the ride of a lifetime.

The work of the Irish Hunter Improvement Society was greatly appreciated, but financing was a problem. A group of us got together with Jed and worked out a breeding incentive scheme, really an extension of the Hunter Improvement Society's. The plan was for a small panel of judges to attend selected shows and pick the best two-year-old filly with strength, bone, and quality, who, when bred to a thoroughbred sire, would produce a quality middleweight hunter, eventer, or jumper (the filly did not have to be a performer herself).

The winners from the selected shows would assemble for the Final at Limerick Show, from which the outright winner would be known as "The Limerick Lady". Further, if these qualified mares return for up to four years in foal to, or with foal at foot by, a thoroughbred sire, they would be eligible to compete for the "Limerick Matron".

At this time the big Aughinish Alumina Company in the Shannon Estuary was sponsoring a couple of horse classes in the Limerick Show. Together with the chairman of Limerick Show, we approached Aughinish Alumina. They received us well, generously agreeing to sponsor the whole scheme.

I said to the company manager, "I really don't know why you are agreeing to this. My wife does not buy any more aluminium saucepans. But you cannot refuse because Aughinish Island is the Irish for 'Island of the Stallion'!"

A name I must mention here is Pat Lynch, the Aughinish representative who, from the inception of the scheme, has done trojan work to ensure its success. In the Irish horse world we are eternally grateful to Aughinish for their generous support of the Irish horse industry.

THIRTY-FOUR

ODE TO A FOX

Slipping silently into the lush grass
Under the thorn hedge
On this evening of
The last longest day of the millennium
I admire the alertness
Of your angular head.
Balance of your brush
And coat of burnt toast.
But when the cobwebs sparkle with dew we will become adversaries
Pitting our will and skills against each other.
I promise you
That our battles will be fair;
Guns and weapons will
Play no part.
You will choose the battlefield
Your call to run and be pursued
Which is your life
Or hide and so to earth and I will say
No shame, call off the hounds
So you can choose another day
To run or hide
For you are Master of this Hunt
In a land where man
Fox, horse and hound were meant to run
And to admire.

—Ger O'Riain

For me this delightful tribute epitomises the relationship that should exist between a huntsman and a fox. It was composed and sent to me by a friend in the west of Ireland with his permission to include it in my book. Ger O'Riain, a true naturalist, loves to study the ways of all wildlife. He is also a keen foot follower of hounds, and delights in watching hounds working the line of a fox or a hare.

The fox is one of God's most beautiful creatures. It is a thrill to watch a litter of young cubs playing outside their hole, observed by the vixen constantly on the alert for any danger, while the dog fox is away hunting for food. When he returns with a rabbit, hen, wild duck, or rat (a favoured morsel), the cubs fight and play furiously for their portion.

There are usually four in a litter. For some reason that I have never understood, the vixen chooses to have her cubs in a simple shallow hole, which she en-

To me, a fox has a special charisma. Catherine Power photo

larges from one made originally by rabbits. Fox cubs are vulnerable to stray dogs, and even to badgers and hawks when they are small, with casualties high.

In the mating season, usually February and March and sometimes as early as January (depending on the climate), a dog fox will travel many miles to find a mate. In a clear moonlit night it is spine chilling to hear a dog fox giving his staccato triple bark, "Ow-ow-ow", and a vixen replying with an eerie, haunting sort of wheeze that must resemble someone being strangled. The Irish used to believe that they would hear the banshee (a fairy woman) wailing when a person was going to die. I believe what they heard was the cry of a vixen.

I find it hard to accept that a creature as noble as the fox should be classed as vermin. The fox plays a necessary part in the balance of nature, controlling rabbits and rats. While my brother John was farming in Co. Cork, fox skins were in strong demand, with a good dog fox worth more than £30. The fox population was decimated. John, who had had a fox covert that was a sure find for the Duhallow Hunt, had a plague of rats within a short time. The fox shooters were coining, using a sort of whistle imported from the United States that attracted dog foxes. A lot of the strong, healthy breeding stock were lost. Fortunately the fur coat fashion ended and a fox skin now is almost valueless.

It is interesting to observe how the fox's lifestyle has changed recently. Whereas they used to be wild animals living far from human habitation and wary of man, their only predator, nowadays they have become semi-domesticated. They have even intruded urban areas, where they feed out of dustbins and household waste. Friends who live in the centre of Birmingham have a litter of cubs in their garden every year, but the adult foxes are miserable specimens, weak and mangy from inbreeding and an unsuitable diet.

To me a fox has a special charisma. I admire his beauty and especially his incredible cunning. I think I get even greater excitement on seeing a fox down the fields on a nonhunting day. Part of the landscape as he wanders through the countryside, his presence is betrayed only by the warning notes of blackbirds and magpies.

A friend phoned me to say he had found an almost full-grown vixen paralysed in the hindquarters and pulling herself along with her front legs, but otherwise perfectly healthy. A fox's bite can be poisonous, so one has to be careful. I offered her a stick that she grabbed instantly. I could then catch her by the back of the neck and put her in a sack. I brought her to my vet Des Barnwell (also our hunt treasurer and keen follower of the hunt).

"Des," I said, "normally I call you to attend a wounded horse or hound so that I can hunt foxes. Now I want you to cure a fox."

After taking her temperature, pulse, and blood pressure—all normal—he said, "I think she probably has been shot and has a pellet in the spine. She may benefit from antibiotics, but it is doubtful."

I agreed to take the gamble. Des put her on a course of penicillin for a week, a capsule once daily. I held her with a stick in her mouth while Anne coaxed some bread, milk, and the capsule down her throat, an expensive and difficult performance. After a few days Anne said we should put her down, but I thought I noticed some movement behind. In about ten days she was bounding around the kennel.

Then one morning I came to feed her and she was gone. Climbing up a corner she had forced a hole in the wire netting roof. I have been asked if I put a tattoo in her ear. My reply was that I never wanted to know whether she was ever caught.

Another day we cycled to Ballintubber to hunt the glen of thick gorse and blackthorn near Slievereagh mountain. It was late in the season and we were on foot. Hounds found a vixen, she circled around for a while and I was suspicious. Inevitably she went to ground in a shallow hole. By the time my whip Tommy and I arrived, hounds had dug her out and killed her, together with a young cub, eyes just opened. I felt sick.

While hounds were held back, I put my hand into the hole and took out three more cubs. I put them in my pocket and we cycled home. We reared them until they were about six months, then released them in Mooresfort demesne, where I knew they would be safe. Two survived and gave us good runs. For several seasons hunting from Mooresfort improved no end; the introduction of fresh blood really worked.

Several friends of mine have had pet foxes, but I have never wanted to keep one. However some individual foxes hold a special place in my memory. Once when we drew Ballinamona Bog, a big dog fox left from the far side. He stopped halfway up Garrett Barry's hill and looked around at us. I could almost hear him cursing us for disturbing his sleep! After giving us a fast four-mile gallop, he got to ground in a badger earth in Wallace's farm in Ballybrood.

About a month later I drew the bog again in the opposite direction. Our friend left the bog, made a big semicircle, straightened out, and made his escape in the same badger earth.

On a third occasion, I had closed the badger earth, but the schemer changed his tactics. This time he took us on a different line to many fresh foxes. Unfortunately hounds changed on to one of them. We never met our champion again. He won that bout and I saluted him!

With the many strange happenings that have been recorded, one is tempted to believe that foxes have a sixth sense. Dick Coffey farmed some sound land at Ballinacree in the heart of our best hunting country and bred some top steeplechasers. Also a popular county councillor, Dick put human values above politics. Dick loved his foxes; Ballinacree covert was never without a fox and he was proud of the record.

Sadly Dick died while relatively young (although his wife Mary carries on the horse-breeding tradition). Two days after his funeral, we had a meet scheduled for Emly with Ballinacree first draw. To keep well clear of that area, I changed the draw completely. As I was recovering from a fall, my whip Tommy hunted hounds. I warned him at all costs to avoid Ballinacree. Hounds found in Ballyhoulihan covert and, skirting the village of Emly, just flew to Ballinacree, through the haggard alongside the house and marked to ground a few hundred yards on. One is left to wonder.

My reader, you may be tempted to ask me, "Given the passionate love that you obviously have for foxes, how can you hunt them?"

This is a complex question to which there is no short answer. I ask you to picture two boxers entering the ring for a title fight. Each one admires and respects the other for his skill and physical ability and resolves to defeat him in fair play. There are strict rules to be observed. They touch gloves as a sign that they accept the challenge in a spirit of sportsmanship and the fight is on. In the first few rounds each man assesses the other's strategy, his strengths and his weaknesses. After a sporting contest the referee announces the winner. Each man accepts his verdict, congratulates the other, and honour is satisfied.

The simile with hunting is obvious. I have endeavoured to breed a pack of hounds with drive, stamina, courage, scenting ability, and a keen instinct that will match those qualities in a fox and if possible outwit him. But the fox has the ultimate advantage of knowing his country intimately. I get the greatest pleasure and satisfaction in watching hounds doing the job they were bred to do, their speed on a good scenting day, and their painstaking perseverance when the scent is cold. Added to this, the thrill of hounds in full cry is magic—it sets followers crazy!

Hounds face their perils too. On a visit home recently I was following the hunt in a car with my sister Gwen. We stopped at a level crossing to see hounds cross the main north–south railway. To our horror a train, travelling at over 100 miles per hour, ploughed through the pack and killed three couple. A foot follower who saw the train coming ran down the line madly, trying to stop it with his hands up—he almost lost his life.

Road traffic also takes its toll. It is usually the best hound, the one in the lead, that jumps off the bank on to the road before the motorist spots him. The electric fence is the latest hazard; on getting a shock many hounds drop their sterns and will not hunt again that day.

A pack of hounds is like a team of athletes. Each one has his own special forté; some excel in pace (but a hound is only as fast as his nose), others in drawing covert, or in hunting on a road or on a cold scent. A huntsman's ambition is to breed the all-rounder, a rare achievement.

Some people believe that a huntsman is bloodthirsty, committed to killing for the joy of killing. I dispute that absolutely. Admittedly a huntsman's first loyalty is to his hounds and he endeavours to see that they are rewarded for their work. But, as with the two boxers in the ring, there must be fair play.

One memory haunts me. Some years ago we were hunting in Kilfrush late in the season and foxes were mating. A small, weak dog fox was following a vixen in the covert by the road. Hounds flushed him out over the road and he circled back in again. They changed on to the vixen who took them over the road and in her turn circled back to covert. Standing on the roadside I spotted the vixen jumping on to the bank in the bushes, not two yards from me. She was frightened, ears flattened, and panting hard and hounds were closing on her. I should have hollered and cheered hounds on, but my heart bled for that little vixen.

"Go on, do something, are you a man or a mouse?" I found myself saying, but I was frozen to the ground.

Then she made up my mind for me. Dodging through my horse's legs, she returned to covert with hounds close. Soon the pack came out again on the small dog fox and within a couple of miles, they got their reward. I felt relieved.

Along with the joy of watching hounds, hunting offers the excitement of riding a quality hunter over our beautiful country, observing nature in the wild, and feeling the rush of adrenaline veins as we risk our necks over the formidable double banks and yawning ditches.

I have shared with you, my readers, some of my joys of hunting, but the best way of appreciating it is to have a go yourself. Even to follow a hunt on foot in company with the bunch of keen car followers will give you a taste of the sport. Soon you will be tempted to ride to hounds.

Some people worry that hunting is cruel. I appreciate their feelings and admire their concern. I will also endeavour to put their minds at ease. If I believed that hunting was cruel, I would not hunt. All the arguments about the benefits of hunting to the economy, the tourist industry, employment, horse dealing, and so on would never compensate for an act of cruelty.

You may well have experienced a serious fall from a horse. Or you may have fallen from a bicycle while going fast down a rough road; the bicycle skids, you hit the road hard, maybe fracture a limb and have the skin torn from your knees and elbows. At the moment of the accident, you do not feel a thing. We learn from doctors and vets that human and animal bodies produce a substance akin to adrenaline that acts as an immediate painkiller. Seconds later you feel intense pain and may suffer in the longer term. I speak from personal experience!

When hounds kill a fox or hare, the same physiology applies, but there is no aftermath. Death is instantaneous. Hounds tear apart a dead corpse. Killing by hounds is the quickest and most humane death a fox or hare can have. Consider the other methods of fox control. Shooting—a direct hit is a fast kill, but how many foxes are only wounded and pine away in agony? Trapping—a fox is rarely killed by a trap; in most cases they may have limbs broken and be in agony until the trapper comes and knocks them on the head. Poison is the most painful death of all as the unfortunate creature suffers severe contractions before it dies.

I was invited to bring my hounds up to hilly country near Rear Cross, where foxes were plentiful and causing lamb and poultry losses. I put hounds into a thick glen, they found, and almost immediately I heard them kill. Pushing my way as quickly as possible down through the bushes, I found a horrifying sight. The unfortunate fox had the gin trap clamped on one front leg and the two bones were held, no skin or sinews left. In his struggle he had pulled the anchor peg out of the ground and was dragging the trap and chain along. Starving, just skin and bone, he must have been in this agony for weeks. Thank goodness hounds found him and ended his torture.

Some years ago Tipperary Community Radio invited me to join a discussion on "blood sports" (a term I hate because it conjures up a completely false and bestial picture of all forms of hunting). One member of the group was a gentleman from Co. Cork, who was spokesman for the anti-hunting movement, a hot character and unnecessarily aggressive. Unfortunately the radio interviewer was not strong enough to control him. Representing a similar point of view was the young secretary of the Cork Branch of the Society for Prevention of Cruelty to Animals (SPCA), along with two friends.

On "our" side was the chairman of the local coursing club and myself. At the end of the lively and at times stormy session, I invited them all to come down to the Royal Hotel and have a drink. It took some persuasion, but eventually they agreed. During a pleasant hour together I related some of the incidents that I have been describing.

Before parting, the SPCA secretary said to me, "Mr Ryan, it seems to me that you are more 'one of us' than 'one of them'."

I replied, "Look, there is no 'us' and 'them' about it. We all hate any form of cruelty and share a common concern for the welfare and fair treatment of all animals." We parted friends.

It is most unfortunate that such hype has built up around the whole spectrum of field sports. I am convinced that it has stemmed entirely from a lack of understanding on all sides. Sadly it is widening the rift between city folk and country folk. Inevitably the divide has worsened since the issue has become political.

We who live in the country have a huge privilege in being able to enjoy the beauty of nature, the purity of the air we breathe, the changing of the seasons, the peace and quiet of the countryside, and the company of the warm-hearted people of the land. I strongly believe that we have a moral duty to share this privileged life with our less fortunate neighbours in the towns and cities. We should hold out the hand of friendship to them. At a local level we could invite them out on farm visits, bring them to our hunt kennels and let their children play with the hound puppies. We could give them a cuppa and a taste of home cooking. We could also encourage schools to arrange such outings. Little by little we can break down the barrier of misunderstanding and let the urban folk realise that we want to be friends. Then it will be easier for them to understand and share our country sports.

In the old days, hunting was the sport of royalty, the aristocracy, and the wealthy. Times have changed. We must explode this myth by showing that the sport is available to all and especially to our landowners and their families, without whom hunting would be impossible.

FIVE

FOXHUNTING—
MORE THAN CHASING FOXES

THIRTY-FIVE

A BUSMAN'S HOLIDAY

One of my regrets is that I did not have a chance to hunt with more packs of hounds—especially in England. It is difficult for a Master to take time off during the season to hunt even with neighbouring packs. Despite such challenges, however, I have managed to hunt with quite a variety and in many parts of the world.

NOT SO FAR FROM HOME

"Master", the late Duke of Beaufort (his car registration plate was "MFH 1"), invited my sister Gwen and her husband Ernest Pearson (they were Joint-Masters of the Suffolk) and myself to hunt with him before the Badminton Three-Day Event. Guest for the event itself was to be Her Majesty the Queen of England, as was her custom.

Unfortunately for our day of hunting, Master had the 'flu, so he could not hunt. His Joint-Master Major Gundry had hunted the dog pack the previous day, old Ted Reid agreed to waive his retirement to hunt hounds in Master's place. We were beautifully mounted on Master's horses, but sport was disappointing. Locals said it was one of Ted's creeping days. However it was a privilege and a beautiful sight to see the Beaufort bitches at work.

After Badminton's cross-country phase the Queen had to return to "Buck House" (Buckingham Palace). For our part, the three of us went to see hounds in kennel, driven there by Master in his Land Rover. The passenger seat was still warm from Her Majesty sitting in it. This is the closest I have been to the Queen!

Staying with Gwen and Ernest, I had a couple of days in Suffolk. It is heavy country in wet weather. You need a horse with breeding to cope with the deep plough. Not a lot to jump, but a good country to see hounds work.

I enjoyed a great day's sport with the Grafton on a horse loaned to me by a friend. It was a lawn meet and the final day of the season. The huntsman was retiring, all of the staff of the neighbouring packs were honorary whips and about 130 followers were beautifully mounted. Hounds got away well to a "holloa" from the first covert. I have never witnessed such a cavalry charge—every man for himself and God help the hindmost! We had three-quarters of an hour at a fast pace. At a check the huntsman held hounds on to the next covert at a gallop, a fresh fox had been viewed away and on we went without a break. Finally he was unaccounted for in thick covert.

At this point many followers left for home satisfied. Those remaining changed onto second horses (I has lucky to have one at all!). Hounds found and we had a glorious run of over an hour, during which the huntsman never touched hounds once and they killed in the open. It was great credit to a pack agreeing to be picked up and carried forward in one run, and then in the second run to get their noses down and account for their fox entirely on their own.

In the course of the second run the Master, Neal Foster, riding a super thoroughbred type, took a purler over a stake-and-bound fence into plough. I was close behind him when a big gentleman in a pink coat crossed in front of me, galloped over Neal, who was struggling to his feet, and carried on regardless.

I said to Neal later, "You were very patient with that thruster. I would have sent him home."

Neal replied, "I could not do that. He is the chairman of the hunt, I'm only the Master!"

A day with the Heythrop was a dream come true. As a huntsman, Ronnie Wallace is sheer genius. The existence of a silken thread (invisible contact between hounds and their huntsman) was never more certain. Quietness was the hallmark of his handling of hounds. He did not need to use horn or voice; his bond with them was obvious.

He seemed to have an uncanny knowledge of the habits of a fox too. He invited me to come with him to the first covert—thick scrub in a glen with a road along the bottom. He put hounds in and then silence. Occasionally he would put his little finger in his ear, and a sound would come welling up from his lungs, "Hp-hp, hp, yi-ieehup", almost inaudibly. That was all.

Then a "holloa" on the road below. I expected him to galvanise into action. As the first fox to go is usually a strong dog fox, I always tried to get hounds away on him. But no response. A few minutes later a second "holloa" in the same direction. Still no response and hounds had not yet spoken.

Frantic, I could not refrain from saying urgently, "Ronnie, you know that a brace of foxes have left."

"Yes, would you hold my horse please, Thady."

He dismounted and pushed his way into the thick covert. I was ropeable. Yet hounds soon opened with great cry, got away well together in another direction and we had a lovely hunt. That evening I asked him for an explanation of his strange behaviour.

He smiled. "We were not allowed into that country where those first two foxes had gone." But he did not tell how he *knew* that a third fox was there.

Another memorable chance to hunt with different hounds came when Anne and I stayed a couple of nights with Brigadier Lyndon Bolton at Alnwick in Northumberland. In the late eighteenth century Lyndon's grandfather had started the Island hounds in Co. Wexford; today George Chapman with Rosemary Skrine as honorary secretary have been showing great sport with the hounds for well over twenty years. By kind invitation of the Master, the Duke of Northumberland whose family own the hounds, we visited the Percy Hunt kennels. They made a fine picture walking out in the beautiful grounds of Alnwick Castle.

The next day we joined the Border hounds on foot. Michael Hedley, the Joint-Master and huntsman, Master and staff hunted on foot and motorbikes as the country on that day was under thick snow and too steep for horses. I hitched a ride on the carrier of the huntsman's four-wheel bike. The Border hounds are impressive—tall, light and lean with quality and great tongue. They got away on a big, leggy fox; I shall never forget the sight and sound of the pack scaling those deep snowy faces. Foot hunting in Kerry is similar, but without the snow! The Border and other packs in that area account for a large number of foxes, providing a great and necessary service to the sheep farmers.

I was mounted for a day with the Devon and Somerset staghounds, thanks to Bertie Hill, who was involved in the three-day event for England in three Olympic Games, twice as a competitor and once as trainer. I had hunted the carted stag with the Ward Union hounds in Ireland, where the stag are bred in captivity specifically for hunting. A red stag (or hind) is hunted only twice in the season. Each one is known by name and, at the end of the run, is returned safely to the herd.

Hunting the wild red deer on Exmoor was a new and exciting experience for me. A stag is harboured (located by professional gamekeepers) the night before. On the morning of the hunt, hounds are kennelled in a farm in the area, while the huntsman takes the tufters—about five couple of steady old hounds, who are too aged to keep up with the pack and who, once they have found, will not change from the chosen stag. On this occasion I went with the huntsman and observed the tufters at work. It took them about an hour to single out the stag and get him away from the herd. Then the pack was laid on the line.

Discipline and control are essential with staghounds. The pack was actually standing on the stag's track waiting expectantly for permission to go. But there was no urgency to get started because a stag keeps his distance in front of hounds; if they check, he will rest and graze until hounds push him on again. Eventually the huntsman cheered them on and they burst through the fence with tremendous drive. There was a long delay while the stag was pushed through a lot of fresh deer. He finally got away out of the deep coombe and on to the moor.

It was surprising to see hounds hunting in almost single file through the heather, so different from foxhunting, where hounds run with a good head (well bunched together). The reason for the staghounds' approach is that a stag's scent is heavy and does not diffuse like that of a fox. A couple of times on the moor the huntsman stopped the lead hounds until the others had caught up, then they were all laid on again. It was a wonderful sight to watch the stag away ahead, hounds racing on, and horses at full gallop across the wild moorland. After about an hour's run, hounds held the stag at bay. He was then dispatched with a rifle, the carcass was skinned, "trophies" distributed, and hounds had their reward.

Stag hunting has an important role in the West country as the most efficient and humane way of culling and controlling stag numbers. Unlike when guns are used for control, there is no question of a stag being wounded and left to die. In addition it offers people an opportunity to observe a wild and noble animal in his natural environment, and to experience the excitement of the chase.

FRENCH STAG HUNTING AND DÉJEUNER

In France stag hunting is something special. Dating from early history, this ancient sport remains as widespread and popular as ever, while its ritual and glamour are meticulously and religiously preserved to this day. Anne and I had the honour of being invited to hunt on two or three occasions with the Équipage par Vaux et Forêts, in the forest of Compiegne, not far from Paris.

With a pack started by her father, Baron James de Rothschild, Monique has been Master and huntsman for many years. Monique, a delightful and forceful hunting enthusiast beyond compare, has a close understanding of the strict rules of *la Venerie* while her knowledge of the ways of the stag and the science of hunting is incredible. Also an admirer of our hounds, Monique was keen to see if the Kerry beagle would hunt well with her French staghounds. She kindly gave us the trip to stay and hunt with her, and learn about the sport.

The format of hunting in France is different from that on Exmoor in that tufters are not used. At the meet the huntsman interviews the two or more foresters who have been out early that morning and report the number, description and location of the deer that they have seen. The huntsman then decides which animal they will hunt. The majority of hounds are used to draw for the chosen stag; the remainder are transported in a van to augment the pack as necessary during the hunt when any tired hounds are picked up.

We had *déjeuner* (lunch) at 12 noon. I had thought some cheese and biscuits would be sufficient, but no, a four-course lunch with wine was served. We then drove to the meet where hounds and horses awaited us. As it was the final meet of the season, it was, by tradition, a combined meet with a neighbouring pack.

After an interview with the foresters Monique decided which stag she would hunt. We mounted our horses, hounds were unboxed, and she blew on the *trompe* (French horn), the particular call or tune announcing the move off. Only the huntsman, staff, and a select number of *boutons* (hunt members), including some elders following in cars, are permitted to carry the horn. It is an essential instrument to help keep the huntsman in touch with the situation—transmitting a message that the hunted stag has crossed a road, entered another forest, crossed a stream, entered a lake, or whatever—because visibility in the forest is limited. It must take a lot of practice to be able to blow the large instrument while galloping through trees and branches.

Incidentally the mouthpiece of the *trompe* (unlike that of the orchestral French horn) has a narrow edge that at first is uncomfortable. The reason for it, as I learned from Monique, is that the mouthpiece beds in to one's lips and will not budge—even when one is galloping through branches while blowing a call. As with the short, regular hunting horn, however, one's lips become muscled up with constant use and do not suffer.

I rode up with Monique. When hounds soon found, Monique recognised the stag she had chosen: he was a *daguet*, a two-year-old with short antlers. It amazed me how quickly the pack settled on one animal out of the herd with little help from the whippers-in. After about four hours of the stag taking us in large circles, hounds lost him completely. In spite of all the assistance from the *boutons* and followers, there was no trace.

The huntsman of the neighbouring pack said to Monique, "We may as well go home. We can do no more."

Monique retorted crossly, "You can go home if you wish. I am going to kill my stag."

She turned her horse around, called to me to follow, and we galloped down the ride. Within half a mile hounds suddenly rushed into a boggy thicket and, miraculously, out came the hunted stag. He was accounted for within another hour. We had been hunting for over five hours, mostly at a gallop. (To be more accurate, my horse had been galloping but Anne's horse and Monique's three that she used alternately were trotters off the track.) I dismounted short of the end because my lad was staggering with exhaustion. I realised then why we had had that good lunch!

The final ritual was then enacted. The stag was skinned while hounds stood around in a circle. The choice cuts were reserved for local landowners. One whipper-in, who had severed the head and covered the carcass with the hide, was teasing the hounds while they bayed with excitement. Meanwhile Monique related the story of the hunt on her *trompe* and each call was repeated by the hornblowers who stood at the opposite side. The whipper-in then threw the hide off with a flourish and hounds had their well-earned feast.

All the hornblowers together intoned the different fanfares of the visiting Masters and noblemen. There was even a special fanfare for a visiting Master of Foxhounds in my honour! Although the French horn sounds great in an orchestra, it does not compare with the sound of about ten *trompes* in unison, played in the gathering dusk with horses steaming and hounds baying. Their rich, glorious music rolled and echoed through the forest. It was magical.

Next morning at breakfast I asked Monique if she was sure the stag that hounds fresh-found was the hunted one.

She almost exploded, "I am not *sure*, I *know*!"

"All right", I said, "how did you know?"

"Two reasons", she said. "First, I recognised his head with the short antlers. Second I noted his slot (footprint) in the clay. The toes of a fresh stag are close together and on a tired stag they are splayed."

I have a lot to learn!

Home again, I sent a couple of good young hounds to Monique, but heard nothing from her. It so happened that two of her hunt followers came to hunt in Ireland and had a day with us. I asked them whether they knew about the two hounds that I had sent to Monique.

They were embarrassed, saying, "We do not know whether we should say it, but they were not a great success."

Upset, I telephoned Monique that evening. "I would not disappoint you for the world. Please come over and have a hunt and I will give you any hound you fancy."

So she came with her sister Nicole who enjoyed a hunt. Monique did not ride (saying, "Who will hunt my hounds if I break my leg?"). The hound they chose was Sailor—a great worker and one of my real favourites, but I would not break my word.

A few weeks later Monique phoned. "Please come out. We cannot catch Sailor in the kennel to put his collar on." This collar was necessary as all hounds wear a collar with the name and phone number of the kennels to which they belong.

Back we went to France again. Sailor was overjoyed to see me, and I put his collar on. At the meet next day, when hounds were unboxed, he came straight up to me and was quite happy, then joined the pack. Although he hunted well, at the end, he was missing. I went with Monique back to where he was last seen, and called and called—I wished I had my own horn. No luck. I came home with a heavy heart.

Three months later, the police phoned the kennels. Sailor was found about thirty miles away from where we had been hunting. He was reunited with the pack and settled in well. The trouble had started when, at one point, the stag crossed the ride in sight of the field. All the followers got excited and blew their own horns, a short-curved variety with a reed. The pack crossed the ride, but the din was too much for Sailor, who stopped abruptly and retraced his steps.

One of the followers asked me, "You have not got your horn?" I replied that I would not dream of using a horn when hunting with hounds other than my own.

HOUNDS OF NORTH AMERICA

Opportunities to become familiar with hounds abroad have also extended to the United States. One of the finest examples of brilliant hound work that I have seen was with Mr Jeffords' Andrews Bridge in Pennsylvania. There had been a sharp frost and dust was flying off the endless acres of plough. After hounds picked up a stale drag (a faint scent of a fox long gone), we walked after them slowly for some time, enjoying their brilliant casting and perseverance, as well as admiring the Master Bob Crompton's patience. Gradually the pace and cry increased as hounds made up ground. Soon we were trotting and then galloping flat out and finally hounds marked to ground. I'd say the fox must have only narrowly escaped with his brush. It had been a fascinating piece of hound work for about an hour and a half, full credit to Bob's Penn-Marydel hounds. They have great nose and cry, characteristics shared with the Kerry beagle.

I get the greatest satisfaction from watching hounds puzzling out the line on a cold scenting day, or when the fox has gone some way ahead. Every hound is desperately trying to pick up the scent, usually working silently because the scent is not strong enough for them to "own" it with their voice. When one hound is sure of what he has found, he gives a whimper, his comrades rush to him and they surge on in chorus. They are doing a job for which they have been carefully bred. To my mind, this satisfaction is even greater than that of following hounds in full flight on a breast-high scent, when hounds do not have to put their noses to the ground to own the fox's scent because the climatic conditions are such that the scent is slowly rising.

Jill Fanning, long-time Master of the Essex foxhounds in New Jersey, took hounds out on foot specially for me to see and hear them hunting, although the season had officially just closed. We started on a grey fox in thick country and hounds worked well. During the hunt I saw a strange sight: hounds were slowly working a stale line and they were closely followed by ten or twelve deer, ears pricked and curious. Hounds never gave them a glance. Buster Chadwell, huntsman for many years, had his hounds absolutely deer-proof—the envy of many Masters.

An exciting day was with Ben Hardaway, Master and huntsman of the Midland pack, mostly American foxhounds who hunt in Alabama and Georgia. Here was another example of the silken thread between hounds and huntsman. The pack ranged wide on either side, all drawing keenly and with an occasional look at their master. On finding they shared Ben's wild enthusiasm, got together well and ran with great drive and cry.

Ben has a lovely story about his farming operation many years ago—to get full value you should hear Ben tell it himself in his delightful Southern accent. To enable his Hereford cattle to stand up to the intense heat, he decided to introduce Brahman blood into them. But Brahman cattle can be wild.

Some time later his farm manager said to him, "Baass, if we done do sometin' 'bout these 'ere Brahman cattle, we are going to lose all our cowboys."

Ben replied, "You go houme and come back to me tomorrow maarnin with a solution to the praablem."

The manager came back next day and said, "Baass, the only solution aah see is we will have to breed slower cows or faster cowboys!"

One year Ben kindly agreed to judge at our puppy show. His co-judge was William Casey, a keen and knowledgeable Kerry beagle huntsman from West Cork. Ben's Southern accent contrasted with William's broad Co. Cork accent but they got on great. I wished I had a tape recorder.

On entering Mr Stewart's Cheshire Hunt kennels in Pennsylvania, one could be excused for thinking one was in England. Nancy Hannum, Master for many years, has maintained the old English foxhound type—strong boned, straight back, not a suspicion of a curly stern, standing almost over on their toes with the pad off the ground. Fortunately this traditional foxhound foot is going out of fashion; for years it has been the cause of toe removal because of infection in the nail. The discipline and kennel routine, as well as the etiquette of the followers out hunting, are strictly preserved on English hunting lines. Joy Valentine gave me a good horse for a day with Nancy. It was a pleasure to watch a disciplined pack of hounds working well, and the country was a gift to ride.

Hunting the wild white-tailed deer in Sonora, Northern Mexico was another exciting experience. Although hounds could riot on mountain lion, fortunately, they did not in my time with them—but more of this anon.

HOUNDS AND OTHERS DOWN UNDER

And so back to a milder climate and some good foxhunting with the Oaklands Hunt in Victoria, Australia. Joint-Masters Catherine and Randall Cameron-Kennedy run a well-organised operation along traditional English lines, in beautiful rolling hunting country. They have bred a superb pack of quality English foxhounds that show great sport. Foxes, which are plentiful, are generally found in rough scrub or small boglands. Unfortunately because the laws of the state forbid any earthstopping, too many foxes escape. With the Cameron-Kennedys for their Centenary Hunt Ball, Anne and I travelled in style from their home to the hunt club in a coach drawn by a handsome grey. Genuine oil lanterns on the coach together with a full moon created a romantic, magical experience.

I had the pleasure of two days hunting with the Oakland. The going is usually hard with some rocky areas. Fences vary from plain wire, mostly panelled, to walls and thorn. The foxes seemed smaller than the ones in Ireland. Hounds accounted for one and marked others to ground. On the first day a hunt member kindly loaned me her eight-year-old Percheron-Thoroughbred seasoned hunter, an excellent performer. The next day I was delighted to ride Catherine's good thoroughbred.

When exercising horses one morning with Catherine in the park land adjacent to the airport, we came across a mob of kangaroos. They took off at speed. I pursued them on the Thoroughbred to try their pace. I was going full gallop and they were still gaining.

Another day Catherine asked me if I would give her huntsman Ben Benfell a lesson on the hunting horn, as he was a bit weak on it. I felt embarrassed since he had been huntsman there for several years. However, as he was delighted for me to help him, he and I, with his wife and young, sat out on his verandah in the sun that afternoon. Now Ben had a large and bushy ginger moustache.

I joked to him, "You would find the horn much easier to blow if you did not have that great gorse bush on your upper lip, and I'm sure your wife would get a nicer kiss from you."

Then we went ahead with the lesson and were both pleased with his progress. That evening was the Centenary Hunt Ball. Ben turned up looking smart in hunt livery . . . and sporting a white, clean upper lip on his dark tanned face. He had shaved off his moustache! Mortified with embarrassment, I apologised on bended knee to his wife. It was the joke of the night.

A more straightforward pleasure was when I had the honour to be invited to judge the Foxhound Show of Victoria held at Sherwood, the Oakland Kennels and Hunt Club near Greenvale. All neighbouring hunts were represented—Melbourne, Finden, Yarra Glen, Lilydale, and Oakland. It was an enjoyable occasion, with Oakland gaining most of the awards. I was elected an honorary member of the hunt, for which I am deeply indebted to the Joint-Masters.

TWO ITALIAN CONNECTIONS

Riding with hounds at exercise along the cobbled Via Appia Antica (the Old Roman Way) past the catacombs and the occasional tall mausoleum—tomb of some old nobleman—felt strangely incongruous. Count "Pippo" Cigala Fulgosi, Master of the Roman foxhounds for many seasons, was our host. Alongside the old road are the ancient hunt kennels and stables, handsome and immaculate, like the horses and hounds.

A day's hunting through the *campagna* was exciting, with good views of hounds. Some of the post-and-rail fences, known as *statsionata* and sometimes combined with a ditch, were awesome; they were made from split chestnut slender spars that were flimsy and tall, but unbreakable. Although it is an open galloping country, hunting is increasingly curtailed, as in so many places around the world, by expanding townships and endless traffic.

An outstanding and remarkable gentleman from an old Roman family, Pippo first came into my life while I was young, when a friend of Dad's brought him along for a morning's cub hunting on foot. We children were in awe of this tall, erect, and handsome young naval officer, perfectly dressed and speaking no English. My next meeting with Pippo was in the Holy Year 1950, when my brother John and I went on a private pilgrimage to Rome. We booked in to a *pensione* on Monte Mario—an area of which Pippo disapproved strongly, but he did not have room for us in his flat. He took us to the magnificent Circolo de la Caccia (the Roman Hunt Club, the oldest club in Europe) in Villa Borghese, where we sipped fine, old brandy from enormous glasses and were served by waiters wearing powdered wigs, knee breeches, and gold buckled shoes—an odd variant from normal pilgrimage routine!

After a distinguished career in the Italian Navy in World War II, Pippo had been awarded the highest naval decoration for outstanding bravery in sinking one of Britain's aircraft carriers. Yet Pippo was not one to brag about his exploits and, although a proud and dedicated subject of his king, he had many friends in England and in Ireland. The war did nothing to injure this friendship;

however, even in 1950, I sensed that he felt keenly the bitterness of Italy's defeat. John and I once touched on some sensitive subject—maybe to do with the poor state of the roads—and Pippo could not stop himself saying, "but we are a poor country, we have lost ze war." I felt I had hurt his pride.

Ambassador Amadeo Guillet, now retired in Co. Meath, told us a story of Pippo's father, a general in World War I. Through a daring manoeuvre, he prevented what would have been annihilation of his regiment, but he was captured by the Germans and due to be shot. On the morning of his execution he came down from his quarters in full uniform. Declining to be tied with ropes, he stood erect in front of the firing party with his back to the wall. He was granted a last request: to give the order to fire. His last words were, "God Save the King and Italy—*Fire*". Pippo too was that calibre of man.

For many years Italy had a royal family whom the people worshipped. Before World War II, the English King George VI and the Queen Mother visited Italy, receiving a warm welcome. To honour their memory, the Rome Hunt Club arranged for a beautiful portrait of them to be preserved in the sanctum of the club, honouring the bond of friendship between two great dynasties. The large portrait remained hanging in Circolo de la Caccia unscathed throughout World War II. To my mind this is an example of true chivalry, especially in sport. Anne and I have happy memories of our visits to Rome.

Retired Ambassador Amadeo Guillet himself is a most remarkable gentleman. After the Allies concluded the North African campaign successfully and defeated the Italian Army, Amadeo escaped and went underground disguised as a farrier. He wreaked havoc behind the Allied lines, and there was a huge price on his head for his capture.

While he was in hiding with one farmer, an English officer called to search the house. The farmer and his wife had a young coloured lad working for them, serving at table while Amadeo was cooking the meal in the kitchen. The couple pressed the officer to dine with them. The young lad was so frightened that he almost dropped the dishes of food. Impatiently Amadeo donned the lad's apron and served the visitor himself!

Eventually the net was closing around him and he decided to get out by joining up with some refugees. After the refugee ship entered the territorial waters of a neutral country, he dropped his disguise and asked to see the ship's captain.

He said to the captain, "Thank you for a pleasant voyage. I am Amadeo Guillet."

The captain knew all about him, but could not lay hands on him in neutral territory. For many years after the war, the "Desert Rats" (Allied Forces in North Africa) celebrated a dinner in London with Amadeo as their guest of honour, the fox they could not catch!

Between the wars Amadeo rode for Italy in showjumping and the military (eventing). After World War II he joined the diplomatic service, working his way up from the bottom to the rank of ambassador; he served in Egypt, India, and several other countries. His autobiography has been published in Italian and he has assured me that the English version will be published early this century. Get hold of a copy if you can—you will not be disappointed.

Amadeo came to stay with us many times at Scarteen, running clinics and helping our farmers and friends to school their young horses. He was extremely fit and athletic. One morning I came in for breakfast and found him in the dining room standing on his head.

He explained, "It is very good for ze brain!"

Pippo too came over to hunt with us on many occasions. He liked to ride thoroughbreds, and it so happened that I had a four-year-old Thoroughbred mare. I had tried unsuccessfully to breed from her, so we broke her in and she turned out a clever hunter. We had a fast run from Mooresfort towards the Galty Mountains and lost in the forestry. There was no sign of Pippo; someone said he had gone home. On arrival home I asked him what was wrong.

He replied, "She would not jawmp."

Shocked, I thought she was possibly overfaced as a young horse in our big country, so I sent her to my brother-in-law to hunt over the easier fences with the Tipperarys. A few weeks later Claude phoned me to say that the mare was in foal!

THIRTY-SIX

TO TELL THE TRUTH

The moment I met Joe Lynam, we became friends. A keen hunting man, Joe has been one of the top marketing experts in Bord Failte (Irish Tourist Board) for years. When I called to his office he explained that the Bord had recognised, as I had, that foxhunting in Ireland was unique, with the potential to become a valuable off-season attraction for visitors worldwide.

Joe outlined a plan that he had drawn up. The Bord wanted Anne and me to go to the United States on a tour to promote Irish hunting and riding holidays. All expenses would be paid, including hotels and travel. A list of venues, hunt clubs, riding clubs, and so on would be selected. A Bord Failte representative would meet us at each venue, having advertised the function in the local press. The whole organisation sounded first class. I was impressed.

"But", I said, "I can see that you hope to fill jumbo jets with American sportsmen. That is the wrong approach. First, Americans coming to Ireland want to meet Irish people, not fellow Americans. Next, the various hunts could not cater for large numbers of visitors at any one time. They could handle the same number in small groups spread over the hunting season. We will be happy to do the job. We do not require any booking of venues or hotels or advance advertising. All we would be glad to receive is our airfares." They were baffled until I explained, "We have had a huge number of visitors staying and hunting with us over the years, and they have always said, 'If you ever come to the States, you must come and stay.' So we will take them at their word."

Getting out our visitor's book, we contacted all our friends. Many offered to arrange venues, usually in the homes of Masters of hounds, and spread the word among members of their own and neighbouring hunts.

And so our itinerary was fixed. We armed ourselves with a load of projectors, promotional films and slides (video had not been invented), and souvenirs and set out for the Big Apple. Were we excited! Occasionally my heart would miss a beat with an attack of nerves. What possessed us to agree to such a task when we had never done the likes before? Then I would think of the crack we would have with our friends and the good job we would do for Ireland, and my confidence would return.

On the day after we arrived in New York, my first port-of-call was the Bord Failte headquarters. Austine Hearst, wife of William Randolph Hearst of the newspaper empire, kindly let us have the use of her big maroon Cadillac and chauffeur, so we turned up in style. Cadillacs were not numerous, especially the maroon variety. And passersby would stare at us. We could read their thoughts: "Probably some foreign diplomat or other."

Austine and her friend Elliwood Baxter were regular visitors to Scarteen, staying for a week and hunting every day. Will came with Austine and Elliwood on their first trip to Scarteen to check us out and, although he did not hunt, he was good company. In subsequent visits he trusted us to look after them. We always looked forward to their visits. We had to remember to bring a trailer to Shannon to hold Austine's numerous trunks. Along with their quantity of hunting gear, saddles, and the like, Austine brought a selection of gorgeous gowns and wore a different one for dinner each evening, putting us to shame! Then they had their city wardrobe for Paris after they left us.

Once when I arranged for them to hunt with the Duhallow hounds, I booked two good safe hirelings from Ned Hannigan. Unfortunately Ned had a puncture and was late for the meet. Elliwood spotted a chap, Frank O'Connor, with two horses.

She asked him, "Are these Mr Ryan's hirelings?"

"Which Mr Ryan?" asked Frank, who happened to be a friend of mine.

"Mr Ryan of Scarteen", said Elliwood.

"Oh . . . Mr Ryan of Scarteen . . . yes, yes, of course."

Frank put their saddles on the two green four-year-olds, and they moved off with the followers. When Ned eventually turned up, he asked Der O'Meara, the honorary secretary, which were Mr Ryan's two ladies. Der found out the "mistake" and was furious. However, all was well as Austine and Elliwood saw the joke, switched to Ned's horses and had a good day. That evening Der phoned me to apologise for what had happened, saying that Frank would never again be allowed to hire a horse with the Duhallows.

I said "Der, please don't do that. I know Frank. The ladies enjoyed the joke; they had the thrill of riding two young horses, nobody had a fall, and all are happy."

During our visit to the States, Bord Failte never missed a chance to advertise our work. A popular television show at the time was *To Tell the Truth*. An individual with an interesting career would be chosen together with two companions—all dressed alike and all using the same name. A panel of three would interview them to identify the individual who truly was in the named career. The two companions could make up any stories and tell as many lies as they wished, but the bona fide individual had to tell the truth.

For our game, two Irishmen were chosen some days in advance. One (we'll call him "Mick") was a theatrical producer and had read up about foxhunting in the library to familiarise himself with it. The other (we'll call him "Pat") owned a pub and was also a boxing referee. He had not had the time for research and knew nothing about the sport. We were taken together to Knoud's on Fifth Avenue, the number one hunting outfitter—exclusive and expensive. There we were decked out with identical borrowed gear—pink coats, white breeches, top boots, hunting cap, stock and pin, gloves, and a hunting crop.

Soon we were on air in front of an interviewing panel, including television personality Kitty Carlisle, and a large studio audience.

The producer introduced us: "This is Mr Ryan, MFH, this is Mr Ryan, MFH and this is Mr Ryan, MFH."

The panel questioned us individually. Mick answered his questions intelligently and convincingly.

When it came to his turn, Pat was asked, "Where is the Quorn Hunt?"

He replied also convincingly, "If you drive about sixty miles west of Dublin you come into the Quorn Hunt country."

I had the greatest difficulty preventing myself from exploding into laughter. Then it was my turn.

Kitty said, "I have an advantage over the other panel members because I have hunted in England. Tell me, Mr Ryan, what is a martingale?"

I gave a correct and detailed description.

Finally I was asked, "Who is the president of Ireland?"

I was cornered. If I said his name I would give the show away.

I said to my fellow Masters, "It's not Sean T. O'Kelly or de Valera. I can't think. What the hell is his name?" The audience burst out laughing.

Then the producer said, "Will the real Mr Ryan please stand up?"

I produced a hunting horn from my pocket and blew the "Gone Away". Kitty failed to guess me, as she said that my description of a martingale obviously had come out of a dictionary! One other panel member also failed, but the third guessed right. If we had defeated the entire panel we would have won $500, but as it was, we won $100. The show was broadcast all over the United States. It also had several repeat showings; a couple of years after we filmed it, a visitor said to me, "Oh, I saw you on TV the other night."

Thanks to the generous hospitality of our numerous hunting friends, we had many successful and enjoyable evenings showing our films of Ireland and sharing memories. One occasion stands out in my mind. Neal Ayer, Joint-Master with Russell Clark of the Myopia Hunt, and his wife invited us to stay and have a session at their house. When Neal and his daughter Helen stayed at Scarteen, they hunted every day. For our visit he had a good plan: he would hire a car and driver from Daimler Hire, who would make all reservations and look after the saddlery and hunting gear. Neal, heavily involved with the United States Three-Day Event team, was known as "Mr 3-DE".

The day before we were due to arrive at their home, I phoned to confirm details, only to learn that they had just had a terrible tragedy. While Neal was playing polo, between chukkas, his pony bucked him off. Neal lay on the ground motionless. Fifi Coles, a great horsewoman, but not medically trained, noticed that he was not breathing. His face was turning purple and his head was at a strange angle. Some instinct drove Fifi to twist Neal's head slightly—a desperately dangerous thing to do—yet he started to breathe again. Later in hospital he had a bone graft to fuse two vertebrae.

When I learned the news from his wife, I immediately said, "Please forget about our party. You are far too engaged."

But she replied, "No way. We urgently need something to take our minds off the tragedy."

So we went ahead as planned. During the evening, news came from the hospital that the operation was a resounding success. I shall never forget the cheering and rejoicing. By an amazing coincidence, the hospital had been built by Neal's father, while Neal himself had been responsible for building the new orthopaedic wing, which had only just opened. He was the first patient in it! I was allowed in to see him next morning when typically he was in great spirits. He was soon back in the saddle again.

Another time we had reason to hire a car and drive to the Bord Failte Office. This was a bit daunting: Anne did the navigating, Joe Lynam watched out for the police, and I did the driving. After completing the exercise without a brush with a vehicle or the law, we were pleased with ourselves. Actually driving in New York is moderately easy because the boulevards run north to south and the streets run east to west (or is it the other way round?).

Dan and Louise McKeon of the Golden's Bridge hounds were old friends of ours. In our travels we stayed with their daughter in St Louis, Missouri, and I took the opportunity of calling to the Benedictine Priory, which had been founded by the monks of Ampleforth. I had a great chat with the prior Dom Luke Rigby (a classmate of mine in school). He was in the process of cutting ties with Ampleforth, thus making the priory independent and autonomous. I felt just a bit sore about this, but of course it was the right direction to take. Now it is a fully fledged abbey as well as a popular and successful public school.

THIRTY-SEVEN

CALIFORNIA, HERE WE COME

On behalf of the Bord Failte, Anne and I did a similar foray to the United States a couple of years later, this time heading west. On the morning of our departure, while Anne was feeding the hound puppies, she tripped over the bucket, cut her leg badly, and had to go to the regional hospital for treatment.

We had an argument. I said I would not do the trip without her. She argued that all appointments had been made and I must honour them. Of course she was right! So I phoned the Bord Failte representative who was in Shannon to see us off, explaining why I had to "go it alone" and that Anne would join me later. He told me afterwards that the conversation had puzzled him—if Anne had kicked the bucket, surely there was no need to treat her leg!

I had an enjoyable brief stay with our old friends in Houston, Lt Governor of Texas Bill Hobby and his wife Diana Hobby. At that time I did not dream that Bill would be one of our "happy family" of Joint-Masters a few years later (chapter 30).

On then to Omaha, Nebraska for an all-too-brief stay with Al and Jean MacTier. A friend of Al's, Van Ketzler, who owned the Dehner Boot Manufacturing Company, was anxious to set up a factory in a country that belonged to the European Economic Community (EEC, now EC). Knowing that Al was a regular visitor to Ireland, he called by to ask his advice.

Al said, "By sheer coincidence, there is an Irishman, Thady Ryan, staying here who might be able to help."

It so happened that the Irish Industrial Development Authority had just built a small factory in my local village, Knocklong, to provide employment in the area. They offered it to Van for his use. Van did not delay; he set up his factory, employed local labour, some of which he brought out to the parent factory in Omaha to learn the trade. The venture was popular in the neighbourhood. What could be more appropriate than an industry making high-class riding boots in the middle of our hunting country?

As the boots were individually handcrafted, it was obviously going to take a while to develop a clientele in Europe. For the first couple of years the boots made in Knocklong were being supplied to customers in the United States. Van wanted the factory to be self-financing, which entailed initial long-term loans. To my frustration the bank was unwilling to cooperate, so Van closed down the factory and returned to Nebraska.

Happily two families who went to Omaha to learn the trade have settled out there, and keep in close contact with the folks at home. For my part, I received from Van Ketzler in Omaha a parcel with the label "Contents: old clothes". It turned out to be a jumble of old shirts wrapped around a beautiful pair of brand new shoes made by Dehner. I wrote back:

Dear Van, thanks for the shirts and socks—Anne will repair them for me. Oh, in the parcel I found some beautiful leather shoes and they fit me perfectly. Thank you very much.

The shoes had come in duty free—a generous present from Van and typical of his friendship.

By good fortune for me the American Pony Club National Cross-Country Championships took place on the MacTiers' farm during my time with them. It was a treat to see an event so beautifully organised in an idyllic setting. The fences were built superbly and the course rode well.

A few years later at dinner in Cahervillehow, I met a charming elderly lady who in her day had been president of the American Pony Club. Recently she had attended the excellent Holycross Gymkhana near Thurles, so I asked her for her comments.

"It was a most enjoyable show", she said, "but a lot of the riding was appalling."

I let her speak for a while, then replied, "Some years ago I was privileged to attend the Pony Club championships in Omaha: I was most impressed with the standard of equitation—immaculate turn-out, correct seat, and the riders were conscious of giving a good impression. But, with respect, I felt that they were lacking one important factor: the 'will to get there'. In Ireland the first thing our young riders want to do is to 'drive on and go hunting'. They are not fussed about what they look like."

Eventually we agreed amicably that both schools could learn something from each other. I do believe that thanks to the good work being done by the Pony Club, along with the increasing popularity of eventing and dressage, the standard of horsemanship in Ireland has improved no end.

After two weeks my solo travel was over (at last!). Anne joined me in Toronto. Our hosts took us on a tour of the Great Lakes and Niagara Falls, a fantastic experience.

Our next stop was Genesee, Wisconsin for a most enjoyable stay with Bill and Pomp Wadsworth. Bill surely was one of the great stalwarts of American foxhunting. On our arrival Pomp greeted us with the news that an English couple by the name of (it sounded like) "Veeaye" were staying and that the husband said he once whipped-in to me in Scarteen. Perplexed, I could not remember anyone of that name. Then, to our joy, out of the house came Tony Villiers, my former amateur first whipper-in (chapter 28), and his wife Rosie. We fell on each other's necks!

With Bill, such a character and an ardent fox hunter, you can imagine the tenor of conversation at the dinner table. Bill told me an amusing anecdote about one of the first astronauts to land on the Moon, Peter Conrad, brother of the lady secretary of the hunt. Before leaving Earth she tried to persuade him to take a hunt button with him. He said it was impossible. Refusing to take no for an answer, she sewed a Genesee Valley Hunt Button into the lining of his tunic. He duly walked on the moon with his fellow astronauts. On their return to Earth they had to undergo intense scrutiny, x-ray, and quarantine, then "Hey, what's this?" The button was discovered. Now framed, it hangs in the Master's study with the inscription: "If there is ever foxhunting on the moon, the Genesee Valley claim the hunting rights."

I have seen that button. And I am delighted that the Wadsworth family are carrying on the great hunting traditions that Bill passed on to them.

Next was Los Angeles and a lovely stay with Harold Ramser, Master of the West Hills Hunt, and his wife Betty. Regular hunting visitors of ours, they were also great patrons of William Frazer, our famous hunt tailor (chapter 31). We visited West Lake Village, a township designed for a maximum of 60,000 people and developed from bare land, some distance inland from Los Angeles. A big artificial lake had facilities for all conceivable water sports. There was also a well-organised riding club run by the two Postel sisters, both large, short, and great company. After our visit there they both came to stay with us. I booked Conor Hanly's good weight-carrying hunter for Joanne, the rider of the two. Many eyebrows were raised and the lads were all angling for a turn to give her a leg up. ("Huh, she won't get very far!") They were all astounded when Joanne turned out to be a fearless rider near the head of the hunt until the end of the day. There was a right party in the pub that evening!

Back in Los Angeles, we had a great gathering in Hal's house, with a lot of interest in our display.

At the end, Hal said, "Does anyone want to ask any questions?"

"Yes, Master," said one of the visitors. "Do I understand from Mr Ryan that if we were to land in Shannon on the Wednesday and hunt on Thursday and Saturday, it would be less expensive than to arrive on Saturday and hunt on . . ."

Hal interrupted, "If anyone has to count their dollars, don't come hunting in Ireland. Are there any more questions?" I think I must have blushed!

Then on to Pebble Beach, where we had a great get-together, reminiscing with Dick and Marguerite Collins and a host of friends. We got a good view of sea otters on their floating kelp rafts, which they never leave. Al and Jo Shreck showed us through some of the Los Altos Hunt country. With the growing popularity of Californian wine, vineyards were proliferating—a huntsman's nightmare!

While staying with Al and Jo, a phone call came through from Al MacTier to say that his company's Lear jet was due to return to Omaha. Would we like a ride? Would we what! Al drove us to the airport and we met the pilot, a delightful elderly chap.

Al said, "You will be in good hands. There are old pilots and bold pilots, but there are no old, bold pilots!"

We took off like an arrow from the bow, leaving the lumbering jumbos away behind. I asked our pilot if we could reduce altitude to get a better view of Mount Rushmore and the presidential rock carvings, but he said sadly no because we would run out of fuel. I had not realised that the higher you fly, the less fuel you use.

It was good to be back with the MacTiers again. They took us to see our first rodeo. I saw that the famous trick roper, Monty Montana, was on the programme. Monty had stayed and hunted with us.

On hearing that there was an Irishman in the audience, he said, "The only Irishman I know is Thady Ryan!" Then when he entered the arena, he rode up to the grandstand calling out, "Where are you, Thady?"

I stood up and gave him a "holloa"! His silver-mounted Western saddle is something special, priceless. His closing act was fantastic. On horseback, he stood in the middle of the arena and opened his lasso into a big long loop. Twelve girls riding bareback galloped past him in line, abreast. He dropped the loop neatly over the lot and galloped on with them—it was unbelievable!

Monty is an outstanding showman. I tried to persuade the Royal Dublin Society to invite him over as an attraction at the horse show. Unfortunately the cost of bringing him over with his troupe and horses was prohibitive.

When my six weeks were up, I flew home. Determined to use the two weeks that she had missed out on, Anne stayed on with friends. She was able to check up on what I had been up to solo, but I have never been able to catch up on what she did in her two weeks!

Looking back, I believe that both our excursions to the United States have borne much fruit down the years. They were also infinitely enjoyable. I can never express adequately my sincere gratitude to all our friends who made them possible.

THIRTY-EIGHT

TARGET—EUROPE!

In 1975 John Kennedy in Bord Failte dreamt up a novel scheme. He picked about a dozen people, each one to be thoroughly conversant with a particular sport or activity that was truly Irish. The subjects included fresh-water fishing, golf, ancient history, art and handcrafts, along with my responsibility—horse riding and hunting holidays. We were scheduled to visit five capital cities. On arrival, after being entertained by the Irish consul, we would be taken to our respective venues, where, as a result of extensive advertising, we should have a large, interested audience.

For weeks beforehand we thoroughly researched our subject with the help of the Bord. Then, armed with a load of projectors, slides, and courage (not the Dutch variety!), we flew out of Dublin Airport.

A WHIRLWIND SPEAKING TOUR

Stockholm was our first stop. As planned, we had a convivial drinks reception with our Irish consul before going to our respective venues. Mine was a riding club in the city, where I had a good crowd, but somehow I felt I could not get through to them; they seemed to lack a sense of humour and were retiring. However after the "business" was over, they relaxed and we got on well.

I was invited by two people to see their horses next day, but I had to decline. "Sorry, but tomorrow we will be in Copenhagen!" This was the only fault that I found in the whole exercise: we should have had an extra day in each location to consolidate our work.

Copenhagen was different. I found the Danes outgoing and warmhearted, with a sense of humour. With good attendance at my venue, we had an enjoyable evening. I longed to have more time with them. The Master of the Copenhagen Draghounds had hunted with us in Ireland; I wish I could have accepted his invitation to come and see his hounds, but no time.

Amsterdam also was most enjoyable. One person who turned up had been a member of a group from the Netherlands that we had entertained for a summer riding holiday some years previously. I had another link with the country, having visited it to judge hunters. On that occasion a big Dutch gentleman had a plain horse that gave me a rough ride.

When I dismounted, the owner proudly said, "This is an Irish horse."

I could not stop myself from saying, "We have far better horses than this!"

He replied, "But I could not afford a better horse and this one satisfies me very well."

It gave me an appreciation that there is also a market for our horses of lesser quality.

After my talk in Brussels I had a few hours to spend with friends near there. Baron Casier had hunted a pack of harriers for many years. His son Philippe was now Master, a keen hound enthusiast, while his father followed in a horse and carriage. The Baron also had a passion for carriages; after the Dutch royal family, he had the most famous collection of them in Europe. He brought me out to see them at his fine moated château. They were an amazing sight, all in immaculate condition in a huge building controlled for temperature and humidity.

On the way out Baron Casier brought me to the place where his son had lost his hare when hunting the previous day. He wanted to see if I could throw any light on the problem. We were literally in a suburb with the occasional strip or square of green grass and dense traffic. I could only think that she had hopped on a bus!

A lady, one of the Baron's ancestors had presented a tract of land to the Belgian Benedictine Monks, whose monastic order is a branch of the English Benedictines at Ampleforth. She also had their mother house *Maredsous*, a beautiful monastery in Belgium, built for them. Monks from there founded Glenstal Abbey, a fine public school near Murroe in Co. Limerick, where our four sons were educated. Because of the family connection, Philippe Casier as a boy visited Glenstal for a holiday. He asked Father Athenasius, the last surviving monk from Maredsous to come to Glenstal, whether any hounds were in the area. Of course he was directed to Scarteen.

Such a grand lad and dead keen, he stayed with us for a few days. While there he took part in the final day's cub hunting in big bank country. Pleased with the hounds' performance, that evening I asked Philippe for his comments.

To my lasting shame he said, "I see that here you hunt to ride. At home we ride to hunt." (Philippe was a purist, and if that was his impression of our hunting, I was deeply embarrassed!)

Zurich was our last call on our whirlwind tour. Actually I went by train to Berne for my appointment, sorry to be leaving the rest of the group in the Swiss capital because we had had a good time together. Actually they were a bit suspicious of my movements. I disappeared with friends at most destinations only to join the group at breakfast. Was I a sailor "with a girl in every port"? I said no way, it was just one of the advantages of foxhunting.

On arrival at Berne Railway Station I called a cab, dumped my load in it, and slumped into the back seat exhausted.

The driver asked, "Where to, sir?"

"The International Hotel, please."

"That is it across the street", he replied.

However, I got a good night's sleep after my final session went off well. Next morning Ruedi Homberger, a charming elderly sportsman and a retired engineer who had hunted with us several times, drove me to his farm in Shaffhausen. There

I saw his two fine Irish heavyweight hunters, now retired, stabled in tying stalls (rather than loose boxes), with a soft neck-rope and block, on a bed of clean straw. From behind the door, Ruedi took a gallon tin attached to a handle, then shuffled the straw with his foot. The horse passed urine into the "potty" that was held out for him, the contents were spilled down the drain outside and Ruedi repeated the performance with the second horse. My eyes were out on sticks in disbelief! Ruedi would visit the horses several times a day to exercise them and make them comfortable, while the straw remained clean and dry.

A SIDESTEP TO ITALY

From there I made my way to Italy on my own account. Travel by air to Milan was the obvious choice, but I decided to go by train so that I could see the countryside. En route I was struck by the general appearance of the Swiss farms—a sense of pride, orderliness, and prosperity everywhere, pretty little houses dotted through the hills and valleys, everything neat and tidy.

Then like a rabbit we went to ground in the tunnel through the Alps. We emerged in northern Italy to a totally different scene. Houses were scattered higgledy-piggledy everywhere, as was the farm machinery, most needing a coat of paint, and fences in need of repair. Yet there was a sense of ease, timelessness, peace, and lack of wealth. I am sure this reflects the warm laid-back Italian character that I love.

After Pucci Rossi, a nephew of Count "Pippo" Cigala Fulgosi MFH (chapter 35), met me in Milan with his sparkling sports car, we drove at high speed over those handsome and lengthy viaducts to Rome to stay with Pippo. Anne also joined us there. Pippo always hoped that Pucci would hunt the Roman hounds, but he simply did not have the time, having inherited several estates from relatives. After a day's hunting with us, he made us laugh.

He said, "Thady, who were those two good-looking young ladies out today?" Jane and Avena, the two daughters of Bill Harrington (the Earl of Harrington, Master of the Co. Limerick hounds), were then as attractive as ever and unattached.

"Did you not speak with them, Pucci?"

"No," he said, "nobody did introduce me." I felt guilty. I had forgotten that Italian etiquette and good manners are paramount.

At that time Pucci was a successful three-day event rider with a great eventing future ahead of him. These days it is pitiful to see him confined to a wheelchair following a serious fall while schooling a young horse. Yet he remains a source of courage, great company, and fun.

Pippo asked us whether we could have another relative, Giulio Pocci, to stay with us in Ireland. Naturally we said an immediate yes. In due course I drove to Shannon to meet him. I pictured in my mind a tall, good-looking, aristocratic young gentleman with a tanned complexion, and I was largely right, although he was rather paler than I'd imagined. On the journey home we became friends but I found him quiet and conversation was difficult.

I told him that by a stroke of luck, we were due to hunt the following day, the first hunt after an eight-week stoppage caused by a foot-and-mouth scare. I mounted him on Spencer, our patent safety. After finding quickly, we had a flyer from Ballyscaddane to Glenefy. There was no sign of Giulio.

I asked, "Has anyone seen my Italian friend?"

Someone said, "He has gone home."

I was bitterly disappointed. Was the country too stiff for him or what? On arrival home that evening, I discovered that he had gone to bed, so I went up to see him.

"What's up, Giulio?" I said.

"Thady, I am not feeling well. Could I see a doctor?"

Heavens, I thought, we have a hypochondriac on our hands. Nonetheless I phoned our family doctor who came at once and went in to examine Giulio. He came out quickly.

"Thady, your friend could die. He has the worst case of jaundice I have ever seen, He must go to hospital at once."

No wonder poor Giulio had been so quiet! Thank God he recovered rapidly! After three weeks of good care at home he was back almost to full strength. He was full of fun, great company and everybody's favourite. A courageous rider, he rode Spencer in the Bank Race at our point-to-point under Knocklong Hill and tasted the water in the famous Black Trench! With his enthusiasm for hunting and eventing, he is now a senior official on the Federation Equestre Internationale and has been technical delegate at the Punchestown Three-Day Event on several occasions.

From a national point of view, I believe that foxhunting has become an extremely valuable off-season attraction and a major source of income. More importantly it has created a Céad Míle Fáilte to sportsmen from all over the world into the hearts and homes of Ireland. In luring people to Ireland it has something in common with another event, the Dublin Horse Show, organised by the Royal Dublin Society, which happens to be the topic of the next chapter.

THIRTY-NINE

THE ROYAL DUBLIN SOCIETY—A LANDMARK IN MY LIFE

The Royal Dublin Society (RDS) must be one of the oldest and finest institutions of its kind in Ireland. Founded to promote and foster agriculture, science, and the arts, it has performed the task admirably down the years. The magnificent façade of its headquarters on Merrion Road reflects its character and lofty ideals. Architecturally it is one of the treasures of the City of Dublin, but for me it represents far more. Looking at it I feel a similar sensation to seeing St Peter's in Rome. It is a sense of belonging. I love the place.

My particular association with the RDS has been through the world-famous Dublin Horse Show. The RDS has given support of inestimable value to the breeding and marketing of the Irish horse down the years. The continuing success of the show as the shop window of the industry fills me with the greatest satisfaction and pride. To the dedicated staff of the RDS, who have played a huge part in this success, I offer all my personal congratulations and gratitude.

The RDS Council decide the policy, which is then implemented by the Executive Committee through the various subcommittees elected by RDS members. I was on the equestrian committee for many years up to my retirement in 1986, when I had the honour of being awarded life membership of the RDS.

One of the most famous names in RDS history was the Honourable Justice W. Wylie. "The Judge", as he was known to everyone, had two major ambitions in his life: to be Master of the Ward Union Staghounds and to be chairman of the Executive Committee of the RDS. To his great satisfaction, he achieved both. One could say he was a dictator in his role of chairman, yet he had the judgement and personality to win the confidence of the Council, the members, and the staff.

The Judge's predecessor, Mr Bohane, epitomised the conservative attitude of Council members. On the opening day of one show, he came into the judges' box in the main arena, spotted a small advertisement for ice cream in the far corner and exploded in rage, "Take that—thing down at once!" What would he say now to see the beautiful flower border of the arena smothered with sponsors' billboards?

The highlights of the year were the two major RDS shows: the Spring (Agricultural) Show in the first week in May and the Dublin Horse Show in the first week in August. Landmarks in the calendar, they set the standard for shows around the country. (How often I have heard it said, "*That* would not happen in the RDS!")

For years Dad was a member of the (all male) Ground Jury, the team of judges of jumping competitions in national and international horse shows. If the hot-tempered Judge got upset over something, Dad was the only person who could say to him, "Ah Judge, don't be cross." When Dad eventually resigned from the jury, I was greatly honoured to be invited to take his place. In this way I entered the world of the RDS.

In those days the double bank and the single bank were famous; people came from all over the world to see them jumped. Hunting experience was a big advantage because one could appreciate the reasoning behind the system of faults awarded. Changing on the single bank cost one fault, hind legs low on the take-off side of both banks or dropping short cost two faults, jumping into the face of both banks cost three faults, and flying each bank cost four faults.

In national competitions, which were jumped in pairs, it was often difficult to judge the banks when both horses jumped together. The arrangement was that one rider wore a red sash and the other a white one. Three judges then worked together: one took white, the other red and a senior experienced judge was referee. So, although the judgement was still a matter of opinion, it was a fair and sporting decision.

The course consisted of six permanent fences only—even in international competitions. The first fence the was a Liverpool (hedge and ditch), second the single bank, third the stone wall, fourth the railway gates, fifth the double bank, and sixth the open water. The stone wall was a contentious fence. If a horse knocked a stone with a foreleg, it cost three faults; knocking it with a hind leg cost two faults. To watch this, a judge stood close to the wall, armed with a red flag and a white one. A flag was held low for a foreleg fault and high for hind leg—confusing when the two horses jumped at speed together. A team of men also stood by to rebuild the wall, which could take ages.

Before the puissance competition was invented, we used stones to increase the height of our champion stone wall until a winner was achieved. While competitors stayed in the arena, at the bell the next horse would start. A regular competitor was John Morrison, a great character from Northern Ireland, who rode a spectacular jumper called Freedom, a big, rangy bay with a wild eye. Morrison would stand on the single bank, then when the bell rang, his groom would bring Freedom alongside the bank, he would vault into the saddle, canter straight to the wall and clear it, then return to the bank. After a couple of turns Morrison would take his coat off! By this time, the Judge would be tearing his hair with fury, but the crowd loved it and cheered loudly. Freedom was frequently the winner.

Among the many famous international horses who have competed in Dublin, Rusty was a handsome middleweight chestnut gelding. He carried Iris Kellet to victory in many international competitions including the Queen Elizabeth Cup in Wembley. In his early years they jumped in the old style: without a clock, it was check, check, check before each jump. In other words, the rider would steady the horse and endeavour to adjust his stride to place him in the ideal position for taking off over the fence. Inevitably, this strategy meant jumping a fence took considerably longer, boring for spectators. When the clock was introduced, Rusty and Iris adapted their style to speed competitions, and continued their winning way—a remarkable achievement.

Another horse I must mention is Goodbye, Seamus Hayes' quality heavyweight hunter type, a magnificent horse with a powerful spring. He carried Seamus to victory in many team and individual competitions. However, he had one weakness; he was unreliable over the open water. One year in the second round of the Aga Khan International Team Competition, the highlight of the week's jumping, Ireland was in the lead and Goodbye was last horse to go. Victory depended on a clear round. I was water judge, the job I was always given because of my fairly calm disposition. There was a hush in the capacity crowd as Goodbye approached the water. My heart was in my mouth. Then, unobservable to others, but no doubt about it, Goodbye *just* touched the lath. I had to be honest. Up went my flag, to boos from the crowd. Ireland had lost the cup. I wanted the ground to swallow me up!

Because Ireland is starved of pageantry, every bit is precious. For some years it was the custom for the President of Ireland to enter the arena on the Friday of Horse Show Week in a horse-drawn carriage, drive around the arena and dismount at the President's Box for the National Anthem. One such occasion almost saw an accident. Our President at the time, Sean T. O'Kelly, was a short, slight gentleman, but his wife was a large, plentiful lady. They entered the arena in their carriage drawn by four white ponies. Unfortunately the ponies took fright from the outburst of cheering applause, turned around 180 degrees and were looking into the passengers' faces. With a heavyweight on one side of the turntable unsupported, her Excellency was almost tipped out. However, completely unfazed, she and her husband recovered their composure and, accompanied by the presidential party, walked across the arena to the cheers of the capacity crowd.

In spite of unremitting pressure and pleading from the RDS it was some years before we finally got the powers-that-be to agree to a repeat of the ceremony. Joe McGrath with his team of beautiful Irish Draught mares, well-schooled and rehearsed, drove the president through the city and into the RDS arena. It was an entirely appropriate display for our horse-loving nation, a great occasion to parade the cream of our native breed before a worldwide audience.

And then the ceremonial parade of teams. A detachment of Irish pipers led each of the eight teams into the arena to the tune of "The Harp That Once through Tara's Hall" or some other rousing Irish air. Halting, they would then salute the President while the band of the Garda Siochana (Police Force) played the nation's National Anthem. When all teams were present, the host nation correctly in the rear, they were led by the three bands in full volume around the arena—the drum major entertaining the crowd by pitching his baton skywards. Thinking of that spectacle still brings tears to my eyes. As a schoolboy without the money for a grandstand ticket, I would climb one of the trees at the end of the arena between the competitor's stand and the Red Cross, thus gaining a ringside view of the whole performance.

Foreign teams were always happy to come to Dublin. They loved the warm welcome, the entertainment, the hunt balls, and the great atmosphere of Horse Show Week. Prize money was of secondary importance, in contrast to today

President Hilary arrives at the Royal Dublin Horse Show with Joe McGrath and his Irish Draught Mares. It was the custom for the President of Ireland to enter the arena on Friday in a horse-drawn carriage, drive around the arena, and dismount at the President's Box for the National Anthem.

when, sadly, money talks. The hunt balls were a feature of Horse Show Week. Once I did three in a row. Never again. I could barely see the horses jumping the following day!

THE SHOW OF A THOUSAND HORSES

As the shop window of the Irish hunter (now sporthorse), the Dublin Horse Show plays an essential part in the industry's operation. Classes are devised to cater for all categories and judging is of the highest standard. Because Britain traditionally has been our nearest and largest market, British judges were always chosen.

Jerry Rohan is one of the best-known hunter judges in Ireland and in Britain too. His father-in-law was sportsman Michael O'Brien, who, for many years, was Master and huntsman of the Bray harriers, as well as being on the jury in the RDS. One evening during Show Week, when Michael and his wife invited me out to dinner as usual, Michael showed me an outstanding six-year-old that Jerry had found for him. I fell madly in love with the horse.

In mock anger I said, "Why didn't he offer the horse to me?"

Michael, who was getting on in years, said generously, "When I retire from hunting, the horse is yours."

About ten years later the horse was pensioned off and Michael was still going strong!

Jerry and I had the job of selecting judges for the Horse Show and recommending them to the Council for approval. I created consternation when I argued that, as the market for our horses was expanding into Europe, we should invite a judge from one of our new customer countries to judge in Dublin. Further, I argued, the continental market was for potential eventers and jumpers, rather than for hunters only. After much persuasion, the Council agreed.

We invited Piero d'Inzeo from Italy to judge the performance championship, a new class I had started. It was really a sophisticated working hunter class in which two judges assess the horses over a course of rustic fences, then each judge separately assesses them for conformation and ride. When Piero judged the ride, the horses went extremely well for him. Growing in popularity since then the class is now divided into three age groups and a championship with good prize money. On occasions the champion has been sold for more than the champion hunter of the show.

At a later show we invited one of the top Holsteiner breeders in Germany to judge the heavyweight hunter classes. Riding a big, quality four-year-old of mine that was slightly nervous, I was apprehensive lest the big man would have hard hands. Unexpectedly he rode on a loose rein and my lad went well. However, his fellow judge, English show rider Jack Gittens, pulled the horse together and asked for a collected and mannerly ride. My lad objected, reared up, and sent Jack out the back door. I led the horse out of the ring in disgrace!

The German judge later said, "There was nothing wrong with that hawrse. He went beau-ti-fully for me. Perhaps that gentleman could not rhide!"

It is most important to help the small breeders and to encourage them to bring their stock out to shows. To this end I started the Breeders' Championship class. It is designed for either non-Thoroughbred mares with foal at foot by an approved thoroughbred sire or for Thoroughbred mares with foal at foot by an approved nonthoroughbred sire. It is judged on points: fifty percent for the mare and fifty percent for the foal.

Qualifying classes are held at shows around the country. At the final in Dublin, big prize money is awarded down the line with a valuable Perpetual Trophy to the winner. Now a highly prestigious class, many shows have included it in their schedules.

The highlight of the show is the Grand Parade of Prizewinners, of which I was commentator for many years. The sight of the arena filled with the cream of our Irish-bred horses is heartwarming. The quality of horses in the Dublin Horse Show is the subject of much discussion among breeders and exhibitors. A low standard is a good sign because it means that the trade is good with the cream of the horses around the country bought up before showtime, and vice versa. Not many owners in Ireland can afford to turn down a good offer just for the satisfaction of winning in Dublin.

The parade is led by a pack of hounds, as it should be because foxhunting must be seen to play a vital role in the sporthorse industry. Following the parade, it is customary for the pack to give a special display. Masters of hounds try desperately to invent a new act to entertain the crowd each time. Once when I had the honour of bringing my hounds up, I jumped on to the double bank and my entire pack came with me. It brought the crowd to their feet. When Evan Williams was invited to bring up the Tipperary foxhounds the following year, he was furious with me because he did not have a suitable double bank in his hunting country to practise on!

Stabling for the 1500 or so horses at the show was always a headache. For a long time the RDS had leased the sales paddocks, their property across Merrion Road, to Goffs Bloodstock Sales Company; this was the only Irish company in the business for many years, who dealt with many of the top racehorses of the world. Ideally situated with a railway siding when bloodstock travelled by train, the stables were used at horse show time. This was a mixed blessing because the horses had to be led across the main road through dense traffic. At one time a tunnel was seriously considered, but soon the problem was solved.

When a large area in Simmonscourt adjoining the showgrounds came on the market, the RDS purchased it and sold the land that had been leased to Goffs. In return they offered Goffs a brand new sales complex in Simmonscourt, which would take over a year to build. So the RDS offered temporary facilities in the various exhibition halls and show rings. This unexpected move by the RDS greatly angered the members of the Thoroughbred Breeders Association (TBA). Soon there was a serious split in the TBA between the "Royalists" (those loyal to the RDS) and the "Pro Goffers". Feelings on both sides ran high.

Meanwhile Goffs purchased a large area down the country at Kill in Co. Kildare, offering TBA members an alternative venue to that available from the RDS.

Parading hounds at Royal Dublin Society Horse Show with Bandoola, 1964. The Grand Parade of Prizewinners—the cream of our Irish-bred horses—followed the parade of hounds. Courtesy of Independent Newspapers, Ltd.

Once when I had the honour of parading my hounds at the Royal Dublin Horse Show, I jumped onto the double bank and my entire pack came with me. It brought the crowd to their feet! J. F. Connor photo

Jonathan Irwin, an astute businessman and able tactician, travelled out on behalf of Goffs to the United States to study Fasig Tipton's famous sales centre. He was able to offer the TBA a superb sales complex at Kill if the members agreed to the proposal. On his return from the United States and to guarantee a winning majority, Jonathan organised a frantic canvassing for membership around the country.

And so the battle lines were drawn. A crowded meeting of the TBA took place. The RDS appointed me as their spokesman, while Jonathan put the case for the TBA. Eventually, in a moment of high tension, the decision was put to the vote. Goffs won the day.

On the way out from the meeting a friend who was in favour of Goffs' proposition said to me, "Well, Thady, you are bolloxed."

I replied, "Just you wait, Paddy."

If the truth be known, the votes of all those recently enrolled TBA members were null and void because, according to the TBA Constitution, members had to be enrolled for over three months before they could vote. Yet it was only afterwards that this was discovered. If this clause had been spotted in time, the outcome might have been different. As it was the RDS built a gigantic exhibition hall that enclosed a magnificent sales complex. The beautifully designed sale ring with a raised oval deck can be used for a variety of purposes, such as concerts, exhibitions, conferences, and even a hound show.

The old pavilion in Clonmel Showgrounds, which had housed the National Foxhound Show for many years, was in dire need of repair, so the Irish Masters of Foxhounds Association decided to abandon it. I thought it would be appropriate to hold the hound show in the RDS during Horse Show week. The

IMFHA agreed to give it a go. The sales ring was the only site that could be made available, and the RDS offered every assistance to adapt it for the job. Kennels were erected in the assembly ring, and an extended floor was fitted on top of the oval deck.

The concept of holding the hound show during the Show Week when so many hunting folk were in attendance was excellent. However there was one major snag. Even in the front seats, the patrons were too far away from the ring. So after two years of trial it was decided to change the venue for the hound show to the excellent field and country fair that was newly established in Adare Manor in Co. Limerick.

Auctioneering firm Messrs Keane, Mahony, and Smith arranged with the RDS to hold National Hunt (steeplechase) bloodstock sales in the new Simmonscourt complex. At the start they sought applications for auctioneer positions. I had done some "selling" at fun auctions at hunt balls and the like so I applied and was short-listed for trial at a hunter sale. I sold two horses! However two other applicants who had long experience at selling were accepted so my career as an auctioneer was terminated.

In due course Messrs Keane, Mahony and Smith amalgamated with Messrs Tattersalls of Newmarket to form a new company, Tattersalls (Ireland) Ltd, under the able chairmanship of Denis Mahony. It was Denis with his big black horse who was favourite to win the East Galway Heavyweight Race in which Michael Higgins, the Master, had persuaded me to ride. I intended to ride Spencer but James Breen persuaded me to ride his young heavyweight Kennedy. ("Master, I would have to carry about two stone of lead and you will not have to carry any!") George Earle, with his quality hunter, was also entered, along with two thoroughbred types.

The going was appallingly deep after heavy rain. After we set off George and I were galloping along, happily chatting in the rear of the field. After one round of the course I noticed that the two thoroughbred types were coming back to us and tiring. I looked into my petrol tank and found it had plenty, so to speak, so I pressed the accelerator, and won the race.

"Why didn't you tell me you were going to win? I could have beaten you easily", said George.

"Then why didn't you?" I replied.

The favourite was down the line. My victory was due to Kennedy's big, plain feet that did not sink into the mud. Of course I then had to buy him, and never regretted it.

Down in Co. Kildare, from bare fields, Goffs erected the most up-to-date sale ring and stabling complex in record time. The two companies were soon in business, working in healthy opposition, but with good relations; Goffs concentrated on the flat scene and Tattersalls on national hunt stock. The thoroughbred industry is well served by both. As with the RDS, Goffs sale ring is adaptable for a number of uses. I have even attended an impressive performance there of the musical *Joseph and his Technicoloured Dream Coat*.

THE QUINNSWORTH CHASE

One day at the Charleville Show I was talking with sportsman Van de Vater ("Van"). As Master of the United Hunt for ten seasons and a dedicated, but modest three-day event rider, he had been extremely popular in both roles.

"Van," I said, "I want to pick your brains. The Dublin Horse Show is a wonderful institution, faultlessly organised and almost perfect in every way, thanks to a team of dedicated workers who take a personal pride in their job, and also to an army of volunteers who give up their whole week to make the show the success that it is. I am proud of them all. However I feel that the show could be criticised for being almost boringly the same year after year, and that it needs an injection of adrenaline to rouse the enthusiasm of the general public. Have you any suggestions?"

Van thought for a while then said, "I agree, but whatever is introduced must have strong foxhunting connections."

Anne and I put our heads together and came up with the idea of an inter-hunt knockout relay race for teams of four riders and a *chef d'équipe* from sixteen hunts over a course of rustic fences wide enough to be jumped by two horses at a time. Teams would include the Master or other honorary hunt official, a male rider over fourteen stone, at least one lady rider, and a special award to the team with a lady riding sidesaddle. In each heat the horses would jump the same course in opposite directions. At the end of the round, the rider would hand over his hunting crop to the next team member. The team whose member was first home would be the winner. Big prize money would be paid to the hunt funds.

After I lobbied some fellow members of the horse show committee, we put forward the proposal. The committee's first reaction was one of almost horror—too dangerous, would take too long, and insurance would not buy it. Finally they agreed to give it a try, but I must get a sponsor. I approached Quinnsworth Stores. Unfortunately the managing director was unavailable; he had been kidnapped and his whereabouts was unknown. I met their financial controller, who was most interested.

"Is this the first time running it?" he asked.

"Yes", I replied.

"Right, you are on. How much money do you want?"

"Three thousand pounds", I said.

"Very good, I can take that decision myself."

I was delighted and so were the committee!

Invitations to compete, together with full details of the fences and competition, were sent to all recognised hunts. Then sixteen teams were drawn and notified in good time for them to rehearse.

On the day before the event, the manager of the Telefis Eireann outside broadcasting unit arranged to interview me. I explained the details of the competition to him.

"Is this the first time this event has been run?" he asked.

"Yes", I said.

"Right we will broadcast it live", he replied.

Numbed with fright, I hardly slept that night. Yet the whole event went off like clockwork, thanks to the indefatigable efforts of Joe Moorhead and his team of stewards. I had made one blunder: I had never conceived that the contestants would ride so fast! The two clock towers (reminiscent of the first steeple chase years ago from Buttevant, in Co. Cork to Doneraile), around which riders had to turn into the finishing straight, were a bit too close. In the semifinal one horse slipped and fell, then the other tripped and fell over him. There was a deathly hush all through the arena until both riders and horses got to their feet, just a bit concussed! The continental bank at the far end of the arena was a spectacle. Two horses apparently galloping straight at each other, but in fact there was plenty of room on top. The crowd went wild with excitement. I have never heard such uninhibited yelling before or since.

The final remark from the commentator was amusing: "Thady Ryan must be delighted with the success of the event, and the great thing was there were no accidents at all." Oh not at all, just two riders and horses lying almost dead on the ground. Thank God it was not worse!

The Chase has become the biggest crowd-puller at shows all over Ireland, England, and the United States—yes, even in New Zealand. A couple of weeks after the inaugural running at Dublin, a lady member of the RDS wrote to them absolutely furious. She was going to cancel her membership in protest against the most appalling display of riding in front of our overseas visitors. Yet she missed the point. It was never meant to be an exhibition of equestrianism. On the contrary it was an exciting performance by genuine hunting folk riding hell for leather for the honour and glory (and a financial reward) for their hunt.

Scarteen Hunt Chase Team competes at Royal Dublin Society Horse Show, 1986. (l–r) Thady, Marie Barnwell, Dicky Power, Phil Purcell. Stuart Newsham photo

THE HURRICANE

My experience of being narrowly defeated for the hunter championship with my good horse Tom Tallow (chapter 33) was a deep wound. It set me thinking. I had always believed that the three judging rings in the RDS for heavyweights, mediumweights, and lightweights were far too small, and a horse with a long stride did not have a chance to show his ability. Coming home from that show feeling sore, I resolved to do something about it.

For months Anne and I worked on a plan to reorganise the judging rings and the entire timetable for the Horse Show. The class judging would extend over an extra day. Rings 1, 2, and 3 would be replaced by one large ring. Ring 4, traditionally reserved for judging of young horse classes, would become the collecting area (as there had never been one before, it meant a big job for stewards to assemble entries). Scrapping the divisions would entail removing the handsome rows of pollarded elm trees between the rings.

At the committee meeting following the show, I submitted our plan to them. It was received with alarm and, I believe, was committed to a bottom drawer. It had been shown to the Executive Committee, who were adamant that those trees must never be removed.

Stan Collen, of Collen Bros Builders in Dublin, an old and trusted friend, had been an ardent follower of the Ward Union Staghounds and used to come down every year with some friends to hunt with us. At the time we had a small problem in our hunting country. There is a bog between two good coverts, Kilteely and Cromhill. Through the bog runs a huge, deep trench with a soft take-off and landing, which always took its toll of horses and riders. I decided to erect a bridge over it. It so happened that Collen Bros at the time were building the large grain silos by the Shannon in Limerick for Messrs Ranks (Ireland) Ltd, an old, established milling firm, now defunct.

I said to Stan, “Next time you have a truck coming down from Dublin, would you drop off for me a couple of twenty-five-foot steel girders?”

“What on earth do you want those for?” he asked.

“I want to erect a bridge over that trench between Kilteely and Cromhill”, I replied.

“O-oh—all right, I’ll have them delivered”, he said, hesitantly. The girders arrived in due course. Keith Reynolds organised the building of a super bridge using railway sleepers.

The following August I was met by Bertie Reynolds, who used to come hunting with Stan and was a demon to go across country. (As a member on the jury in the RDS, he also kept everyone in good spirits.)

“Oh,” said Bertie, “I hear the ’Tans are finished. They can’t jump their ditches, they have to build bridges over them.”

The story had got around among all my friends. I had a miserable show!

But retribution was to come. The following hunting season, Stan and party came down with their horses as usual. The meet happened to be at Kilteely and the fox took us to Cromhill, over the new bridge. No sign of Stan and his good four-year-old. On the way back to draw Kilteely again, we came across Stan in grievous trouble. His horse was partially submerged in another trench and had to be roped out.

But Stan, that is only a tributary of the trench with the new bridge", I said with glee. But I'm away on a fresh fox again. Sorry!

My wound had festered for nine months. At a committee meeting before the show the following year, Stan asked at my request, "What has happened to Thady Ryan's plan?"

Copies had been issued to all committee members and a discussion took place. To my disgust and fury Stan criticised all the points I had made.

Professor Mullany stood up and said, "Mr Chairman, we expected that Mr Ryan would open a window and let in some fresh air, but we did not anticipate this hurricane!"

There and then it was decided to submit the plan to the Executive Committee for consideration. Stan and I were directed to study the plan at length and report back after the Horse Show.

After the meeting I attacked Stan with the words, "I thought you were my friend. Why did you hammer me so hard in committee?"

He replied, "I just wanted to find out were you dead serious about your proposal because I think the concept is excellent."

At an autumn committee meeting, looking out on the three rings, I noticed that all the elm trees around the perimeter had been pollarded (trimmed), but those between the rings—the trees that would have to be removed—had not.

Hugging Stan, I said, "We've won, we've won!"

Stan and I spent long hours discussing all the points I had made. Eventually we decided on an alternative plan built around two big rings (instead of one), with classes timed and tailored to fit accordingly. At the following horse show, before a final draft was decided, Stan organised a team of intelligent girls to work separately, one to each ring. They were to record on paper an exact log of progress to include every detail of time spent for a break, for prize presentation, for start and finish time for each class and so on. The "new" timetable would then be compared. We hoped it would work as we could not afford to make a mistake.

One important duty that remained was to solicit the reactions of as many long-standing exhibitors as possible to the proposed changes. Nat Galway-Greer, who had shown more horses and won more championships than any other exhibitor over the years, was one of the best-known dealers in the country. I was detailed to sound him out. At first he was all against the change.

"Many riders have difficulty enough in controlling their mounts in the present rings. Give them a larger ring and there will be a disaster", he argued.

I replied, "Nat, are you saying that your horses would be unsafe in a larger judging ring?"

We had a good laugh and he agreed to the change without further ado. All of those interviewed, almost to a man, were eager for the new-look horse show. It was implemented the following year.

FORTY

JUDGES DIFFER AND . . .

I have enjoyed judging shows of both horses and hounds. Although the role is an unenviable one, it must be said that a judge is invited to give his or her unbiased opinion on the order of merit in the class; the Show Committee has chosen this judge because it has confidence in his or her knowledge of the subject and good track record. Inevitably as a judge one is criticised unmercifully by the spectators!

JUDGING HORSE CLASSES

Long involvement with the RDS and many years hunting hounds inevitably led to invitations to judge horse shows in Ireland, England, and further afield.

Judging in England was always a pleasure. Many owners can afford to buy the best and keep a good horse for the joy of winning show championships year after year. So one has the chance to ride horses of superb quality, which are beautifully schooled and mannered and which one has never seen before. Following a show career, the horse is usually retired to the hunting field.

My greatest thrill was judging hunter classes one time at the Horse of the Year Show in Wembley with Master (the late Duke of Beaufort, MFH from chapter 35). Being a junior judge I was doing the ride, while Master was responsible for the conformation and action in hand. I knew only one horse there. From his photos in *Horse & Hound*, I recognised Prince's Grace, a magnificent gelding that had been the reigning champion at major shows for some years. Now, I thought, I am going to have the ride of my life.

I was bitterly disappointed. He rode a tired horse, lacking any spark of excitement or get-up-and-go; he had gone stale, probably from over showing. In all honesty I had to give him a low score. In contrast Master gave him almost top marks because he was just about faultless in conformation. The result was that he finished in about fourth place.

In the following issue of *Horse & Hound*, the show correspondent Pamela McGregor-Morris slated me:

> It was a crying shame that such an outstanding champion should be demoted from his rightful place at the height of his career. Obviously the Irish judge had not recognised what he was riding.

I bit my lip, but did not change my opinion. Two years later, at lunch in the judge's pavilion in the Dublin Horse Show, I was called over to another table to be introduced to a charming elderly English lady.

She said in a rather croaky voice, "Ryan? Ryan? You are the man who put Prince's Grace down the line in Wembley two years ago? Well done, you were absolutely right. I don't know what people saw in that horse. He could not move a yard!"

"Oh," I said, "I have a friend at last" and thanked her profusely.

The next time I met PMM, I accused her of slating me.

"Oh Thady," she said, "I would never do such a thing." We were old friends, so we had a good laugh.

Another horse I shall always remember was the outstanding heavyweight His Grand Excellency. I would rate him among the greats, including the Dublin champions Mighty Fine and Mighty Atom. He gave me a thrilling ride when I was taking him through the normal routine—walk, trot, canter, and gallop on both reins. It was like driving a supercharged Rolls Royce (I believe, not that I have ever driven one)! I was enjoying myself so much that I asked him to do one more round. He said, "No" and took me back to his place at the top of the line. In his long career as a show champion he had never been asked to do such a thing before. It was a mean trick, so I laughed and gave him best.

There was a similar incident in the Working Hunter Competition at Burghley Horse Trials. I had the thrill of riding Cornishman. (Ridden by Mary Gordon-Watson, he was the most outstanding and famous three-day eventer of his day.) He was one of my three winners for the championship. I asked each of them to jump a couple of fences again, a most unusual request, and all three knocked them, so on points Cornishman was my champion. I don't think that Mary never forgave me for causing her and her brilliant horse to be so humiliated!

Judging the Lloyds Bank In-Hand Championship, open to all breeds, was a new experience. There, one is looking for the best of breed; in other words, the horses are not being compared with each other. I had never known Welsh cobs before, but the stallion on show looked such a magnificent specimen that I placed him first over some beautiful two- and three-year-old hunter types. I felt better after the show when I learned that my champion was Black Magic, a well-known winner around the country.

Another horse I shall never forget was David Tatlow's Bunowen, a high-quality middleweight that had been "knocking at the door" as reserve champion several times that season. He was a bit strong in the hand, but such a magnificent mover, and could he accelerate! I placed him up top and he carried the champion rosette at many shows from then on.

Hickstead International Jumping Festival, established by Douglas Bunn on his farm in Sussex, was another lasting memory. I was honoured to be the invited foreign representative on the jury and a guest of Douglas Bunn for the show. In between international competitions was a display by a pack of foot beagles. They were a beautiful sight, about eighteen couple of beautifully matched quality hounds. In those days the grandstands were tubular temporary ones. As the pack paraded around the arena, I noticed that the second whip had something fixed to the heel of his boot. I was suspicious.

Sure enough on the second time around hounds picked up the scent—the thing on his boot was a rag soaked in aniseed. Hounds raced away in full cry, giving a grand display of hounds hunting, albeit on a drag. However, the Master had not allowed for the strong wind that blew the scent under the grandstand into the collecting ring, where the horses were warming up for the next jumping competition. There was chaos. The huntsman was left in the centre of the arena blowing his horn and not a hound in sight!

I thought to myself, "Serves you jolly well right, making fools of your hounds."

Seamus Hayes, Ireland's leading international showjumper for several years, was competing at the show and also staying with Doug. As he and I were not drinking men, after dinner each night we would disappear and go for a breath of fresh air around the jumping arena.

On the last night of the show Doug said, "I don't know what mischief you two Irishmen are up to. I'm coming with you to find out."

So the three of us went for a stroll together in the moonlight. Seamus was explaining to Doug one of his theories that I believe makes a lot of sense. The theory goes that, when starting his round, if a horse is over-collected and all tensed up, he feels no pain on hitting a fence, so he gets careless. On the other hand, if he is ridden on a light rein and sympathetically, he will avoid hitting a rail because it hurts.

Doug said, "A load of rubbish!"

After a couple of moments Doug let out a yell of pain. Seamus had given him a hard blow in his solar plexus.

"Ye felt that, Doug di'nt ye because ye wern't 'spectin it. Next time ye won't feel it because ye will be 'spectin it."

"Get away, you so-and-so murderer", shouted Doug.

For years Dad had been on the jury of Balmoral Show in Belfast. On his retirement I was invited to take his place, which I did. Granville Nugent, Master of the Newry harriers, was president of the jury for a long spell. His formal and resonant voice over the public address system will be long and fondly remembered.

Another jury member was Colonel Cunningham, president of the Royal Ulster Agricultural Society and longtime Master of the County Down staghounds. I asked for his thoughts on hunting the carted stag compared with the wild deer. Most of the followers hunted for the ride, with runs of fifteen to twenty miles not uncommon, but I knew that the colonel enjoyed the hound work. In an intriguing reply, he explained that it was like playing both hands in a game of poker. On the one hand, he was breeding stag to outwit his hounds and, on the other hand, he bred hounds to outwit the stag.

When he retired, his daughter Anna MacIlveen carried on the Mastership. She was *chef d'équipe* of the Co. Down staghounds team when they won the Quinnsworth Chase in the Dublin Horse Show.

One year I was invited to judge the ridden hunter classes at Balmoral Show together with an elderly judge from England. The only two entries in the four-year-old heavyweight class were a big, quality chestnut gelding and a plain grey. Having placed the horses in a provisional order, one of us would start at the top of the line in alternate classes, so it was my turn to ride the big chestnut. When I went to mount him, two extra men came into the ring and stood one at each side of him. I began to have my doubts.

When giving me a leg-up, the owner said to me in an undertone, "I'd advise you get into the saddle as quick as you can, sir."

Heavens, what was I in for? Barely in the saddle with no feet in the stirrups, I had picked up only the snaffle rein when the horse bolted like a bullet from a gun, knocked the two assistants, and galloped madly around the big ring. We did three circles at top speed. Spectators tried to stop us by waving coats. Pandemonium! Eventually the horse tired, came back to me and halted in a lather of sweat. I got my feet into the irons, collected both reins, and we walked on. He had great action in all paces, as well as a good mouth, and he gave me a super ride.

Back in line, I said to my co-judge, "I think you had better not ride him today."

He said, "There is no point in you riding the grey. He is useless."

After some deliberation we gave the red rosette to the chestnut. The owner of the grey was furious. We excused the chestnut on the grounds that he was only four and probably had never been ridden by anyone other than the owner. I told the owner to get all his friends to ride the horse before the championship the following morning. Next day when my co-judge and myself rode the horse, he went a dream. We made him reserve champion.

That was the third week in May. The top horses from Balmoral then usually go on to compete at Dublin Horse Show in August. That August there was no sign of our reserve champion.

I asked Roly Cunningham, "What has happened to our good Balmoral winner?"

"Oh your name is mud", said Roly. "The horse went to Ballinahinch Show in the north and bolted with his owner. He has ended his life in a tin."

I was sorry to lose him. I'm sure he would have settled down to make a great huntsman's horse.

At one Balmoral Show, the organisers laid on a steam traction engine display as an entertainment. A huge monster of an engine led the parade, chuffing away happily until it reached the governor's box. There it hit a soft spot, with the weather extremely wet, and it started to sink.

"Don't worry, ladies and gentlemen," said the commentator. "The next one will pull it out"

The next one was slightly smaller. It was hitched on and both engines remained stationary, chuffing and sinking.

"I want 300 able-bodied men into the arena please", said the commentator.

Two long ropes were laid out, 150 men to each.

"Pull!" shouted the announcer, and they hauled the engines out of trouble.

When I travelled north to the Balmoral Show, I was always struck by the obvious prosperity of the farms once we crossed the border into Northern Ireland. Fields and fencing were in good order and new machinery everywhere, compared with the impoverished conditions down south. Farmers in the north received massive grants funded by the British Exchequer. Now with the Irish economy booming as a result of European aid, it is reflected throughout the country.

Co. Clare, with its wealth of limestone outcrop, is noted for its horse breeding. In contrast, Co. Galway's fields have a covering of loose stones, which farmers down the years have used to build stone wall boundaries. The story is told of a land agent who was trying desperately to sell a farm for a client. He was showing it to a would-be purchaser.

The prospective client objected, "This land is too stony for me."

"Ah, you are wrong", said the agent. "Those stones are like gold. They warm up in the summer and prevent the ground freezing in the winter."

"Well, how is it that the farm next door has no stones? They are all in heaps."

The agent replied, "You see, that poor chap has not had time to spread them yet!"

Year after year I was invited to judge the horse classes in Ennis Show. I used to object because I felt that it was not fair on exhibitors always to have the same judge, but the committee insisted. At one show I started judging the class, which had about ten horses. After I had ridden a couple, I was suspicious that one of them was not sound of his wind. I asked the vet in attendance to check him.

Meantime a young dealer whom I knew came running in out of breath, "I have two horses in this class, and we have had a breakdown. Can you please allow us to bring them in?"

"All right," I said, "but be quick."

While I was riding I saw the two latecomers entering the ring. These two fine young horses were obviously better types than what I was judging already, so I told the owner to go to the top of the line and I would take stock of them later. I asked the vet about the grey.

"Oh," he said, "You are right, he is definitely making a noise, but that is not your only trouble. Those two latecomers are only three-year-olds and the class is for four years and upwards. What is more, one of them has just won the three-year-old class in the led-horse ring next door!"

I called up the owner. "Look here, John," I said, "your horses can't be three-year-olds and four-year-olds on the same day. Now go home."

He replied, "Sir, I would prefer to win the four-year-old class, and I will give back the red rosette to the steward next door."

Also judging at Ennis Show was Eamon Moloney, who has been on our Hunt Committee and has hunted with us for years. He was judging the cattle classes with his brother-in-law Pat Raleigh, a noted cattle judge, but regrettably not a hunting man. There were two entries in the Hereford bull class: one had been champion in the RDS Spring Show, a magnificent animal; the other was what is known as a speak-easy (not up to licensing standard and should have been castrated).

The owner of the champion was leaning over the rail with the lead rope in his hand watching the previous class (commercial bullocks) being judged. His big bull stood placidly alongside him, chewing the cud. By chance the ring in the bull's nose was worn out and dropped on to the ground. Discovering that he was free for the first time in his life, the bull started charging at the bystanders, including his owner, who was trying to catch him.

"Roll, Paddy, Roll!" people were shouting. (The word is that if a bull charges you in a field and you have no chance of running away, you should lie down on the ground and roll towards the bull. He cannot get you with his horns and is so puzzled by your antics that he will leave you alone. However, I have had neither the occasion nor the inclination to try this out, so I cannot guarantee that it works.)

Someone had the bright idea of letting out a couple of bullocks to distract the bull. All three animals were driven into the tractor trailer that had brought the bull to the show, the two bullocks were taken out, and the ramp was closed up. Then the Hereford bull class was called. The stewards would not allow the Dublin champion to be exhibited, so the owner, not to be outdone, drove the tractor trailer and bull around the judging ring, followed by the farmer pulling the "spake-aisey" behind him. What were the judges to do? After much discussion, they gave the red rosette to the Dublin champion. The other exhibitor was wild!

Lady Daresbury, Boodly to her friends, had the awesome responsibility of finding and schooling horses for Lord Daresbury (Toby) and the Co. Limerick Hunt staff. She was showing a young horse in Ennis one year.

As I was mounting him, I asked her, "What is his background?"

"Just a four-year-old, my dear."

I was barely in the saddle when he put in a buck and a twist and the two of us were on the floor laughing.

"Terribly sorry, my dear. Never saw him do that before, my dear!"

Boodly was the kindest person imaginable and immensely popular. Few people knew the great extent of the charitable work she did all over the country.

I had a most embarrassing experience after Toby offered me a day's hunting in the big, heavy country beyond Charleville on the borders of the Duhallow. I was on one of Toby's best hunters. Hounds found in a big thorn covert, the fox left quickly, and we had a short circular run over tall narrow double banks and back into covert.

One of the followers came up to me and said, "Your horse is bleeding badly."

Looking down, I saw that he had over-reached badly. I went straight up to Toby.

He said, "Go to the groom and get my second horse."

Although I remonstrated, he insisted and so I put my saddle on a beautiful grey. You won't believe this, but the incident was repeated. On a short run and back to covert, this time a sharp stump of a thornbush went right into the horse's fetlock from the bottom and he was bleeding profusely. This incident was in November and those two horses did not hunt again that season.

I hate borrowing a horse. It is far better to hire one. Actually when one thinks of the number of horses hired out to visitors, many of whom have never jumped banks, it is incredible how few get injured. The hirer is not liable for any loss or injury; the owner carries the entire risk.

For many years judging of showjumping was a man's domain. Lady judges were unheard of. At one time the Showjumping Association of Ireland decided in its wisdom to appoint lady judges in Dublin, so all shows followed suit. I encountered this new way of doing things at Cork Show, one of my perennial duties, which I always enjoyed because the show chairman was Noel Tanner, chairman of the Muskerry Hunt.

After three of "us men" on the jury stood down after a big competition, two lady members took over. It was a pony competition, where a small fat white pony, ridden by a boy, who was obviously too big for him, was next to jump. (I was reminded of two farmers watching the lady's hunter class in Dublin. Pointing to a large lady on a small horse, one said to the other, "What do you make of that one?" His friend replied, "I'd say the joint is too big for the dish!")

Boy and pony cleared the first fence. The second fence was a double: they knocked the first element and demolished the second. The gong was sounded and rebuilding caused a delay. As the two lady judges started gossiping, they did not notice that the boy had retired. Then the fence stewards signalled that the course was ready, and the starting bell was sounded. The boy on a white pony started to jump the first fence. The judges pressed the eliminating gong, announcing that he should have started his round again at the second fence.

The boy rode up to the judge's box in a fury and said, "It's a different bloody pony!"

Nowadays, "we" have to admit that the ladies are doing an excellent job.

JUDGING HOUNDS

Judging hounds is a different ball game. Judges have their personal preferences for type and do not always agree. At one hound show in New Zealand, I spoke with a judge selected from the kennel club list, remarking that a common fault in many kennels is a broad chest, with front legs too far apart.

"Oh," he said, "but this is essential in any hound or dog that hunts by scent, to enable them to get their noses to the ground."

My first experience of judging was the County Carlow Puppy Show, where my co-judge was a professional huntsman. Of course I was nervous, and dressed correctly in a dark suit and bowler. With a lot of Beaufort blood, the Carlow were beautiful foxhounds, all quality and level (the Carlow bitches being famous throughout Ireland and England). Placing them in order was a challenge.

I must have done reasonably well because the Master Mrs Hall ("Missus") said to me afterwards, "Well done boy, good show, but next time, remember, black shoes with bowler hat!" My new shoes were brown.

Judging was followed by presentation of prizes, a sumptuous tea, and a speech of thanks from the Master to puppy walkers and farmers. (This is the normal practice. At another puppy show, a Master's wife was entertaining the visitors. She said to an elderly farmer, "Have another sandwich, Mr Walsh." "No thank you, mam. I have fed very well", he replied. "Then what about a slice of cake?" "Ah no thank you, mam. Don't press me, I could put my finger on the last bit I ate!")

Well-known throughout hunting country, Missus was masculine looking with an Eton crop, and highly regarded as a huntsman and judge of hounds. She was always invited to stay at Badminton for the three-day event and was a close friend of the English royal family. She arrived at one royal breakfast to find one of the sisters was already there.

"Morning, Elizabeth", she said warmly.

"It's Margaret, Missus", said the younger princess.

Missus replied, "Oh, I never know the difference between you two girls!"

I have also been invited to judge at three major hound shows in the United States: Bryn Mawr, Virginia, and Mid-America. It is a privilege that I have enjoyed immensely.

Before the Mid-America Hound Show, Anne and I treated ourselves to a little holiday. After watching an impressive steer-roping contest and doing a little sight-seeing in Santa Barbara, we flew to Los Angeles with Sandy and Heloise Power in their private plane. From there Anne and I flew on to the Grand Canyon, where

Tom and Elsie Morgan (right), Joint-Masters of the West Waterford, judge the Scarteen Puppy Show, 1980. Captain Harry Freeman Jackson, ex-MFH of the Duhallow, is on the left. Mary Tarry photo

Judges at the Virginia Foxhound Show, America's largest, in 1995. (Front row, l–r) Thady Ryan, Coleman Perrin, Captain R. E. Wallace, Captain Ian Farquhar; (second row) Katie Schuttle, Jake Carle, Epp Wilson, C. Martin Wood III

we stayed the night in a hotel right on the edge of the canyon. The whole area—the gigantic canyon itself, the Colorado River, the exotic colours, and weird rock shapes—beggars description. Our cameras were running red hot.

Next morning, we flew on to St George, where the plane had to be serviced. We then hired a car and had a most spectacular drive through strangely coloured smaller canyons. One rock mass resembled a colossal organ and pipes. I longed for a car with a sunroof so that I could stand up through the roof to film the scenery as we travelled.

We handed in the car at Salt Lake City and flew to Jackson Hole to be met by George and Janna Stevenson. They drove us through wild swamps and forests, getting close up to buffalo, gazelle, moose, numerous elk, and even an arctic fox. Although we also got near three grizzly bears they, were in a spacious caged area in Discovery Park.

The next day, Mary Hutz and Paul Gilroy collected us. Professional outfitters, they run a vast safari-type adventure camping holiday business for trophy hunters and wildlife photographers. Everything, but everything, has to be carried on horseback away up to the camp sites in the mountains. Two hundred horses, mostly heavy types, are used, loaded with colossal backpacks that carry three weeks' supply of food—all in large tin containers for protection from bears—and even the wood-fired kitchen range. How I would love to go on one of their trips!

After a couple of nights with Mary and Paul, we were picked up by helicopter and brought to the fabulous Silver Tip Ranch—surely the high spot of our holiday. George Ohrstrom, who owns the ranch in a partnership, flew up from his home in Virginia to be with us. The ranch house and buildings are all beautifully constructed log cabins set in a clearing in the forest. We feasted sumptuously; a Kiwi lass was in the housekeeping party, so we got preferential treatment!

As no motor vehicles are allowed, one has to come in either by chopper or on horseback and wagons. The pet of the place is an 18 hand mule—a real character and a lovely smooth ride. In 1988 when a huge forest fire was approaching the ranch, they got helicopters to drop water constantly on all the buildings and surrounding trees. The horses were loose and stayed under the trees, and the fire passed right over them. All inhabitants took shelter under special aluminium covers. The roar of the fire travelling at forty miles per hour must have been terrifying. It destroyed over one million acres and wildlife losses were high, more from starvation than fire as there was nothing left to eat. Now gaunt charred tree stems are everywhere. The new seedlings were already almost a foot high.

We hated leaving, but needs must. We "choppered" to the airport and flew to Kentucky to be met with open arms by Jack and Ruby Rhodes. Next day it was down to work at the Mid-America Hound Show among a host of old and new hunting friends.

I have felt most at ease with the American foxhound and the Penn-Marydel (a breed that originated in three states, Pennsylvania, Maryland, and Delaware) classes because of their similarity with the Kerry beagle. The cross-bred classes are an additional challenge because in the same class you will find some hounds that take after the American breed and others that take after the English foxhound.

"HOUNDS, PLEASE"

In chapter 21 I mentioned that I had sent several hounds to the United States. It was in 1961 that I sent Famous, a bitch in pup that had some of my best bloodlines, to Jack and Ruby Rhodes in Kentucky. Jack gave Saintly, a daughter of Famous, to the Long Run Hunt. The Master, pleased with her progeny and wishing to continue the Scarteen line, commissioned two hunt members to call to Scarteen while in Ireland for the Dublin Horse Show. I sold them, I think, two couple. They turned out well and I am pleased to hear from the present Master, Charles McLaughlin, that their bloodlines are still evident in the Long Run kennels.

Recently Norman Fine sent me his article, "In the Tracks of Mountain and Muse," published in *Covertside*, the American magazine of which he is editor. Norman and his wife, Joan, were among our earliest hunting guests at Scarteen

Mountain and Muse, as sketched by Benjamin Ogle Jr. (1775-1844) of Maryland. The blood of these Irish hounds, sent to America in 1814, is in most of the important American foxhound strains. Courtesy of Museum of Hounds and Hunting, Leesburg, Virginia

(chapter 30). The article intrigues me no end. I had no idea that these two hounds sent from Kerry to the United States in 1814 were so highly prized for their hunting ability. Nor had I appreciated the extent of their influence on several breeds of the American foxhound.

There is one anomaly in the article that puzzles me. To my mind the owner's sketches of Mountain and Muse bear little resemblance to the true Kerry beagle. As I mentioned in chapter 21, Irish patriot and politician Daniel O'Connell (the Liberator) had a pack of hounds at his home Derrynane in Co. Kerry. I have been fortunate to find in a private collection a beautiful oil painting of Daniel O'Connell with one of his hounds.

Daniel O'Connell, "The Liberator," with his Kerry beagle (photograph of an oil painting). Grandfather's brother, Clem, married a great granddaughter of Daniel O'Connell.

This photo clearly illustrates the head and build of what I believe is the true Kerry beagle: It shows the high occipital dome, the long, low-set ears, the deep jowl, and apparent throatiness around the larynx, the hare foot with full pad on the ground and strong toes. All are true characteristics of the breed and show a strong resemblance to the French hound, the Grand Bleu de Gasgogne, from which I believe they are descended.

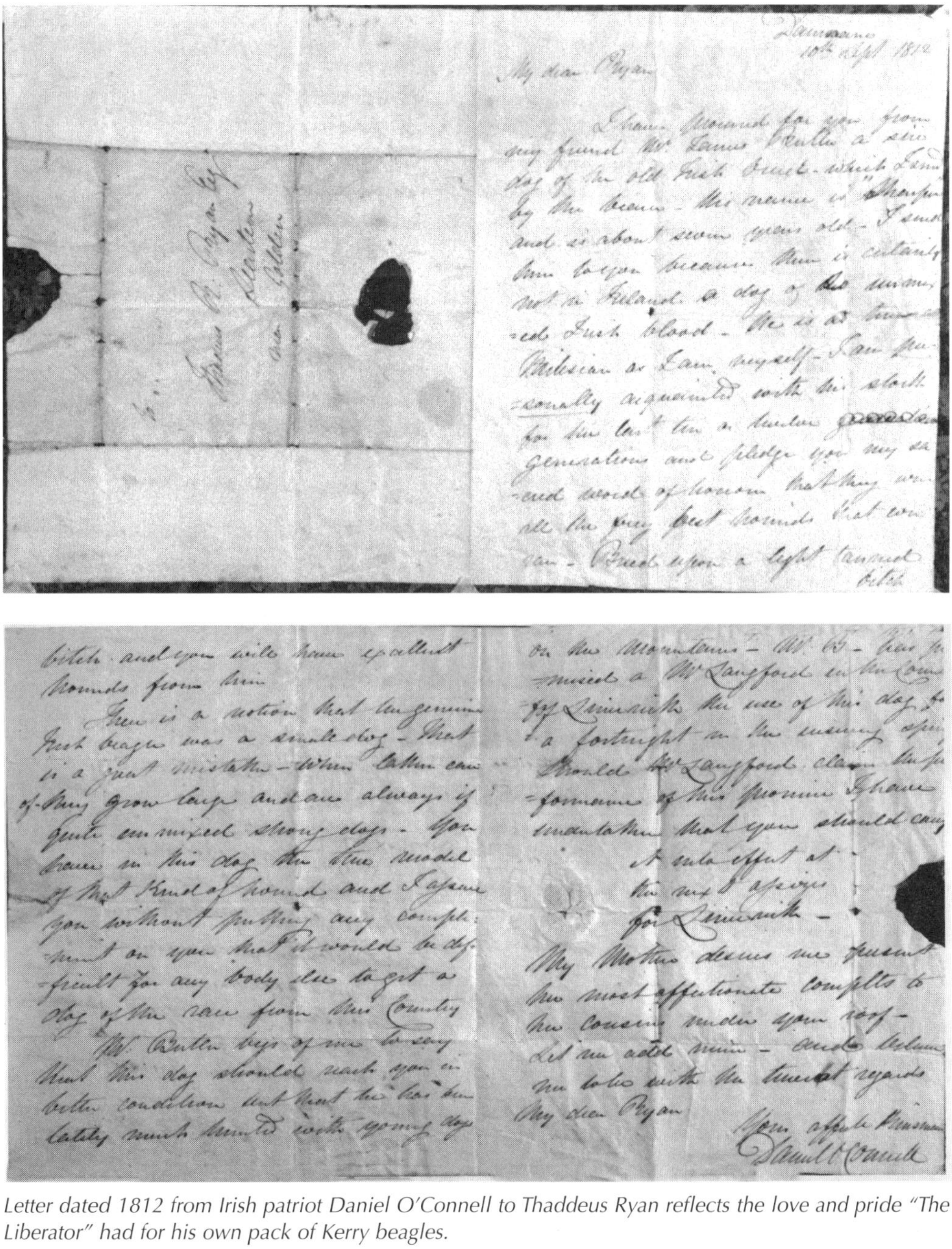

To [illegible] Ryan Esq [illegible]

[illegible] 10th Sept 1812

My dear Ryan

I have procured for you from my friend Mr. James Butler a sire dog of the old Irish breed — which I am [illegible] by the [illegible] — His name is "Champion" and is about seven years old — I send him to you because there is certainly not in Ireland a dog of the [illegible] real Irish blood — He is as true a Milesian as I am myself — I am personally acquainted with his stock for the last ten or twelve generations and pledge you my sacred word of honour that they were all the very best hounds that ever ran — Breed upon a light tanned bitch and you will have excellent hounds from him.

There is a notion that the genuine Irish beagle was a small dog — that is a great mistake — When taken care of they grow large and are always of quite unmixed strong dogs — You have in this dog the true model of that kind of hound and I assure you without putting any compliment on you that it would be difficult for any body else to get a dog of the race from this Country.

Mr. Butler begs of me to say that this dog should reach you in better condition but that he has been lately much hunted with young dogs on the mountains — Mr. B — has promised a Mr Langford in the County of Limerick the use of this dog for a fortnight in the ensuing spring. Should Mr Langford claim the performance of this promise I have undertaken that you should carry it into effect at [illegible] for Limerick —

My Mother desires me [to] present her most affectionate compts to the Cousins under your roof — Let me add mine — and believe me to be with the sincerest regards My dear Ryan

Your affecte Kinsman
Daniel O'Connell

Letter dated 1812 from Irish patriot Daniel O'Connell to Thaddeus Ryan reflects the love and pride "The Liberator" had for his own pack of Kerry beagles.

An 1812 letter from Daniel to my great-great-grandfather Thaddeus Ryan reflects the love and pride he had for his hounds (see photo). Many of the old families in those days kept hounds, as illustrated by a 1759 letter from Standish Grady of Elton House to my ancestor John Ryan of Ballykeveen. Obviously all three families exchanged hounds.

So where do Mountain and Muse fit into this picture? With due respect to the artist, it is possible that the sketches were stylised, as was the custom at the time. Compare the works of the painters Herring and Stubbs. They stylised their horses—giving them finely chiselled heads, long elegant necks, and light bone—to highlight their superb quality and breeding, but I am sure that the horses did not look exactly like that.

Another explanation is possible. Willie O'Neill and the late Fleur Shea in Cahirciveen represented the two schools of thought among hound breeders in Kerry; they would hardly speak to each other! Fleur favoured the stronger type of Kerry beagle while Willie liked a lighter type altogether. (Who knows, could they have stemmed from different breeds in France?) Co. Cavan has Kerry beagles of the lighter type. They are long in the leg, light of body, with a high-pitched note, and fast. Perhaps Mountain and Muse stemmed from this strain.

One line of support for this idea is that my son Chris has bred a couple of bitches to a Cavan dog. The progeny are on the light side with flatter heads, high-set ears, and quality. They are great hunting hounds, but with the high note. (On the subject of note, I like to compare a pack of hounds to the string instruments of an orchestra. The range of note graduates from the high pitch of the violin through the mellow strains of the cello (my favourite) to the deep booming of the double bass. All three make up the total symphony.)

One common denominator among all the Kerry hounds, both in Ireland and in the United States, is their high-powered hunting passion, almost to the point of being wild. Mountain was a typical case, a brilliant hunting hound, but so independent that at one point he was destined to be put down. Fortunately he was reprieved and proved to be an outstanding sire.

Before last cub hunting season, when hounds were in long roadwork, Chris wrote to me: "My young entry are very promising, already they are entered to everything, except fox."

One further observation. I have often wondered from where did the American hound (particularly the Penn-Marydel) get the typically French head. I was therefore most interested to learn from Joseph B. Thomas's *Hounds and Hunting through the Ages* that:

> French Hounds were imported to Louisiana probably in the Seventeenth Century by an early ancestor in America of Mr Percival Rosseau, the famous limner of Sporting Dogs.

So it is no wonder that the Scarteen Kerry beagle crosses so well with the American. I am proud of our common ancestry.

Without hunting, what would we talk about!

I was embarrassed at one show. The Rolling Rock had a large entry. In my opinion all these hounds had a common fault: their shoulders were rounded and lacked freedom, and their extension came from the elbow. I had to be honest with myself, so the Rolling Rock hounds were first to be asked to leave the ring. In the bitch classes after lunch, the Rolling Rock huntsman withdrew his entire entry.

That evening I discussed the matter with Bill Brainard, long time Master of the Old Dominion and an acknowledged expert in hound breeding. To my great relief, he agreed with me entirely. Actually I found the same fault with the Orange County hounds, and mentioned it to their Master. It is a fault that, once introduced to a kennel, is difficult to eradicate. I experienced it myself one time. A good-looking and good-working doghound that I found in Kerry had the shoulder problem, but I thought that my bitches had shoulders good enough to nullify the fault. I was wrong and had to draft his entire progeny.

On one occasion a pack showed an attractive doghound, who was correct in every way and had tremendous freedom. His coat was long, showing obvious Welsh ancestry.

I said to his keen young huntsman, "Would you do me a favour? Would you take your hound out and clip him? I can't see what I have."

"Yessir", he replied hesitantly, blushing.

I told him I was only pulling his leg, then made the hound reserve champion doghound!

It is the custom in the United States to show hounds on a lead. To my mind this is not fair on the hound because he cannot demonstrate his natural movement and agility. I have always encouraged huntsmen to train their hounds to show themselves off the lead using small bits of biscuit. Hounds love the game, as do the spectators.

A huntsman said to me one time, "Oh we could not show our hounds loose. We would lose them."

After one show we had an interesting seminar on handling hounds in the field. Among the panel members were Bill Brainard, Wilbur Hubbard, Bill Wadsworth, Ronnie Wallace, and myself. Ronnie emphasised the importance of quietness. Many hunts suffer from a noisy huntsman who likes to show off his horn-blowing ability. In others, the whippers-in are too busy cracking their whips and putting hounds onto the huntsman unnecessarily. They seem to think that they must be seen to be doing something all the time. All this noise aggravates hounds and causes them to lift their heads.

What a joy it is to watch a huntsman who has the silken thread. Only a few huntsmen have this gift. My son Chris has it, Ronnie Wallace is an excellent example, and Ben Hardaway is another. I shall never forget watching Ben drawing some open scrub country in Georgia. The pack fanned out about 200 yards on each side of him. Occasionally a hound would lift his head and look to Ben just to be sure he was there then the hound would resume his work.

When hounds found a fox, Ben would explode with excitement, cheering hounds on. This is excusable (for the huntsman only) and hounds share his wild enthusiasm.

At the seminar one of the audience stood up asking, “Do the panel think that it is necessary for hounds to kill foxes in order to remain keen?”

Wilbur Hubbard (Master of Mr Hubbard’s Kent County hounds) replied, “My hounds hardly ever kill a fox, and yet they are as keen as mustard.”

Next morning Ben and I were first down to breakfast. I asked him what he thought of Wilbur’s theory about not killing.

He replied, “Waal, if Wilbur’s haans are happy with what they’re doin, let ’em do it!”

Ben Hardaway, MFH, Midland Fox Hounds (Georgia) and Ted Casey, West Cork (center) judge the Scarteen Puppy Show, 1981. Tommy Dwyer, kennel huntsman (left) and Thady Ryan, MFH, exhibit hounds. Galty Mountains are in the background. Mary Tarry photo

FORTY-ONE

WHO WANTS TO BE A MILLIONAIRE? I DO . . . DON'T . . . ?

Al and Jean Mactier came from Omaha, Nebraska to hunt with us regularly. As president of Conagra, the third largest supplier of flour to the United States market, Al was expanding the milling business and searching for a trade name for new products in horse feed and dog feed. Over his years of hunting with us he was impressed by the history of the Ryans of Scarteen and their famous hounds. Such a long tradition of sportsmanship would be hard to come by in the United States, yet he felt sure that the nostalgic concept would appeal to sportsmen and women of all ages there.

He asked me whether he could use my name for the product; he suggested Ryan's Choice. My first reaction was one of shock. What would my family think of us becoming commercialised? Then I realised that, on the contrary, it would be an honour and recognition of the esteem with which people regarded an old Irish tradition. Al explained that there would be considerable financial benefit for me from the agreement. When I consulted the family, they were all in favour.

The general plan was that Anne and I would travel to Nebraska, stay with Al and Jean and be available to Conagra at their headquarters in Omaha to take part in a television test commercial. In all I made three trips, two with Anne and one solo, all expenses paid. Al insisted that my recommendation for the product must be truthful, so he sent over small quantities of balanced dog ration and of horse feed, attractively labelled "Ryan's Choice", for me to feed to my horses and hounds. I can truthfully say that both were consumed eagerly!

For the television commercial the first performance was to promote the dog feed. I was given a script to learn off by heart. The producer put an advertisement in the local paper:

> Wanted, a number of dogs, any breed, for a brief film career. Please attend at (a designated location) at 10 A.M. on Monday.

Well, an assortment of dogs of all shapes and sizes turned up. Soon a fight started between a great Dane and a German shepherd; one of the cameramen who helped to separate them had his jeans torn off. Obviously such a gathering was going to get out of hand, so the party was adjourned. The producer booked an old English sheepdog to turn up on the following morning.

Take 1. The scene was a clearing in the woods, beautiful sunshine. I stood by a table with a bag of Ryan's Choice dog feed on it, the handsome old English sheepdog alongside me. A big square number "1" was held in front of the camera then I started my spiel. After a few minutes the producer called, "Stop". A cloud had obscured the sun.

Take 2. The story began the same, way then the cicadas struck up a din and interfered with the sound recording.

On the third attempt, an aeroplane passed over.

On the fourth attempt, all was set. I started off . . . and forgot my lines! Eventually we succeeded in our effort.

Al asked me had I ever ridden "Western." Of course the answer was "no". As there would be a big market for the horse feed in the West, we boarded the company's Lear jet and flew out to a friend's ranch in Wyoming. We slept in a true log cabin up in the hills. The nights were still and clear; one could almost touch the stars. It was a comfort to see the Plough up there, just as we could from Scarteen, only it seemed so much closer.

At cockcrow next morning, I joined the cowboys up on the hills, the Big Horn Mountains in the background. The cameras were positioned at vantage points. I saddled my mount, a well-mannered cob with quality. I could barely lift the Western saddle onto his back, it was so heavy with two folded blankets under it—they obviously had not been used for ages and were solid with caked sweat. The day's job was to move a mob of five hundred Angus and Hereford steers on to another block some miles distant. The sunrise on the well-grassed hills and scattered trees was spectacular.

Cattle driving in Wyoming—my first time in a western saddle! Larry Dale Gordon photo

Using no dogs, we rounded up the beautifully conditioned cattle and got them on their way. After a few hours the chuck wagon turned up with large pots of delicious, hot, brown beef stew, spuds, veggies, and dessert. The ten or so cowboys, great company, made short work of it.

Arriving at the overnight stand, I spotted one big steer lying away on his own. He looked sick. I pointed him out to one of the lads.

"Aah guess he'll die", he said.

"Hey, he is worth about six hundred bucks. We must do something for him, penicillin or whatever", I said.

"Aah guess no. He got (some disease)."

Next morning, when we rounded up the mob for the second drive, the sick beast was dead.

"What happens now. Can we shift him with a tractor?" I asked.

"Aah guess no", he replied. "See them birrds up there? Aah guess they will deal with him." The vultures were gathering already.

Next day, some drafting was to be done. The mob were just gathered when an almighty blaze of lightning and a deafening thunderclap shook the land, followed rapidly by torrential rain; the cattle scattered madly in all directions. I was whisked into a big station wagon as I was precious and must not get my clothes wet. Poor Anne was mounted and was drenched!

But the hot sun soon returned, and we witnessed an interesting display of "cutting out" by one man on an experienced horse. Once the lad had chosen a particular steer to separate, the horse did the rest with almost no help from the rider; they were drafting the Angus from the Herefords.

I asked one of the lads, "How do you amuse yourselves in free time at the weekends?"

"Aah guess caalf ropin'."

"But", I said, "you've been doing that all the week."

The three days had been a thrilling introduction to the Wild West—fabulous country, great people, a dream come true. But it was all over; we boarded our "arrow" and sped back to Omaha.

The story did not have such a happy ending. Al retired after fifteen years in office, business slumped, and the whole concept of Ryan's Choice was abandoned. Although I was presented with a quantity of superb coloured slides that bring back fabulous memories, I was not destined for Millionaire's Row!

FORTY-TWO

SAYONARA

In my view, while foxhunting is the greatest equestrian sport, eventing runs a close second. When it comes to *competitive* equestrian sport, eventing is at the top. Known originally as "the Military" because it was considered essential to forming the character of young officers, it is a comparatively new sport that is becoming increasingly popular. It is a natural progression from foxhunting in that both make almost identical requirements of a horse—soundness, quality, athleticism, courage, stamina, speed, and above all an equable temperament. Because the requirements in a rider are also similar, the majority of competitors have started their riding careers in the hunting field.

My own eventing career was brief, culminating in the disaster with my super horse Villain at Punchestown (see chapter 32). Moreover I had neither the time nor the means to continue competing. Nevertheless I inevitably became involved in the organisation and soon found myself on the council of the Irish Olympic Horse Society. As chairman of the Selection Committee, and later as joint *chef d'équipe*, my responsibilities were daunting.

When I took on these roles, my mind went back to a dramatic incident in the Rome Olympics. Anne and I were there as spectators only, staying with Count "Pippo" Cigala Fulgosi, MFH. On the final day of the three-day event, the Irish team were poised to win a medal. The showjumping course was open for inspection and the technical delegate was to be there at 9 A.M. to walk the course with the *chefs d'équipe* and riders. Harry Freeman-Jackson, one of the Irish competitors, waited in vain for ten minutes. Finally, as he was second in line to compete, he walked the course alone, and then went to the stables to saddle up and warm up his horse. Once the technical delegate eventually turned up and began walking the course, he decided that one particular turn was too sharp. He planted a compulsory turning flag to give a better approach to one of the fences.

With the competition underway, Harry jumped the particular fence as he had planned, without going around the new turning flag. The crowd yelled at him, and he thought they were cheering him on. He did a beautiful clear round, but of course he was eliminated. I rushed around to join Harry as he was walking back to the stables. He was heartbroken and inconsolable, feeling he had lost the medal for Ireland.

I used to have nightmares about this incident, which highlighted the weight of a *chef d'équipe*'s responsibilities. The technical delegate had broken the rules because the course could not be altered once it had been declared open. So first, the Irish *chef d'équipe* had grounds for an objection to the elimination but he did not draw on them. Secondly, he should have informed Harry about the flag. In my observer's role at those Olympics, I became only too aware that a *chef d'équipe* must be alert to all possible contingencies.

Competitors in the top flight were scarce on the ground. Eventing is an expensive and time-consuming sport, far more so than showjumping. In early days it was truly an amateur sport. Prize money was negligible—admirably, people participated for the love of it. I felt that it was a bit of a "closed shop" and that we should make every effort to help and encourage our young, talented riders to compete at top level.

MAKING IT HAPPEN

With time pushing on, we had our sights set on the Tokyo Olympics to be held in 1964. The shortage of funds that dogged us all the way made us all the more determined. Lord Harrington, chairman of the Irish Olympic Horse Society for a number of years, did trojan work organising fundraising events. Support around the country was great. The Government helped but kept the purse strings tight.

Also scarce were suitable horses and riders. A lady in Co. Westmeath applied to put her horse in training for Badminton. Some Olympic Horse Society council members said that the horse was not suitable. However, I insisted that if the horse had any reasonable potential, the lady should be given a fair trial, if only to prove that we were open to accepting all with a fairly good chance of success. After much pressure on members, it was agreed that Maureen Hogan and I should go up and inspect the horse.

It was a long drive. We were well received with a delicious lunch, although conversation was difficult over the constant yapping of a houseful of Yorkshire terriers. The horse was a tall, unattractive black gelding, not exactly a showpiece for our breeding industry, but he had an extravagant jump. Thinking "beggars can't be choosers", we recommended that he should go to Badminton. (His owner, suffering greatly from asthma, was advised to drink goat's milk as a cure. Much later, after she developed the leading herd of milking goats in the country, her asthma was cleared.) I told her that if she put up a good show in Badminton, she might be considered for selection for Olympic training. She completed Badminton and, to my dismay, sold the big horse after the event!

Our next concern was a trainer. After answering an advertisement in *Horse & Hound*, Brigadier Lyndon Bolton from Alnwick, Northumberland came over for an interview. He stemmed from an old Co. Wexford family, the "Boltons of the Island"; his grandfather had started the family pack of foxhounds by that name. We fell for the Brig right away. No one could resist the mischievous wink in his eye! We explained to him that his salary would be small, a blow to him as he needed the money. However, the joy of training the Irish team was something that he could not resist. He was well qualified, having hunted as much as military service allowed and competed in Three-Day

Events, with good placings on at least two occasions at Badminton. His mental and physical ability belied his years and he was always in good humour. With his military background he was a brilliant communicator and soon our squad were welded into a happy family.

The squad was comprised of Captain Harry Freeman-Jackson, MFH, Master of the Duhallow Foxhounds riding St Finbar, John Harty with San Michele, Tommy Brennan with Omar van Landeghem's Kilkenny, Tony Cameron with Black Salmon, and Reserve Rider Ginnie Freeman-Jackson with Sam Weller. But that was it. We had no adequate second line of reserve, a weakness of which we were all too conscious.

About this time another old Amplefordian, Major Eddie Boylan, told me that the army had a good-looking young horse, inexperienced but worth seeing. I fell immediately for the tall, quality, dark brown lad with a foxhunter's eye and tremendous scope over a fence and in all his paces. I bought him, then sold him at cost to Eddie on the condition that if he did not make the grade, I would buy him back as a hunter.

Though not a full Thoroughbred, Durlas Eile had been bred on the best old steeplechasing lines by Phil Sweeney (a brother of Fr Sweeney who "led the stag hunt" in chapter 27) in Thurles. Despite the horse's lack of experience, the Brig agreed that he had the ability and that we must have him for our squad.

Now we were in a dilemma. If one of our horses went lame, we had no spare of the same calibre. We needed Durlas Eile but our riders were a team and we could not upset the balance by bringing in a new rider. I begged Eddie for his horse, but he refused point blank unless he was to ride the horse himself. I shall never forget agonising all night over the problem with the Brig in a small pub in Drogheda. Eddie's father, Brigadier Boylan, had been a bosom friend of Lyndon's, and Lyndon was bitterly disappointed to the point of anger with Eddie. In hindsight maybe we should have accepted him. However, as chairman of the Selection Committee and joint *chef d'équipe*, I was scared to break the bond that welded us together. I still worry over that decision. Yet although we were leaving behind a gem, we left as a happy family.

Our next obstacle was transport. Even if flying with one of the major airlines had been within our budget, they were all booked up already. We eventually got a quote from a small American charter company, Shannon Air, who would take us on an old DC6 adapted for cargo. Its cargo previous to us was a load of monkeys from India! We got on very well with the Irish captain. I made several trips to Shannon to discuss details, payload, flight times, and the like. We were to fly over the North Pole with just two refuelling stops, one at Keflavik in Iceland, and the other at Anchorage, Alaska.

Final training in Phoenix Park went well. Horses and riders were extremely fit and healthy. Both our trainer and our vet, Professor Martin Byrne, were well satisfied.

As "D-Day" approached, our excitement was almost at fever pitch. The horses stayed overnight at the airport. They all had previous flying experience.

Some weeks before departure, Curragh Bloodstock kindly flew the one who had not flown before to Newmarket Sales and home again for free. I had heard the story of a British eventer that went berserk in the plane. Thereupon the captain attempted to shoot him and missed. The horse lived to compete for many more years.

On the lighter side, I was worried about possible language difficulties in Tokyo. I wrote to Linguaphone in London to ask whether they had a course in Japanese.

They replied, "We have. How long do you have to study it?"

I said three weeks.

"You will need three years to become reasonably proficient." I gave up the idea.

A JOURNEY OF UPS AND DOWNS

D-Day! Our plane was late calling to Paris to collect Trish (daughter of Sir John Galvin, who later provided Loughlin for our team in Mexico: chapter 43), her husband and her two horses for the individual dressage. We waited interminable hours, checked and rechecked all our gear. We were very close to maximum payload. At last the plane arrived, and the ramps were put in place. My first anxiety was to have Fr Sweeney, then curate in Knocklong Parish, bless the plane and all the horses and personnel—we were most grateful for the blessing later. The horses climbed up the ramp and into the fuselage, walked into their positions and the crates were assembled around them. Peat moss was their bedding. While loading was in progress, a wagon and trailer came out to the plane laden with cardboard boxes.

"What on earth is this?" I demanded.

It turned out to be a generous present from John Power and Son Distillers: one bottle of whiskey, one of gin and one of vodka for every member of the

Boarding at Shannon for the Olympic games in Tokyo. (Thady is Chef d'Équipe of the Irish team.) (l–r) Harry Freeman-Jackson, John Harty, Tommy Brennan, Tony Cameron, Brigadier Bolton (trainer) on ground with Hilda and Cliff Cameron.

party. We would be able to extend Irish hospitality to all our new friends! Secretly I was worried about the extra weight, but our captain was happy.

All our gear was stowed away, including the grog. Our seats were bolted down in position towards the rear of the plane. Hugs, goodbyes, and God bless all round and we boarded. A final wave and the door was closed. I was sore leaving Anne and the rest of my family standing on the tarmac. I would not see them for the next five weeks. The four propellers turned slowly and the old engines roared into life. We gathered speed—Anne said later she thought we would never leave the ground—finally at the very end of the runway the plane struggled upwards and we were airborne, away on an unknown adventure.

Literally sharing the stable with our horses on the plane was a wonderful experience. It created an unbreakable bond between horse and rider that we all shared. It also gave us courage and confidence through all our trials to come.

Gale-force winds with sleet greeted us as we landed in Keflavik Airport in pitch dark. By then sleep had overtaken most of the group. Refuelling complete, we taxied out on to the runway, accelerated rapidly . . . and stopped. We turned about, went back to the starting point and tried again. Same result. The captain came back to tell us that at maximum revs the manifold of number two engine had got loose and (in layman's language!) the flames hung around the engine instead of going out the exhaust pipe. The necessary repairs were carried out in the lee of a hangar. John Harty, Sheila Kessler (one of our supporters), and myself went for a run and felt the better for it. After a two-hour delay we eventually took off safely.

As Anchorage had recently suffered a horrendous earthquake, only two runways were operating—a long one for the big jets and a shorter one for the likes of us. I was aware that we were approaching to land at a very high speed. After a long run-in the plane stopped abruptly, the tail lifted right up off the ground and bumped down again. Most alarming. I wondered if our pilot was sober! As it turned out, a pipe had burst, all the hydraulic oil had leaked out and the "airbrakes" would not function, so the pilot had to make a last-minute decision to land on the long runway. We just missed a big jet taking off.

Spare parts had to be flown up from Seattle, so we would have to wait much longer than just one hour for refuelling. There was no provision for offloading our horses, and anyhow quarantine restrictions would not have allowed it, so they had to stay on board.

We were treated to a gourmet dinner. I asked for caribou steak, a real delicacy, but unfortunately for me caribou is protected, so cannot it be marketed. Instead I had a scrumptious king salmon dish.

Getting into conversation with a charming young fire warden, who was also a forestry officer, I begged him to take a couple of us in his car up into the forest. I longed to see and hear the wildlife of Alaska. John, Sheila and I set off with our new friend, and we did come close to a moose with her calf, but it was not safe to leave the car. Sadly, no bears! We then drove through the city, where we saw the devastating earthquake damage. Great, wide, bottomless clefts split the roads. A big house had sunk so that its chimneys were now level with the front door of the house next to it. Colossal office blocks were just split in two. Almost all buildings were damaged.

Back at the airport we learned that in our absence a monster bull moose had come out of the woods on to the tarmac. The autumn colours of the maples around the airport were just spellbinding. Most of our party took a bed provided for us in the airport hotel, but I could not resist the walkabout as I thought I would never visit Alaska again.

After an eleven-hour delay we were airborne again on the last leg of our journey. The scenery as we crossed the roof of the world was just magic. Hour after hour of the most spectacular views of jagged, ice-capped mountains and glacier-filled valleys. They were dangerously close—we could not fly any higher because of faulty pressurisation. The icicles that had formed in our "stable" melted as we started our descent. I had to ask Cliff Cameron to put down his umbrella in case it frightened the horses!

In spite of weariness we were all wildly excited to be in Tokyo. There was a welcoming party to greet us in the person of Shozo Tanaka and his friend. Shozo, who owned a stud farm in Co. Tipperary, was a most generous host to us throughout our stay. Best of all his English was excellent.

Our horses had been standing in their crates for fifty-seven hours—surely a record. They walked down the ramp just a little bit stiff, as if they had had a long day's hunting. Otherwise they were extremely fit and well. Their form was a great tribute to our trainer, vet, and grooms. After the horses were loaded into big horseboxes, we had a tortuous drive of about three hours winding our way up into the mountains.

KARUISAWA FOR THE THREE-DAY EVENT

It was dark on our arrival at Karuisawa. Our horses were made comfortable in their brand new stables in the quarantine area. We gathered outside the golf clubhouse, our base. There we had to endure a lengthy speech of welcome by the camp commandant—all in Japanese and without an interpreter. As we were hours behind our scheduled time of arrival, all we wanted urgently was sleep! We were housed in comfortable cabins surrounding the clubhouse, which was expanded to contain dining and lounge areas. I chose to share a cabin with the Brig, and soon we were out for the count.

We awoke next morning to see the most beautiful scenery of strange trees and our own "private" volcano steaming away happily, within walking distance. If the breeze blew towards us, it was enveloped in its own vapour.

Our interpreter, Tatuji Sueki, a delightful young man attending university, met us after breakfast. For a whole week I could not get him to smile. Every morning he would meet me in the hallway, laden with presents—one for each member of our group—ranging from shaving kits, toiletries, and perfumes, to miniature plastic dolls.

One morning Sueki said to me, "Today we have photograph. I would like you to meet me here at 11 A.M. with Harry Freeman-Jackson and your daughter."

"But Sueki," I said, "I do not have a daughter here."

He was surprised: "But, Ginnie—she not your daughter, no?"

"No, she is Harry's daughter," I replied, and he laughed. The ice was broken at last. From then on we were on the best of terms.

The stables were about five minutes' walk from our lodging, beautifully built with fresh, untreated timber. The horses soon discovered this delicacy! A few days after our arrival, a near calamity occurred. In the British team, Richard Meade's good little horse Barberry developed a severe colic and was near death's door. Gloom spread through the camp, showing the camaraderie that existed among all the teams. I thought straight away that the colic was caused by a surfeit of fresh timber, but discovered that Barberry was the only horse that had not chewed the stable doors. To everyone's immense joy, he responded to treatment and was back in work within a few days. Exercising facilities were excellent and included a track up the mountain alongside the ski-tow rail, as Karuisawa is a popular ski centre in winter.

With training progressing well, our horses were healthy and getting really fit. Our supply of raw carrots, which St Finbar relished, was running low. Early one morning, I drove Shozo's car to the vegetable market near the station and bought a bagful. In unlocking the car I dropped the keys. Unfortunately they fell through a drain grating. I could just see them about two feet down on a bed of sludge!

I approached a couple of rail workers and tried to explain in sign language my predicament. I needed a length of wire to hook on to the key ring. Eventually they understood and produced some wire. After watching my fishing exploits with great interest, they gave a great cheer when I landed my prize. Was I relieved! We had free use of Shozo's car, a great blessing that enabled me to get Mass on Sundays.

Our team at exercise in Tokyo: (l–r) Tony Cameron, Harry Freeman-Jackson, Tommy Brennan, Ginnie Freeman-Jackson, John Harty, Bill Carroll (Chef de Mission).

With the Games fast approaching, tension in the camp was rising. I decided that, to get people to relax, the Irish would throw a party.

The Brig was horrified. "You can't do that, such a thing is unheard of."

But I persisted and we had a great evening. Di Bowly and the other ladies of our group produced some delicious finger food. The Irish coffee was extremely popular! The Russian team were the only ones to abstain. They turned up, their *chef d'équipe* thanked us politely for the invitation, and they withdrew.

We set off in jeeps to inspect Phases A and C (roads and tracks) through glorious mountain and woodland scenery. Our little army driver drove as if possessed by a devil and we were nearly thrown out in the rough going. The Brig shouted, "Slow" but of course the man did not understand. The Brig then rolled his papers into a tight baton and brought it down hard on the driver's head. Although it nearly knocked him out, it had the desired effect!

When walking the steeplechase course, I discovered that the take-off ground at one fence was like a bog. I could push my stick down about two feet. I reported this problem to the technical delegate. Within a short time, hundreds of little men with machines removed the "clay" from the spot and replaced it with gravel and sand, making a safe take-off.

In most Olympic Games because of the large area and suitable terrain required, finding a suitable site for the Three-Day Event presents a problem. For the Tokyo Olympics the Three-Day Event was located at Karuisawa about eighty miles from the rest of the Games. This was a bonus for all the three-day teams. We lived like a big happy family in luxurious quarters away up in the mountains. What a difference from life in the Olympic Village in the heart of the city with the intense heat, together with the lack of oxygen for the additional millions who flooded the city; in the heat of the day many people wore oxygen masks.

We had our own opening ceremony and lighting of the Olympic flame. Then the parade of teams. I was proud of our lads. The voice of the lady commentator as Tommy came past still rings in my ears: "Kill-kenn-ee, Tommie Brenn-ann, Ier-land."

The cross-country course was not overdifficult. The fences were beautifully built and well presented. As there had been a lot of rain, the going was soft—a bonus for Irish horses! Never in the history of the Olympic Three-Day Event had the scores of the first four teams been so close. Italy won the Gold. If the last horse to jump on the final day had knocked a pole, we would have won the Bronze, but he went clear and we were fourth. It was agonisingly close.

Some years earlier we had been hunting at Ballinacree on a really wet day, with mud everywhere. As we approached the road to go home, an apparent stranger opened the gate for us. Then I recognised Carlo d'Angelo, the best-known Italian horse dealer who bought the cream of our horses.

"What in the name of fortune brings you here?" I said in astonishment.

"Oh, I have been beezi", he replied.

He told me later it was on that visit to Ireland that he had bought the entire Gold medal–winning team of horses.

Pippo Cigala must have been delighted. He said to me one day, “Thady, my greatest wish is to see Italian riders riding Italian-bred horses, but until that time, dey must ride Irish horses because dey are dee best.”

Medals were presented and that evening a lively and excellent dinner was enjoyed by all. Saki flowed freely but watch it—it is a mildly pernicious drink! Bill Roycroft recited that rollicking poem “The Man from Snowy River”. You have to hear it rendered by an Australian for full value. Tommy got chatting with a Russian rider. They were both in high spirits. Tommy demonstrated what he claimed was an Irish custom, a glass of whiskey “down the hatch” and the glass thrown back over the left shoulder. The Russian thought this was great. Also mesmerised was a little Japanese waiter carrying a huge pile of plates. He stumbled and the plates crashed to the floor. A “referee” was called to restore order!

EXPLORING TOKYO

On the following day we travelled by train to Tokyo while our horses were trucked to stables near the city. My room in the Olympic Village overlooked the central railway station. The musical horns and the incredible acceleration of those high-speed trains were unforgettable. We were able to see quite a lot of the Olympic events.

Every evening Shozo took us out on a jaunt. We went to a Sukiyaki dinner in the revolving restaurant on top of the gigantic Post Office Tower. At one point the potted palms started waving. We were experiencing a minor earthquake.

Another time we went to a Geisha house—a bit apprehensively! We danced with delightful young girls adorned with exotic pure silk gowns. We then sat on the floor, each facing a girl. A number of minute dolls were positioned in two piles with a small china bowl between us. We were then blindfolded and, using chopsticks, we had to put the dolls into the bowl. The first person to get all the dolls into the bowl was the winner. Inevitably the girls beat us. It was harmless and childish fun.

On another enjoyable evening we visited a musical show. It was an absolute extravaganza, three separate stages, with a different show on each. The popular musical instrument is the *shamisen*, a hollowed-out log with strings from end to end. The strings are plucked and the music resembles that of a banjo.

Although extremely hospitable the Japanese will seldom, if ever, entertain in their own homes. As I wanted to experience a Japanese home, I asked Sueki as a great favour: could John and myself visit him one evening?

Very embarrassed, he said, “We are very poor and we could not offer you anything adequate.”

I said we just wanted to visit his family. Eventually he agreed.

I said, "Sueki, what does your family consist of—parents, brothers, and sisters?"

"Oh, there is my mother, my sister, and my girlfriend."

"And your father?" I asked.

"No, he died a few days ago."

"Oh, I am so sorry," I said, "perhaps we had better cancel the whole idea."

"No, no," he said, "my father was very ill and he is better off dead." I felt a slight shiver down my spine!

So it was arranged that John and I would come to see him by train. At the third station Sueki met us and we walked to his house. We took off our shoes and entered a small living room sparsely but tastefully furnished. In the centre was a coke brazier—no chimney, just a hole in the roof. By the brazier there was something; at first I could not make out what. It turned out to be a tiny, wizened old man, his wrinkled skin stretched over old bones. We bowed to each other in greeting. This was Sueki's grandfather. His mother and the two girls were delightful. Only Sueki spoke English. Then we had supper. First course was a small piece of smoked fish wrapped in seaweed, the second course was a jerkin wrapped in seaweed, then (I was anticipating the joint) an apple and a glass of wine. That was the meal!

Sueki's sister played the piano and we sang "It's a long way to Tipperary" in Japanese. Inevitably the Cherry blossom song, a sort of national anthem, followed. They were so kind and friendly and we really enjoyed the experience. We were probably the only visitors to the Olympics to have the privilege of entering a Japanese home.

For the showjumping final, the main arena was just a sea of colour. The fences were beautifully built and presented; each one was a veritable flower garden in itself. Finally while the arena was being cleared, the crowd were entertained by a large group of dancers, who were dressed as horses in exotic outfits and gave a unique display to music.

On my tape recorder, Di Bowly recorded the most moving commentary on the closing ceremony. Back in Ireland she was a beloved field secretary to the Duhallow Hunt and accompanied Harry and Ginnie at all major events. She was the soul of kindness and support to all and sundry.

The closing ceremony was surely the most dramatic moment of the entire Games. The teams of all the nations marched into the arena to our appointed positions, led by a flag bearer. All the while the massed choirs gave us their best. The President of the International Olympic Council then officially announced the close of the Olympic Games with an invitation to all present to assemble again in 1968 in Mexico City. The Olympic flame slowly faltered and finally died. Darkness enveloped the arena with just one spotlight on the Olympic flag. The choirs sang the sombre and magical Olympic hymn, bringing tears to thousands of eyes. The flag was lowered and borne around the arena on the shoulders of six naval ratings, illuminated by the single spotlight—then total darkness.

Suddenly, a breathtaking explosion heralded the most astounding display of fireworks imaginable. The entire sky was ablaze with every possible hue. The authorities had planned that all the athletes would march in an orderly fashion out of the arena. Instead the exit became a near riot as everybody rejoiced in boisterous mood. We walked to a big park in which the greatest feast of exotic food for all tastes was laid out in such a way that there was no queuing, and a surfeit for all—a miracle of organisation. Eventually, we joined our buses and returned to the Olympic Village, feeling weary after standing or walking for hours on end.

As a last request I asked Sueki could he get me a little souvenir. I had my eye on the small tie clip, depicting the Olympic rings and the rising sun, which all officials and stewards wore as part of their uniform. Sueki presented me with his own one.

I said, "No, you must keep that as your own souvenir."

Yet he insisted and said he could get another one. I treasure it to this day. My parting with Sueki hurt. I wonder what he is doing now.

Sayonara, time to go. We were due to load at 9 A.M. There stood our old faithful perambulator alone on the tarmac. After our previous experiences, the thought of the long trek home over the North Pole was slightly daunting. However I remembered Fr Sweeney's blessing, and said a wee prayer.

Our crew were late, so we started loading. We erected the crates slightly off-centre to allow a bit more room to walk up and down. I hoped that it would not upset the balance of the plane. The captain assured me that it would be okay.

Take-off seemed easier, with no grog and fodder greatly reduced. The flight was largely uneventful. The one exception was when we hit some severe turbulence. The plane would drop several hundred feet suddenly, and equally suddenly would elevate. Our captain explained that we could not fly above the storm because of poor pressurisation; we could not go below it because we would hit the mountains; we could not fly around it because we would enter forbidden Russian airspace. So we had to go through it!

Touching down at Shannon was a magical relief. We felt endlessly grateful for all the prayers that had been offered for our safe return. I heard later that the charter company's policy was to buy up second-hand planes from the big companies and flog them for as long as they would stay airworthy. Our plane ended its days on blocks somewhere in England. It had breathed its last and the company had gone bankrupt!

FORTY-THREE

MAÑANA . . .

Soon our sights were set on the Mexico Olympics in 1968. We engaged retired Sergeant Major Jock Ferrie as trainer for our three-day event team. Well over six feet tall and built in proportion, he rode like a lightweight, with sensitive hands, a powerful voice, and a commanding, yet gentle, manner. Every horse went well with him. Most importantly he got on well with our riders.

Suitable horses were scarce. Our short list was: Sir John Galvin's Loughlin with Penny Moreton, Sir William Blunden's Jenny with Juliet Jobling-Purser, Diana Willson on her own Chianti Rosso, and Alan Lillingston on his own Biddlecombe. Our spare with John Fowler was to be Mrs Kjaer's March Hawk. Harry Freeman-Jackson, long-time Master of the Duhallow hounds, and I were joint *chefs d'équipe*.

Training went according to plan. My big worry was the altitude in Mexico, close on nine thousand feet. Advice from the Veterinary College was that horses would be at their lowest ebb after three weeks at high altitudes, so we should either go out just a few days before the event and come home straight after it or go three months early.

We had already booked to travel in an Air France 747 with the Polish showjumping team; no other plane was available or affordable. The French Equestrian Federation kindly offered to put up our team for a month in the French Alps, where they were training, so that we could get acclimatised, but we could not afford the time nor the expense. So we were committed to travel out three weeks before the Games. Worried, I warned our trainer Jock to watch the horses carefully. He and Professor Martin Byrne VS certainly did a great job. They had our horses 99 percent fit and able to cope well with the rigours of the journey.

I was determined to have our own freshly crushed oats for our horses. I found an old hand-operated oats crusher in excellent order, which I borrowed. The legs were removable, but it was heavy (I was not popular!). It was to be the job of Jimmy Willson (Diana's husband) every morning. He was delighted, as were our horses!

Compared with our Tokyo exploits (chapter 42), the flight and all arrangements were excellent until we arrived in Mexico at around 2 A.M. in torrential rain. I did not notice a gap of about six inches below the partitions in the big, articulated trucks. We drove across the city to a cavalry depot, which was our quarantine area. The trucks were too high for the overhead cables and had no ramps, so an unloading bank was excavated. It promptly flooded. In reversing, the first truck was crooked to the bank, the driver attempted to straighten it, and skidded to and fro. On my insistence they took the cab from the second truck, tackled it to the first, and pulled it out.

The first truck took a chance in the compound and, with a man on the roof with a pitch fork holding the cables clear, they made it to the regular unloading bay. We got the horses off, only to discover that one of our showjumpers had got a foot caught under the partition and a whole slice of hoof had been torn away; Jenny had gone down and skinned her hip. While we were dressing them, one of our grooms came running in to say the second truck was stuck in the same boghole. I could not believe it.

When I approached the Mexican veterinary major who was in charge of the whole operation, I lost my temper, wrongly I'm afraid. When we finally had all horses stabled, I asked the veterinary major to take me to a dairy or somewhere to get some hot tea and sandwiches for all our lads as we were dead tired and wet.

"Oh there is nowhere open where we could get such a thing", he said.

I was furious. "Come on, there must be an all-night restaurant in Mexico City"

We drove in and found one. While the tea was being prepared, we had a cup each ourselves and I cooled down.

"Major," I said, "I must apologise sincerely for being so angry."

He replied, "Oh it is all right. We are a simple people and we do our best and I have read in ze papers dat ze Irish do explode sometimes." We became good friends and he could not do enough for us.

GETTING TO KNOW OUR NEW HOME

Keen to visit our "permanent home" for the Games, next morning I hired a small Volkswagen and Jock and I set off on the long, twisty road to Avandaro. Jock slept. I was admiring the beautiful scenery and cactus-covered hills (good covert for a fox!) and unconsciously drifted to the left of the road. Jock awoke to see a huge truck coming straight for him. He let out a roar and we just avoided a collision!

The track for the cross-country phase went through an upmarket golf course with a stream wandering amidst attractive scenery; the stream featured in many of the fences. The golf club buildings were our headquarters. It contained numerous three-berth cabins with all mod-cons and each one had a huge plate-glass window looking out on the most glorious view. The excellent new stables were within walking distance.

Some years earlier a chap called John Tritton up in Co. Donegal asked me if I could spare a few hounds for his brother Patrick, who hunted the wild deer in Mexico. I happened to have a litter of three couple, all of which had appalling feet—toes flat and spread like a hen's claw—and I was going to put them down. He could have them as a gift. Patrick was delighted. He kennelled his hounds by the pyramids, where he hunted hares before trucking them up to

Sonora in northern Mexico to hunt the white-tailed deer for a couple of months in the season.

He and his wife were responsible for travelling the Olympic Torch across part of Mexico State. Patrick is a wild and likeable chap, mad keen on hunting. He and Bill Clyde had rented a beautiful bungalow that was actually in the cross-country course. One night they gave all our Irish group a fabulous dinner; it had to be in the dark, so that we could not see the fences! After the meal everyone was in high spirits. John Fowler, while chasing someone, crashed through a glass door. He was in a bad way. Juliet and I took him to the hospital at about 2 A.M. The doctor turned up in his pyjamas and not in a good mood. After John was laid out on the operation table, the myriad of pieces of glass were removed without local anaesthetic. Then he was bound up with brown secondhand bandages from the sterilising chest.

The golf course was adjacent to the small village of Valle de Bravo. We were warned strictly not to eat any tortillas, although they might tempt us, nor any raw fruit or veggies until after the event, or we would risk getting the painful Mexican tummy. Harry, Jock, and I shared a cabin; Harry's bed was alongside the window. We got to bed late one night after a tequila party in the village. During the night I was woken up by the sound of deafening thunder, but strangely no lightning. Instead it was Harry who had fallen out of bed and was wedged against the big plate-glass window, which he was hammering with arms and legs. I had to wake Jock to help put him back in bed. At breakfast next morning Harry completely denied the whole episode!

Life in the "camp" was pleasant indeed. Our horses were working well; we were getting excited. The weather pattern was identical every day. Roasting sun (so horses had to work early) until 11:30 A.M. when clouds would gather, then an unbelievable thunderstorm and tropical rain for a couple of hours. By 3 P.M. the blistering sun would be back again, causing steam all over. The small stream would break its banks and flood water would be everywhere. Next day it would be back to normal. All *chefs d'équipe* implored the technical delegate to get the organisers to start the cross country at 7 A.M. instead of 9 A.M., so that it could be finished before the rain. But they would not budge: "It will be all right, it never rains in October"!

A couple of days before the start, we had a huge disappointment. Biddlecombe broke down. Poor Alan was devastated, indeed, our whole group was. So we substituted March Hawk and John Fowler. However, my "boss" Colonel Bill Rea, assistant *chef de mission* in charge of our equestrian teams, had nominated Tommy Brennan as reserve rider—in those days only one reserve rider was allowed for both the eventing and showjumping teams. I argued that March Hawk was a small horse, too small for Tommy, and John had trained him from the beginning, but Bill was adamant. There was unease in our camp for a while, but it soon cleared. In the event, Tommy and March Hawk gave their best and everyone was satisfied. Tommy had the experience of the Tokyo Olympics under his belt, so he was technically more qualified than John.

On the day before the opening ceremony we all bussed down to the Olympic Village in Mexico. Early next morning, I was wakened by gunfire. I thought it strange to have army manoeuvres on that of all days. It was reported that a crowd of students were staging a peaceful protest to highlight the gap between the rich and poor in the country, and that the army had shot seven students. Later, thirty-five were confirmed dead. Tragic.

Mexico is a country of contrasts—the extremely rich and the extremely poor. I saw an example when I took a taxi from the Olympic Village to the quarantine stables and the driver got lost. I knew the way, but did not correct him because we were going through a slum area on the outskirts of the city. On the side of a hill, two big rocks about eight feet apart had some rusty corrugated iron sheets as a roof and some sacking as a back wall. It was the family home for parents and about five young children, and typical of many. The family had been lured in from the country on the false expectation of a well-paid job. Admittedly the children looked healthy. It was said that they were clothed and fed by the authorities, but not given any money because they would just use it for drink.

Mexicans are lovely, warm-hearted people, similar to us Irish. About a week after our arrival, Brigadier Grose, *chef de mission* of the English teams, said to me, "Thady, how are you getting on with these people? I find I cannot get cross with them."

I'd known the brigadier since Tokyo days. I replied, "James, there is no point in getting cross with a Mexican, or an Irishman for that matter. It gets you nowhere!"

True to tradition of disorganization, the city council decided to install an underground rail system in the city, beginning in the first week of the Olympics. It caused traffic chaos in the ancient Metropolis.

THE GAMES BEGIN

The opening ceremony was spectacular. Representing one's country and marching in company with many hundreds of international athletes gives one an explosive feeling of camaraderie and pride that is hard to describe. Tokyo and Mexico must be among the greatest highlights of my life. But it was good to be back "home" in our little enclave in the hills.

All of our team did a highly creditable performance in the dressage and were well placed. We were proud of them. Then the cross. As we had forecast, the rains came. Our interpreter, Fernando Soler, a charming young man who had a holiday home in Avandaro, told me that he had never seen the stream as flooded as it was that day.

Penny was our first to go. Loughlin was a handsome horse, almost thoroughbred and a bit of a handful for Penny. I had implored Sir John to allow us to send him hunting, and to compete in a variety of events. However, he said that when he had given a number of horses to the United States Three-Day

Colonel Bill Rea and Thady Ryan with the team in the Olympic stadium. Bill was Chef de Mission, *in charge of our equestrian teams. Four years later, Bill and I were two of twelve men appointed by the Minister of Agriculture to be founding members of the* Bord na gCapall *(the Irish Horse Board).*

Event team, too many had been injured in training. Loughlin could have a go at a single one-day event, no more, so Penny was on a super, but inexperienced horse.

I was at the start of Phase D to check each one. After Penny and Juliet had started, a French rider who had finished his round came up to me and said, "You are Irish? I am so sorry for your loss." I was shocked and speechless. He went on, "You do not know that you have lost a horse?"

Fence seven was a maximum post and rail, a ditch with a take-off rail, then another rail into a wood. Instead of overalling it, Loughlin had gone far too fast, tried to put in a short stride, and hit the second rail hard. He broke his back and had to be destroyed. Poor Penny was crushed, with several fractured ribs, and lay unconscious in hospital for a few days. Thank God she made a complete recovery.

Juliet and Diana got around successfully just before the flood, then chaos reigned. Horses and riders were half drowned, having to be rescued with ropes (outside assistance, against the rules!). At least three who "finished" the course had missed out one fence completely.

Objections were coming in so fast that the organising committee announced, "We will accept no more objections. There are too many."

The flood was at its highest when Tommy started. Fence 5 had three parts: a maximum post and rail, one stride to another rail and a drop of about five feet into about eighteen inches of water, then up the bank and out—a nice fence. When Tommy came to it, only about a foot of the first rail was showing, the second rail was only just showing, then about five feet of raging torrent carrying branches and rubbish. Little March Hawk came to it with ears pricked, cleared the first two rails, and stumbled on landing in the torrent. Both horse and rider disappeared completely. Surfacing with water pouring out of the little horse's nose and ears, they jumped up the bank. Tommy remounted, but after two more fences, they had to retire. *What* a courageous rider and *what* a game little horse!

And so the Irish team was out of the competition. However, Jenny and Chianti had got around, and both were clear in the showjumping to finish seventh and twenty-seventh individually. A great performance.

March Hawk and Tommy Brennan are in right trouble at the rain-swollen stream in Mexico that, in decent weather, was intended to meander scenically through several of the jumps on the course.

Tommy is still in trouble!

On the evening of our final day at Avandaro, with typical Mexican generosity, the golf club members laid on a fabulous farewell dinner party for the teams and supporters of the twelve nations. During the celebrations, held in a huge marquee erected on the lawn, there was an absolute downpour and we were up to our ankles in water, but nobody cared.

Each team was invited to get up on the stage and sing a national song of their country. Of course the Germans excelled, and the English, Italians, and others were great. Then it was Ireland's turn. We could not decide on a song: "you know the words of one song, but not the tune, I would know the tune of another but not the words" and so on. Eventually we settled for "It's a Long Way to Tipperary", a British marching song. I was embarrassed!

We had four days before the closing ceremony. Fernando offered to accompany us on a fishing trip. Four of us flew with him to Merida on the point of the Yucatan Peninsula, then by bus to Valladolid and by boat to a tiny island called "Isla Mujeres" (remembering *j* is pronounced as *h*; the name translates as the Island of Women). There we spent two glorious warm moonlit nights sleeping in hammocks slung from the waving palms. By day we went game fishing, catching mostly barracuda. Outside a restaurant was a turtle that had been turned on its back to be killed by the broiling sun. After that it is eaten. That put me off turtle soup!

The region around Merida is crowded with historic Aztec ruins and is still being explored. We saw a well-preserved arena for pillotto, a game something like basketball. Using only their elbows, shoulders or head, players had to drop a heavy leather ball through a big stone ring about ten feet above the ground. The Emperor had his throne at one end. Both teams had a good incentive to win because the losing team was sacrificed to the Sun God.

Back to Mexico for the moving closing ceremony. I had thought Tokyo was perfection, so I did not bother recording Mexico, but I had assumed wrong. During the ceremony about three hundred *mariachi* players came in and were supposed to fill the big arena with music. However, with musical talent a general characteristic of Mexicans, the players were drowned by the beautiful singing of the massed choirs, along with the audience themselves, who were singing their hearts out. It still echoes in my ears.

At the poignant climax of the ceremony, the long Olympic flag was lowered in dead silence. The six naval ratings received it, but it had a twist in it. In their confusion they twisted both ends instead of just one and the twist remained! Suddenly the magic spell of silence was broken. The whole assembly exploded with laughter. Somehow it was a fitting end to the Mexican supreme effort to present the best and most enjoyable Olympic Games ever.

AN IRRESISTIBLE DIVERSION

Domingo, a friend of Patrick Tritton, had a big sugar-refining business on the West Coast of the United States. One day Domingo's lawyer informed him that he owned a big cattle ranch in Sonora, northern Mexico. He flew in to inspect it, fell in love with it, handed over his sugar refinery to his son and became a rancher! Patrick used to bring his hounds up there for a couple of months each year to hunt the wild white-tailed deer. He invited four of us to join him.

After flying by regular airlines to Hermosillo, we flew to the ranch (not far from Nogales on the United States border) in a private two-seater piloted by Patrick. Horses (or "cow ponies") and hounds were waiting for us at the airstrip. We rode to the ranch house and kennels in the most gorgeous scenic landscape imaginable—rolling hills of prairie grass, dotted with cactus and a few groves of trees.

Domingo made us welcome. We were introduced to cumaro, a far more potent firewater than tequila and distilled from a different variety of cactus. That evening our cow ponies—strong small cobs with quality—were driven to a corral some distance away in the area where we were to hunt next day.

Rising early we drove in beach buggies to the corral. Our mounts were tacked up (with English saddles) for us already. Mine was Dollar, a young roan who could really gallop and was a delight to ride. The first thing I did was to adjust the girth to release the wrinkles in his skin and loosen the throat lash and curb chain, which were far too tight. Hounds, a mixed bunch, but looking well, had come on in a truck. Patrick still had one of the hounds I had given him. The hound had never been lame in spite of his splayed flat toes. It was amazing considering that some of the terrain—what they called their Apache country—was just jagged sharp rocks. So much for the tight catfoot fashion in Peterborough!

We first rode to the nearest water hole, where our ponies filled themselves (like camels), being extremely thirsty as they had had no water in the corral. Never shod, their hoofs were hard as steel because of the intensely dry conditions.

We found deer, and hounds hunted well with good cry, but discipline was not great. They changed stag frequently, so did not account. I don't know what would have happened if they had closed on one because no one seemed to carry a gun or a hunting knife.

We stopped hunting at 11 A.M. because of the baking sun. That afternoon we watched a young pony being broken in. He was put in a small pen, blindfolded, and saddled (Western). Two lads on their ponies stood close to him, one on each side. Then the third lad mounted him, the blindfold was removed, the gate was opened, and all three (tight together) galloped madly down the dry riverbed. The two outside riders separated and the young pony was made to gallop on his own. When he was exhausted, he was ridden back to the pen. End of first and last lesson, "next please". I don't think Monty Roberts would have agreed!

The following day the "meet" was on the landing strip. As arranged, the small plane landed, I said goodbye to the Master and all my friends, changed planes at Hermosillo, and went back to Mexico City. Of course I could have gone home with our riders the day after the closing ceremony. But with the head groom for both teams perfectly capable of looking after the horses for the extra week, I could not resist the temptation to hunt stag in northern Mexico.

Next day our Air France charter 747 arrived. We loaded up without incident and had a super flight home to Shannon. So ended one of the most exciting, unique, traumatic, and enjoyable adventures of my life.

I still feel sore that, in the two Olympics in which I have been involved, we did not win a medal. "I'm sorry, Ireland. Is there anything more that I could have and should have done?"

Hunting the wild, white-tailed deer in Sonora, northern Mexico, was another exciting experience.

SIX
SOME FINAL THOUGHTS

FORTY-FOUR

THINGS THAT MATTER

In this chapter I want to share with you, my readers, my personal feelings on matters that should concern us all deeply.

Living in a materialistic world, it is all too easy to forget the real purpose of life. That purpose is to achieve the happiness of eternal life and to help others to do likewise. The struggle against the powers of evil will test us to the end, but God has promised to be with us always and if we keep our trust in Him, we will achieve our goal.

This does not mean that we cannot enjoy our legitimate pleasures. My favourite has been foxhunting! Those of us who are able to enjoy the countryside with all it has to offer are especially privileged. I have had the added support and friendship of all my fellow parishioners in Knocklong Parish for which I am truly grateful.

In my childhood, before the days of electric lights and heaters, our church in Knocklong Parish was cold. In the wintertime the sacristan would hold a candle with shivering hands, to give the holy old parish priest, Canon Ryan, some light to read the long prayers before Mass. The grease would spill all over the book, making Dad frantic! We could scarcely hear the Canon and Mass took a good hour and a half—tough on all the children and old folk.

But Great Aunt Helen (Auntie), a saintly and warm-hearted old lady, had a story that brought a lighter side to it. St Peter stood outside the Gates of Heaven, checking people as they came in.

He asked one old man, "Where do you come from?"

"The parish of Blackrock in Dublin", he replied.

"Oh," said St Peter, "go back to Purgatory, you are not ready to come in yet. Who's next?" He asked the old woman next in line where she was from.

"The parish of Knocklong, your Honour."

"Oh come in, come in, ma'am. You have done more than your share already."

Another story is of a parish priest celebrating Rosary and Benediction in honour of our Blessed Lady in May. Halfway through the Rosary, he received an urgent sick call.

He turned to the sacristan, "Let you carry on the Rosary, I'll be back soon."

The sick call took longer than expected. When he returned he found the sacristan carrying on gallantly, "The forty-fifth glorious mystery, St Peter stabs Pontius Pilate in the back . . . Our Father . . ."

In those days Knocklong's three galleries were almost full for the two Sunday Masses. Some people came by horse and trap (the rings where the horses were tied are still in the wall by the church) or by bicycle, but most came on foot. The fields had well-worn Mass paths. Hail, rain, or snow, the parishioners would not miss Sunday Mass.

Every year we had a parish mission or retreat usually given by two priests from the Redemptionist Order in Limerick. Wonderful preachers, one was elderly and appealed to the old folk, the other was lively and forceful, responsible for the sermon on Hell fire and brimstone. As the mission tended to coincide with hay making, it was hard on the horses working long days in the meadow, then galloping with a full trap to reach the evening mission in time. The church would be *packed*. In most houses and cottages around the country, the family Rosary was said every evening. Devotion to Our Lady was part of our lives.

The Catholic Faith was strong in Ireland. People cherished the memory of generations past, the thousands of missionaries who went abroad to preach and give their lives for God. In most houses throughout the country you would see a picture of the Sacred Heart and old photos of family members as priests and nuns. The young people grew up imbued with the strong Faith of their parents and many answered the call to the priesthood and religious life. Ireland is the one beacon of light in the darkness of a world gone mad.

What has become of our Faith? Our churches are less than half full. Vocations are at an all-time low and marriages are getting scarce. People talk glibly about "partners" and "de facto relationships" instead of spouses; cohabitation seems to be the norm. This despicable litany of horrors is endless. Sin seems to be a thing of the past.

As a direct result of all this we have broken marriages, solo parents, fragmented families, children without a father or mother, abortion on demand, and euthanasia. We have lost sight of the dignity of human life, we are becoming a Godless generation. Pleasure is our goal.

We cannot blame our young people. What a sorry world they have been born into—no family life and no parents to care for them. It is no wonder that they turn for refuge to drink, drugs, sex, and suicide. There is something terribly wrong with society if a mother as well as the father must go out and work to support the family. Her place, her *vocation* is in the home, caring for and loving her children. Albeit there are many cases where the mothers need not go out to work, but they are living beyond their means and neglecting their children. There is a huge responsibility on governments to recognise that the family is the strength of a nation and that their welfare should be the first priority.

In her numerous apparitions around the world our Blessed Lady has stressed that the crime of abortion causes the greatest sorrow to her Son and Herself. It is difficult to comprehend how any man or woman can deliberately kill a young human being—don't call them embryos, they are God's created children from the moment of conception—and now they are being used for "spare parts". Undoubtedly practitioners know what they are doing. Recently a group of senior surgeons were debating at what age a young baby should be given a painkiller before he or she is extracted piecemeal from the mother's womb.

Our Lady has said in tears many times during her apparitions that, in spite of Her Son's ultimate sacrifice on the cross to save the human race, the number of souls who get to Heaven will be tragically small. God forgive me but I cannot help thinking that abortionists and their assistants will be at the head of the queue for Hell. We must pray for God's mercy on them.

In "developed" countries, materialism has stifled all the moral standards that have guided governments and lawmakers down the years. Lust for power and wealth have dulled people's consciences. Insidiously the Devil is manipulating the media in all its forms to implement his wicked plan to defy God and bring the human race to eternal damnation. In the wrong hands the Internet's capacity for evil is as yet unfathomed.

But don't let us despair. There is a solution to this apparently irretrievable situation. We must bring God back into our lives. He has promised never to abandon us, and that He will be with us to the end of time. But He will not force us. He has given us free will and is waiting for us to ask Him for His help.

In the right hands, man's incredible inventions—telephone, radio, television, and now the Internet have infinite potential for good in spreading the Gospel and making people aware of the dignity of life and the enormity of the privilege He has given to us in making us co-creators with Him of human life, and so perpetuating the human race. He ordained that a man and a woman as husband and wife should be completely bonded together in the sacrament of marriage, each giving the other their entire being. As a reward for this ultimate giving, they experience a moment of sheer physical pleasure, happiness, fulfilment, and love. When one realises that this sexual act is an intrinsic part of God's sacred plan for procreation, one can see why it should be treated with the greatest reverence and respect and that it should take place solely within the state of matrimony and with the intention of procreating children.

Sadly owing to the frailty of human nature, this sexual pleasure has been exploited and commercialised beyond belief. It is practised as a normal source of pleasure outside the state of matrimony. As such, not only is it sinful, but it is the major cause of abortions and numerous other evils.

We have a serious obligation to instill in our children the sacredness and dignity of human life and the reality of God's infinite love for each and everyone of us. This should be the basis for religious instruction in our schools.

We need to hear more on these lines from our pastors in all churches.

What a fantastic and historic event the seventh World Youth Day turned out to be in August 2000 when two and a half *million* young people from all over the world assembled in Rome to pray in response to our Holy Father Pope John Paul's plea. It was the largest pilgrimage ever to be seen in the Holy City. They are the Christians of tomorrow and a symbol of hope for generations to come.

We have in Pope John Paul II a wonderful, courageous, energetic, and holy man. He is truly a man of God. In calling the Second Vatican Council, Pope John XXIII opened a window to let in some welcome fresh air, not anticipating the hurricane that ensued. It was left to our present Holy Father to cope with the aftermath. Despite being heavily criticised for being out of date and lacking understanding of modern living conditions, he is only too well aware of the powers of evil at work in the world. Our Faith, with all that it entails, is being put to the test as never before. We must not weaken, and Pope John Paul is committed to guiding us along the road that leads back to God.

What can you and I do to help the people of this troubled world? The answer lies in prayer and good example. God knows I am no saint, but I try to do my best. My Faith has stood me in good stead, and I long to see the love of God experienced by all those around me. My grandfather's favourite prayer, which I say every day, was:

> Oh my God teach me to love Thee and to serve Thee with my whole heart and to do all things according to Thy most Holy will.

Do try to make it yours too.

FORTY-FIVE

PARISH BONDS

As befits an MFH, I was always deeply involved in the life and activities of our parish. In the same way that hunting hounds through the country gave me the opportunity to get to know all the farmers and the sportsmen, so sharing life and activities with all my neighbours and experiencing their warm-hearted friendship has been one of the greatest joys of my life.

In the previous chapter, the physical character of Knocklong Parish seems to have been portrayed in a poor light, yet thankfully, that is now far from the reality. In place of the old building on top of the hill is the "new school", a well-designed, comfortable, and attractive building. It is an example of what a modern national school should be. Sean O'Shea, as headmaster for many years, did a wonderful job. In another sphere, Sean jealously guarded his position year after year as steward of the Number Board at the hunt point-to-point. His position as headmaster has been taken ably by Ger Power, who is maintaining the excellent academic record and healthy spirit of the school.

In the succession of excellent teachers, it is difficult to mention names. But one must not be forgotten. Mary Fitzsimons, whose father was headmaster for some years, followed on as head teacher for a long period and was honoured with a Papal Award for her trojan work. As our choir master she will long be remembered for her loyalty to that lovely old hymn, "The Old Rugged Cross", which she trotted out on every possible occasion, be it for feastdays, funerals, or weddings, but we loved her for it.

Knocklong Church, now over one hundred years old, has had a new lease of life. Because it needed extensive restoration, the two side galleries had to be removed. I miss them as our family always used the front two seats of the right-hand one. Nowadays there seems to be enough room for the congregation in the church without them. With central heating, excellent lighting, and tasteful decoration, it must be one of the finest country churches in the diocese.

To commemorate the Marian Year, the parish decided to build a shrine to Our Lady at the Chapel Cross. David Barry offered a site for it at the corner of what used to be known as "Kirby's Big Field". To design the shrine I asked architect Chevalier Sheehan in Limerick, who specialised in designing churches (for which he was awarded his "title") and other important buildings, including Limerick's fine regional hospital.

With tractors and trailers, we drew loads of that special reddish stone with chips of marble through it that is found behind Glenbrohane village on the way to Ballintubber. We were fortunate in having a gifted stone mason, Tom O'Donnell, who lived alongside Scarteen. He followed Chevalier Sheehan's design with meticulous care and produced a simple and most beautiful shrine.

Next we needed a statue and wanted the best. In answer to prayer, we imported direct from Italy a magnificent statue of Our Lady in carrara marble. With great joy we positioned it carefully on the shrine and begged Our Lady to bless our parish. As one comes out of the church on a fine day, the view of the shrine with Slieveneagh Mountain in the background is stunning.

Shortly after all this, while on a visit to Lourdes, I asked the parish priest if I could have some relic from the grotto. It so happened that, to insert the bronze plaque in the grotto, chips of rock were taken out. The plaque is inscribed, "Je suis l'Immaculée Concepzione." The chips were almost all gone; they were to be alloted only for Marian shrines. I brought one home with glee. It is set in a mount of white marble with the inscription:

> Piece of actual rock on which Our Lady stood during her Apparition at Lourdes.

So the shrine is special.

One of the biggest events in the country just after World War II was the Rural Electrification Scheme. We had to do a lot of canvassing for it as we had to have about eighty percent acceptance before the company would take on our area. Although some people were scared of it and did not want to change from their old ways (hard to believe that now!), fortunately, we just made the required percentage. It transformed life in the country. Our good neighbour Tommy Fitzpatrick in Lackelly palled up with two experienced electricians and wired our house for us. They did a good job, not an easy one in such an old house.

At one time one complete branch line would black out for no apparent reason. The company kept replacing fuses, but still it would happen with no warning. Then one day someone was walking across a field where the cables turned a corner and the corner post had a staywire. He spotted a big bullock having a grand scratch under the stay wire. The cables would start swinging, the high-voltage wires would touch with a bang and a flash, and—problem solved!

Another excitement in the area was the Thatched Cottage Scheme. To bring life and employment to isolated areas with scenic or sporting potential, the Government would build a small group of traditional thatched cottages. Such cottages became extremely popular among tourists who wanted to rent them (self-catering), meet the local people and sample Irish country life. For a few years a group of seven cottages built close to Knocklong were successful, with Eileen and John Carroll in charge. Then occupancy started to drop off because the area did not have enough local attractions, so they were sold individually. The owners today are proud of them, maintaining them beautifully to provide a colourful attraction.

Without a mains supply, a big problem was ensuring a clean water supply for all families in the area. Although the Government could not afford to install the mains, it devised a scheme under which householders would group together and do the work themselves under supervision. When the job was completed to standard, a fairly generous grant per house would be paid to the group. So the "Scarteen and Ballyscaddane Group Water Scheme" was formed.

This was exciting! County engineers planned the scheme, taking careful levels to ensure that all houses would have equal pressure. To start with we had twenty-five houses accepted. We located a water diviner, who found a good supply at a reasonable depth in the plot I had given to my sister Gwen (where she then built a delightful small bungalow, "Scarteen Beag", Irish for "Little Scarteen"). To reach some of the more distant houses, we had to get a contractor to erect a six thousand-gallon high level (twenty feet) reservoir on a height across the road from Gwen's house. Then the pipe-laying started. We hired a chap with a large disc plough and winch to open the trench. Mickey Dea was a wizard, quickly learning the art of joining the plastic piping and the multitude of fittings, meters, and the like, and he did most of the plumbing in the houses.

The landowners themselves did the manual labour with shovels and housewives fed us as we progressed. With the whole operation a great community effort, the job was completed in a remarkably short time. Several other groups came to inspect and learn from our successes and mistakes. Maintenance was a bit of a headache at times, so after some years we handed over our scheme to the county council. They have since connected it up to the major Knocklong mains, which also supplies the village of Hospital, while "our" spring and reservoir are used as a booster supply whenever required.

Another huge asset of which we are proud is the new cemetery. The old one on top of the hill near the castle was full to overflowing. I approached Maude Donovan and her son Pat, who had the pub up the road from the church. After lengthy and amicable discussion with our parish priest, they agreed to sell a section of land, between their house and the church, to the parish. The new cemetery is now beautifully planned and maintained, with all plots bought and carefully numbered.

Our family has one of the plots. Formerly the Ryan family vault in Emly Graveyard had been our place of burial since we lived in Ballyvistea. Our darling Claire was interred there and the vault is now sealed. I was hoping that we could have her in our new plot in Knocklong, but the cemetery had not yet been completed.

These are some of the projects that have kept us busy down the years. Our family has always had and, please God, will continue to have a worthwhile input into the life of our parish. We have valued highly the strong links that we have enjoyed with our farming friends throughout the country. I am convinced that, God willing, this will always be the case.

FORTY-SIX

A MOMENTOUS DECISION

One day John said to me, "Dad, I would rather not take over Scarteen and the hounds from you. I would prefer to do my own thing."

By tradition as eldest son it was his prerogative to step into my shoes. However his wishes and happiness were more precious than tradition. There had also been precedents, such as my grandfather. It was obvious that Chris was the one to take over in John's stead, as all the family fully agreed. Willing, able, and eager to accept the challenge, Chris became the owner of Scarteen and Master of hounds.

I thank God for our united family every day. All five of them are devoted to their old home. John and Hugh put in several years of hard work getting the farm back on its feet, and when Chris joined them, they became a close-knit team, helping each other out on every possible occasion. Chris and his wife Sue give a great welcome to the rest of the family whenever they come to stay. With farming, hunting, Equigrass, schooling young horses, and most importantly bringing up their family, they are doing a wonderful job.

Now Anne's and my future had to be pondered. It was now 1985. We had both agreed, years before, that when one of our boys took over Scarteen, we would get right out of his hair and not interfere with his life. We looked seriously at a small farm on Newtown, the hill behind Caherconlish, about sixteen miles from Scarteen. An old ruined stone house there had a fabulous view across the whole of our hunting country to the Galtee Mountains and one can just see Scarteen on a clear day—tempting indeed.

Then I thought to myself, I am being selfish. After years of devotion and hard work for me, my darling Anne deserves better than this. Anne had given up her family and her country for my sake. I resolved that, with her agreement, we would retire to New Zealand.

It was a momentous and traumatic decision to take at our time of life, but the more I thought about it, the happier I felt, and of course Anne felt likewise. The one person that I was really worried about was my dear sister Gwen. She and I, the last of our generation, are close. However, generous as ever, she accepted my decision—even though it hurt her deeply. Our mother, who had spent several years in Gwen's care at Scarteen Beag, moved down to John at Burton Park (her old home) for her final days, so Gwen lived alone.

A wonderful character came into my life when we were all at lunch in Scarteen and a horse-drawn caravan came down the avenue. Usually the "travelling people" camped on the roadside close to our gate, but they never ventured down the avenue. Going out to investigate, I met a delightful, slight elderly lady with a disarming twinkle in her eye.

In an English voice she asked me, "Are you Mr Ryan, the Master of the Scarteen hounds? Can I come and spend the night? My good friends Tom and Elsie Morgan of the West Waterfords recommended me to call to you."

Of course my answer was "Yes". Any friend of Tom and Elsie's would be our friend too.

From Somerset, Susan Paulet was a descendent of Admiral Paulet RN and closely related to the Marquis of Winchester. After deciding that she had paid enough taxes to the British Crown, she handed over her farm to her niece, got a friend to build her a caravan (just a large box on pneumatic wheels), tackled up her working mare, and took to the road. Also crazy on hunting, Susan visited many of the foxhound packs around England before crossing to Ireland.

We parked the caravan on the lawn near the house and put the mare out to grass in the field by the avenue. Next morning when Susan went out to feed her, she found to her dismay that the mare was dead in the field. With no "engine", poor Susan was grounded. She stayed with us for the hunting season!

Susan quickly became one of the family. Gwen used to take her in the car to follow the hunt twice a week—this was bliss for her. Once when they were crossing a branch line of the railway, the man in charge assured them that there was no train due. Suddenly an unscheduled train appeared and brushed the tail of Gwen's car without doing too much damage.

"Stupid man," exclaimed Susan, "he could have killed us."

At the close of the season Susan bought a quiet skewbald horse (naturally she called him "Magpie"). Taking to the road again, she made two more trips to England and Scotland to visit her friends. Eventually travelling became too much for her and we persuaded her to retire in a small mobile home. We parked it close to Mickey Dea's house, near Scarteen, where Mary (Mickey's wife) looked after her as if she was her mother.

Then while Susan was airing her clothes by her stove, they caught fire and the mobile home burned to the ground. She was lucky to escape.

Another time she said to me, "Thady, tell Tommy to put me down and feed me to the hounds; I'm no use any more."

I replied, "Susan that would be a waste of time. You have not got a pick of by Carmel and Raoul Westbrook meat on your bones."

She spent her final few years happy and in good health, lovingly cared for by Carmel and Raoul Westbrook in a small home for the elderly near Ballylanders.

Irish humour can be bizarre. I am mindful of the story of the elderly couple living alone.

Mary says to Paddy, "Will ye go'ut into the garden and fetch me in a head o'cabbage, the bacon and spuds is cooked. Don't be long now, 'tis getting late."

She was telling this story later to her friend Joan. Paddy had gone out for the cabbage. Ten minutes passed, twenty minutes, half an hour. Mary had wondered what was keeping Paddy. She had gone out and found him abroad in the garden, an' he *dead*.

"Oh," exclaimed Joan blessing herself, "that was a terrible thing to happen. What did ye do?"

"Oh", says Mary, "I just opened a tin of beans instead."

Another factor in our decisions over retirement began long before when Arthur Stirling painted a portrait of Dad while they were prisoners of war together in Germany (it now hangs in the hall at Scarteen). Later he wrote to Dad asking him whether his niece Nonie Millar could come to Scarteen as a paying guest for a season's hunting.

Dad replied, "Yes of course, we would be delighted to have her."

The extra bit of income would be welcome too. And so Nonie arrived with her small hunter mare and her collie Jenny. She was a delightful girl, blonde, always in good humour and with a broad Scottish accent. She loved the hunting and visited us for many years.

Out of the blue I received a letter one day from a firm of solicitors in London informing me

> that their client Miss Nonie Millar of Tinker's Cross, Braintree in Essex had just deceased. In her will she had bequeathed her house and lands to Thaddeus Ryan MFH of Scarteen in Co. Limerick, or his survivor.

I was overwhelmed. Dear Nonie, I knew that she had been fond of our family.

Going straight over to Essex for the funeral, Anne and I met some of Nonie's relatives and the solicitor. When the obsequies were over, the solicitor brought us to see the little house. On seeing it my heart missed a beat. It was a gem, a listed house of great character, stone built and nestling among mature hardwoods and a profusion of attractive shrubs. It had obviously been tenderly cared for by Nonie over the years. Both inside and out, it was in perfect condition and ready to walk in to.

Anne and I set off for home and some hard thinking. Our plans for retiring took on a new perspective. But could we settle in Essex? The thought was bewildering. We discussed the proposition with the family. They agreed entirely with us that for us to retire to live in Essex was out of the question. And so with a heavy heart I instructed my solicitor to put Tinker's Cross on the market. It did not realise quite as much as we had expected, but enough to make most of our plans for retiring to New Zealand achievable.

FORTY-SEVEN

AMBITION ACHIEVED

From now on our sights were fixed distantly on New Zealand. It was close on thirty years since Anne and I had left its shores to make our life together in Ireland. In all that time, I had not been back, and Anne had visited her family on only three occasions. Our children had done something to keep up the connections. Some years earlier our son John had been to New Zealand to study dairy farming for two years, gaining his diploma from Massey University. Our daughter Rachel went next in answer to an advertisement for a director from a group of parents in Palmerston North, in the lower North Island, who wished to have a Montessori school.

At her interview, Rachel agreed to take the post on condition that the school must be available and affordable to all children, whatever their colour or financial status. This meant that her salary would be considerably lower than what the group had planned originally. Although to earn enough to live on, Rachel initially had to take a job as waitress on three nights a week, she was happy and successful in her work. Starting with three pupils, she handed more than forty-nine pupils to her successor after three years. She then bought a small, attractive little house in the Glen, not far from Nelson at the top of the South Island, where she became coordinator of the Montessori Teachers' Association of New Zealand.

Yet while Anne and I had been living in Ireland, a lot of had changed on both sides of the world. We were about to take a huge gamble. What if we did not like "the Kiwis"? What if "the Kiwis" did not like us? I decided I must go there on a reconnaissance trip to reassure myself that we were making the right decision.

So in 1986 we went to check our emigration plan against the reality. After a few weeks, we were absolutely happy with it. It was just wonderful to meet Anne's relations and our old friends again, although inevitably many were missing. The "dream home in New Zealand" that I had in my mind was a small house on about fifty acres of rolling grassland with a trout stream running through it and a view of the mountains. I wasn't asking much, was I!

We were tempted to retire in the Nelson area to be near Rachel. However, as we were going to be involved with horses, we thought that Nelson would be a bit too isolated. There were two mountain ranges and seven hours of driving between there and the province of Canterbury, where many horse activities took place. So we decided to confine our search to South Canterbury, where most of Anne's relatives and friends lived.

Back home in Scarteen, we got busy. When we were married in 1953, I had been keen to introduce the Irish Draught breed to New Zealand if ever the occasion arose (see chapter 33 if you are wondering why I would wish to take them to the other side of the world). Now we had the opportunity. I was determined to bring out a son of the legendary Irish jumping sire King of Diamonds. I contacted the owners of all his sons on the register but most were either not for sale or not suitable for some reason. Only one was possible. He belonged to Tom Nyland up in Co. Mayo. Tom and his wife had stood many a good sire in their yard.

We drove up to inspect Kingsway Diamond. He was just what I had hoped for, a big noble, chestnut horse standing 17.1 hands with great bone, power and presence, wonderful freedom, and outstanding jumping ability. Most importantly he had a kind and generous character. All these were the attributes of a traditional Irish Draught. He was not cheap, but I wanted to bring the best out to New Zealand.

We had secured our stallion. Now I wanted to find a two-year-old pure Irish Draught filly also by King of Diamonds. My reasoning was that the traditional plan for breeding top-class sport horses was to breed a thoroughbred sire to an Irish Draught mare. However there were no pure Irish Draught mares in New Zealand, so we were restricted to breeding the reverse way. As some of my old friends in Ireland said it would not work, to play it safe, I thought I would also bring out a filly. Once again we searched Ireland for a high-class filly, in vain for a long time. Finally we heard of one down in Kilmanagh, Co. Kilkenny, belonging to Tom Purcell. She was an absolute beauty. I had to have her!

Tom had been breeding top-class Irish Draught stock for years. He had two fillies, a grey by King of Diamonds and another by a different sire.

I said to Tom, "How much do you want for the grey?"

Kingsway Diamond, by the legendary jumping sire, King of Diamonds. I planned to introduce Irish Draught bloodlines to New Zealand by breeding him to Thoroughbred mares there.

"Oh she is not for sale. She is the only filly by the King that I have had out of my old mare. All her other progeny were colts, several have been sold abroad and two are stallions."

"Go on, Tom," I said, "put a price on her. I want her."

"No, I won't sell."

After further pressure he said, "All right, I won't take less than £3000 for her."

I said "Right, I'll take her."

Poor Tom was in agony. "No", he said.

Anne said to me, "For goodness sake, give it up. You are torturing him."

I had one last go. "Tom, would another £500 make a difference?"

I was crazy. It was an unheard of price for an unbroken two-year-old filly.

After some thought Tom said, "I'm only a small farmer and I could not afford to turn down that sort of money."

So the deal was clinched, and I have never regretted it. She has given us some super stock. About four years later, when visiting Ireland, I called to see Tom. He also looked happy.

"Hop into the car", he said. He took me to a yard at the end of his farm.

There in a stable was the most beautiful filly I had ever seen. She was by a son of the King out of the old mare.

"Tom," I said, "promise me something. Don't ever sell that filly, not even to me!"

I could not resist buying another two-year-old three-quarter Thoroughbred filly by Carnival Night, the leading eventing and hunting sire and successful racehorse by Prince Richard (by Hyperion) and bred by the Queen of England. Michael Leonard from Newcastle West, one of the best judges of young stock in the country, had bred the filly. Her dam was an outstanding halfbred hunter mare and she herself was everything you could wish for in a high-class brood

Kilmanagh Banrion (by King of Diamonds), an Irish Draught filly, would be bred to New Zealand Thoroughbred stallions.

Thady Ryan shows his prize-winning registered Irish Draught mare, Banrion (by King of Diamonds), imported from Ireland, and her foal, Coolfree, by Malakelhawa (New Zealand Thoroughbred). Michelle Thompson photo

mare. Her breeding would be invaluable in New Zealand. But we were left with reduced funds to buy a house!

I phoned John Cottle, one of New Zealand's leading international showjumpers and the only horse contact I knew in that country. I remembered him competing in Dublin Horse Show some years earlier. On that occasion he took a great fancy to the Irish hunters and longed to introduce them to New Zealand. So he was delighted to hear of my plans for the stallion, something he had wanted to do for years. He would solicit members to form a syndicate to help with the financing.

In the meantime while on a cycling and camping holiday, Rachel met up with an absolutely super young Kiwi from Taranaki country in the North Island. Grant Williams had been an eel fisherman for years, an interesting and lucrative solo career. Anne and I "fell for him" instantly. Rachel and Grant were married by Fr Brendon Keeghan, a friend of Rachel's from Wellington, in a charming little chapel close to Lake Rotoiti. It was such a happy family wedding. Our son Mark, who had a job in Perth, Australia, was able to join us and of course Grant had a host of family connections and friends. We had photos down by the lake shore. Idyllic.

We gave Rachel the job of looking out for a suitable property for us in the future. I thought it would probably be about ten years before we moved out from Ireland, but I was wrong!

A TURNING POINT

While we were cub hunting at Darragh I was struck down with angina. I literally threw the horn to Chris and told him to carry on. Poor chap, he was the one member of the family that could not get a note on it. He asked me if he could use a horn with a reed in it.

I said, "Over my dead body!"

He has now got a far sweeter tone on the horn than I ever had.

This turn in health was surely one of the most sensitive turning points of my life. I had been hunting our family pack of hounds, with all the responsibilities that that entailed, for forty years—surely the envy of any young MFH. Now I must abandon it all and accept a complete change of life. In retrospect, however, it was time to get rid of the old wood and let the fresh growth take over. I was blessed to have Chris to continue the great traditions handed on to him in turn by his father.

When Mr Nelligan, the leading heart surgeon in the Mater Hospital in Dublin, examined me. He said I had two options: a bypass or a lifetime on expensive pills.

I asked him, "What are my chances of surviving the operation?"

He replied, "98 to 1."

"Then what am I waiting for? Let's get on with the op!"

He was glad about my determination because many people say to him, "Well, what do *you* think, doctor?"

The day before my operation, a couple of patients asked me, "Aren't you nervous?"

I replied, "No, I have had Confession and the Sacrament of the Sick, and I believe that if God wants to take me, I am ready to go to Him."

Besides, I knew that Heaven was being bombarded with prayers and Masses from all my family and friends. Our family solicitor in Heaven, our darling Claire, was also interceding for me.

My double bypass operation was an unqualified success, thank God. I was home within ten days. I am endlessly grateful to Mr Nelligan and his team.

In the bed alongside mine was a grand young chap from Co. Wexford. A chain smoker, he was in real trouble after his operation. One has to cough to clear the congestion from the lungs, excruciatingly painful until the chestbone that was sawn apart and laced up with wire has knitted together again. Every day the physio would pummel my friend's chest unmercifully to clear his smoker's congestion and he suffered agony. Take heed all you smokers! I am glad to say that when I was leaving hospital, he was recovering well. But I don't think he would ever "look a cigarette in the eye" again.

THE FLIGHT OF THE IRISH DRAUGHT SIRES

Our three horses, the stallion Kingsway Diamond and the two mares Kilmanagh Banrion (Irish for Queen) and Night Errand, went over to Newmarket in Suffolk to do their three weeks' quarantine. Inevitably news of our emigrating to New Zealand got into the *Horse & Hound*. I received a letter from a friend in England as follows:

> I was most interested to hear that you are taking an I.D. sire out to New Zealand. We also are sending out an I.D. stallion called 'Laughton's Legend', and he is due to fly to N.Z. on Feb. 15.

That was the day our trio were due to leave. Even after confirming this with the International Bloodstock Transport Company, I could not believe my ears. The first time that the Irish Draught breed was ever introduced to New Zealand, and two stallions, unknown to each other, were going out on the same plane. It must be the greatest coincidence of all time!

There was a second coincidence. Some years earlier I had been invited to judge the Irish Draught Society (Great Britain Branch) Breed Show. At the time the quality of the breed in the United Kingdom was low, so I was desperate to find a worthy champion. Finally I decided on the yearling colt. I did not like his shoulder action, but otherwise he was quite an attractive horse and the best I had. Little did I think that the next time I would see him would be in New Zealand.

Heidi Brace from Massachusetts was with us while we were planning the move for the horses. She was the second of two excellent horsewomen whom Julie Ulrich of Virginia, a top instructor in the United States, sent over to help with my hunters. First had been Elin Payne for one season, a super girl who could turn her hand to anything and no day was too long for her. When we asked Julie for "another Elin", she reluctantly sent us Heidi, who turned out to be a pure miracle. Now she longed to go to New Zealand. Was there any chance that she could travel with the horses? The charter company said that if I could recommend her as capable, she could go.

I replied, "You could not get anyone better."

She and the horses all travelled happily. I have never been able to find out whether Kingsway Diamond or the "rival" stallion actually touched New Zealand soil first. Edwina Morris who imported Laughton's Legend maintains that he did, and of course I claim the honour for Kingsway. There has been a healthy rivalry between us ever since.

John Cottle kept the horses for a few months, with Heidi in charge of Kingsway. John agreed to stand him at stud at Clevedon Equestrian Centre for three seasons with Dr Ivan Bridge, a leading veterinary surgeon supervising and operating artificial insemination. Later Kingsway came south to Dr John Shaw, veterinary surgeon in Prebbleton Farm Stud near Christchurch. In his off-season periods he holidayed on Heidi's small farm, only about twenty minutes from us, where the two became "bosom pals".

Back in Ireland I could no longer hunt nor do much on the farm. Anyhow Chris was proving well able to fulfill his responsibilities. We were still to find a place to live in New Zealand. On our reconnaissance visit, Anne and I had gone around with several land agents inspecting possible properties, but without reaching any decision. We commissioned Rachel to continue the search for us. She sent us photos of one twenty-acre farmlet in an area called "Kerrytown"! However, there were complications over titles and boundaries, so we went no further.

Then Rachel phoned. "Dad, I've seen it. Buy it."

I said, "Right, darling, if you say it is okay, we're on!"

Photos and location looked attractive. I phoned our solicitor and instructed him to buy the property.

FORTY-EIGHT

"MASTER, ARE YOU LEAVING US?"

Martin Ryan, correspondent of our weekly newspaper the *Limerick Leader*, phoned to ask if it was true that we were emigrating to New Zealand. He would like to publish the story. Could he call and have a talk? Finding me in the drawing room with my special friend Chips, a terrier, alongside me, he captured the moment with his camera. When it was published, the photo had the caption, "Master, are you leaving us?" And so the news went out, causing shock waves among many friends.

"Master, are you leaving us?" Chips and Thady are photographed by Martin Ryan shortly before their departure for New Zealand, for a story in the Limerick Leader.

The Limerick Show Society organised a farewell party, advertising it in the *Irish Field*, in the Dunraven Arms in Adare. A huge number of friends came from all over the country. Tom Purcell, from whom I had bought the Irish Draught filly, came with his wife all the way from Kilkenny and gave us a lovely present. I was touched.

The Scarteen Hunt too laid on a special party in Emly. The Golden Thatch was packed to overflowing. Bidding goodbye to all my farming friends and hunt followers hurt me most of all. They wanted to make us a presentation.

"No," I said, "you gave me the most beautiful present a couple of years ago, Peter Curling's outstanding painting of Tommy, myself, Jacko and hounds at Knocktoran Bog. It is customary to make a presentation to someone on leaving or retiring, but I did not take the hint!"

However the committee insisted. They presented Anne with a reclining armchair and myself with a selection of power tools and a lathe.

Another occasion will remain always in my memory. Our nearest neighbours entertained us in the old school at Knockcarron, where they gave us a special gift, an engraved penstand and biro. It has pride of place by our telephone and is a constant reminder of all our old friends.

This painting by Peter Curling was presented to Master Thady by the Scarteen members in 1982. It shows Thady, Tommy Dwyer, and hounds at Knocktoran Bog, probably the best covert in the Scarteen hunting country. Knocktoran was the home of Napier (Napper) Webb, hunt treasurer and Field Master for many seasons, and his wife, Mary, who rode sidesaddle and hunted hard.

The Scarteen Hunt Committee presented the Curling portrait to Thady Ryan at Mooresfort, November 21, 1982. (l-r, front row) David O'Meara, David Russell, John Harold-Barry, Michael Kennedy, Dicky Power; (back row) James Purcell, Nora Russell, Arthur Moore, Beatrice Hurst, Thady Ryan, Maureen Hogan, Gwen Pearson, Tom Purcell, Semon and Beverly Wolf, Percy Harris, Sir Hugh Walker.

I called to one special friend, Mrs Stanton, who had been a keen hunting farmer at Cromhill and had walked innumerable hound puppies down the years. I shall never forget her closing remark.

"Master, you are not really leaving us, are you?"

It tore my heart out.

Chilli and Chips, our two terriers, were a big worry. It was going to cost £500 each to bring them out to New Zealand. We could not possibly afford it. The charter company who had flown our horses out heard of our dilemma.

They told us, "You have given us a lot of money already. Next time we have a flight to New Zealand, we will take the terriers free for you."

We were thrilled! We left the terriers in the charge of an agent who did the paperwork and provided the two crates. Then the saga started. There was a mixed cargo on the plane, including two Congo buffaloes and three hundred pedigree angora rabbits from Germany. In loading, one buffalo died of stress and the staff had to redistribute the cargo. Inadvertently they placed the terriers alongside the rabbits.

When we met them on their arrival in Auckland, it was discovered that Chilli had torn her way out of her crate, into the nearest rabbit crate, and killed the two monster inmates. The terriers were supposed to travel fasting throughout the trip, but Chilli arrived full and comfortable. The story soon spread around New Zealand and improved in the telling.

Chips on the other hand was too law-abiding. An outstanding character bred by John Harold Barry (now chairman of the hunt), he had been so small as a puppy that he taught himself to sit up to look over the grass. He passed on this habit to many of his progeny. He was brilliant at his job of bolting foxes. His most outstanding performance was near Eyon Hill while we were cub hunting. Hounds marked a fox to ground in a drain made of concrete blocks. It was nine inches high, six inches wide, and there was water running out of it.

I said, "Leu in, Chips."

He looked at me as if to say, "You must be joking."

I said, "Go on, man" and in he went.

For over half an hour there was not a sound from the drain. Our foot followers spread out over the field listening.

Eventually one of them called to me, "I think I hear Chips, Master."

I ran to the spot. Sure enough there he was marking his fox about eighteen inches down. After getting him out we dispatched the fox and gave it to the hounds. I then paced the distance—seventy-five yards from where he had gone in!

In our preparations for moving ourselves, we had a stroke of good fortune. As usual on these occasions an antique dealer turned up on the off chance of picking up a bargain while we were choosing which pieces of furniture that

Thady and Chris, father and son. The passage of years has eased the pain of handing the horn over to Chris, and I can once again enjoy the companionship of the pack. It was the cause of intense happiness for me when, upon our departure for New Zealand, all three Joint-Masters agreed to carry on with Chris as senior Master. God bless them.

Chris and Sue at Scarteen did not wish to keep. About thirty years earlier at a house auction we had bought a large Victorian-style glass-fronted bookcase. It barely fitted into the hall and looked squashed.

The dealer said, "How much for it?"

I said, "What will you give me?"

He bid me £2000. My heart missed a beat.

I said, "That is an insult. I will not take less than £3000."

He gave me £2900 in cash. We had bought it for £16. He too probably sold it later for a handsome profit. With ours we bought some nice pieces that we really liked.

The cheapest way to move our furniture and other effects was to hire a freezer container that had come from New Zealand with frozen lamb and would otherwise have to return empty. Although we hired a firm of professionals to pack all the items, I made one mistake. An old oak tree had fallen in a storm. I had it cut into slabs and packed some of them at the bottom to bring out, as a souvenir, for mantel shelves. Soon of course the container was airtight. During the five weeks of travelling, dampness from the timber wrecked some good books and other pieces.

And so April arrived. Time to say goodbye. Driving out of Scarteen for the last time was heart-rending. Then I mused over the countless Irish families in years gone by who saw their loved ones boarding a ship for Australia or some other foreign parts, knowing that they would probably never see each other again. They would have had months of hardship and discomfort ahead before they arrived in a land of strangers.

Talking of emigration, the story is told of a poor, struggling family in the west of Ireland. Two uncles who had emigrated to the United States had good jobs. Come Christmas, Uncle Dick would always send a big parcel of goodies home to the family. This time there was a new pipe for James, a smart hat for Mary, a pretty dress for Joan, a pocket knife for Sean, and a packet of brown flour. After the family opened the parcel excitedly, Mary added some white flour to the packet of brown and baked a loaf of soda bread for the tea. A week later a letter arrived from Dick, and James read it out:

> "'Dear Family, I hope you are all well after the Christmas. I hope you got my parcel safely. You will be sorry to hear that poor old Mick passed away a week last Saturday. His last wish was that his ashes should be sent back . . . to . . . to . . . Ireland a-and' . . . Oh gor we have him ate."

How lucky we were! Three days of comfort in a fast plane. I was bringing my beloved home to her own country. We were going to be united with our children. God *is* good to us.

And as I mused, the pain of parting eased and we thought excitedly, "New Zealand, here we come!"

FORTY-NINE

SCARTEEN, NEW ZEALAND

Meeting Anne and myself at Auckland Airport were Sebo and Kit Huisinga-Bruins, whom we had first met at the County Limerick Hounds Puppy Show. They brought us to their lovely home in Hamilton, in the upper North Island. Originally from the Netherlands, the couple could spend only six months of each year in New Zealand due to its immigration laws so they alternated between there and a small attractive house in Ireland overlooking Lough Derg, Co. Tipperary. We were not due to take possession of our new house until May, so we had a few days with them.

After Rachel joined us at Hamilton, we drove down the North Island in a little Honda Civic that Anne had bought the previous year. After travelling across to the South Island on the ferry, I felt we were almost home, a slight thrill I still get when we disembark in Picton. Then we drove for seven hours along the beautiful Kaikoura coast to the garden city of Christchurch, the largest city in the South Island. From there across the dead flat Canterbury Plain, and some old familiar landmarks crowded into view—Mount Hutt (a major skifield), the mighty Rakaia River, the broad Rangitata, Mount Peel, and Four Peaks Range and finally to Orari Homestead, where an old school friend of Anne's gave us a huge welcome.

We were burning to see our little house, so it was into the car with Rachel without delay, a right turn in Winchester, then a second left along dusty shingle Te Awa Road for a mile.

"Is this it, Rachel?"

"No Dad, further on."

"Is this it?"

"No, it's on the other side."

"Is this it?"

"Yes."

We stopped the car.

I hesitated. "Not this one surely?"

I was pulling her leg cruelly. The little house was irresistible. Poor Rachel almost broke into tears.

I gave her the most loving hug that I possibly could. "However did you find it? You could not possibly have even conceived anything more perfect, my darling."

As we say in Ireland, the house had a "come-hither" about it. Straight away I knew this was our home, Scarteen, New Zealand. A small bungalow, about one hundred years old, it had a veranda on the front and one side with traditional curved sheet iron roofing. It also offered a fantastic view of the mountains—they might have been the Galtees only on a larger scale. We were all overjoyed.

The previous owners, who had bred angora goats, had divided the eight acres into seven paddocks—all beautifully fenced with a race (passage) down the middle and water laid on to operate the small irrigator. The house looked directly on to the shingle road about thirty yards distant. In between, the vegetable garden came up to the front door and there were numerous goat pens and a berry cage with great blackcurrants. Highway One was about a mile away as the crow flies, the attractive small town of Temuka was five minutes drive away, and Timaru with its busy port, just twenty minutes. It was an ideal location, close to a shopping centre, yet away out in the country.

We moved into our home on 1 May 1987. Adriane and Alister and other friends loaned us some basic furniture until our container arrived a few weeks later. My 12-bore shotgun and .22 rifle were in that container. Before leaving Ireland I had got an export permit for both guns from the Garda (Police). The officer advised me to go directly to the local police barracks in New Zealand to get an import permit, and then "we would be right".

So, calling to the police in Timaru some time before the container was due to arrive, I asked to see Constable McCarthy who was in charge of firearms. He looked a big Irishman in every sense of the word! My interview went like this.

"Constable, I am bringing my shotgun and rifle into New Zealand. My wife and I have bought a small property and are going to retire."

He foraged for a large book. "What make are the guns? If the names are not in this book, you cannot import them."

Fortunately I remembered the names, which he found in his big book. "Now you can't bring them in unless you have an import licence."

"Well, that is why I came to you, to get an import licence."

"Now you can't get an import licence unless you have a firearms certificate. To get that, you have to sit an exam, and the next exam will not be for another three months."

Although I was getting frustrated and impatient, I knew there was no point in getting cross. I tried another ploy.

"Did you say your name was McCarthy?"

"Yes."

"With a name like that you must have some Irish connections?"

We started tracing his family around West Cork. Within half an hour, he had dropped his defences and I could have brought in the entire contents of Dublin Castle if I wanted to. This was my first taste of the countrywide bureaucracy in New Zealand. I was surprised to find it because it is so alien to the Kiwi character.

I encountered bureaucracy again when a customs inspector asked me, "What is in the box labelled 'Trophies'?"

I told him, "A fox's mask and a hare's mask."

"Oh," he said, "they will have to be fumigated."

"Look," I said, "the fox was killed by the Scarteen hounds in 1929 and the hare was killed by the Ampleforth College Beagles in 1939. They could not possibly have rabies!"

However, it was the wooden mounts that he was concerned about, so they were duly fumigated.

Moving from our big rambling house to a small bungalow was a psychological shock. Yet when we had all our furniture and treasures positioned where we wanted them, the house really felt like home. It has a small and efficient log burner in the big sitting/dining room, which keeps the house beautifully warm in cold weather.

After some months we still felt restricted for space, especially if friends came to stay. Going through the small village of Winchester, I spotted an ancient old hut with a tattered notice hanging on it: "For Sale". On inspection we found it consisted of two rooms with a passage between them, but what caught our eyes was the quality of the doors and panelled ceilings: the floors were covered with sheep dung!

"Will you sell?" I asked the elderly owner.

"I will", he said.

"I'll give you a couple of hundred dollars for it", I said half-jokingly.

To my astonishment he said, "Right, take it."

I was dumbfounded. "Look, I said $200, not $2,000."

"Oh I heard you all right. Take it away." I could not believe our luck!

Take it away was meant quite literally. It is common to see a complete house on a huge trailer being transported by road, preceded by a police car and a "Wide Load" notice (with most private houses in New Zealand being built of wood). If the house is too large, it is cut into portions with a chainsaw and reassembled on its new site. So our little cottage was an easy job for the haulage contractor. In no time he had planted it on piles just five yards from our back door.

We then bought a bigger house not far away. As it had been empty for years and was riddled with borer, we got it for $200 also, demolished it, burned the useless bits and got the world of good timber, sheet iron, and bricks. From those materials we could build a veranda onto our new cottage. It is now a comfortable two-bedroomed little gem with all conveniences and a superb view of the mountains. Note: Friends and relations are always welcome to come and visit us!

Next it was landscaping. With the help of great neighbours we removed all the goat pens, re-sited the vegetable garden and made a second driveway past the house to our grass yard. We cut out a gravelled sweep in front of the house and with all the top soil built a large crescent-shaped mound, which shelters us from the road and the east wind—we call it "Galteemore". Getting ambitious, we created a large pond, Lough Gur. Without thinking, I put the clay from the lake on top of the good top soil of the mountain, so many of the shrubs perished. However, thanks to a fantastic rate of growth there, we are now sheltered.

A previous owner had built a large galvanised iron shed. I thought a couple of stables were a first priority if we were going to have mares and foals, so I built two good-sized timber loose boxes in the shed. However, I was soon to learn that horses are always out, even mares are foaled in the paddocks. The stables have never been used!

A new mailbox on the roadside by our entrance was essential. I constructed a white box with a green roof, surmounted by an almost life-sized, wooden Scarteen fox, traced from the hunt card. It is the only fox in New Zealand! I refuse to put our name on the letter box. If people cannot recognise Scarteen by the fox, just too bad.

A couple of years after our arrival, the Taoiseach (Prime Minister of Ireland), Charlie Haughey made his first official visit to New Zealand. The Irish consul invited Anne and myself to a reception for Charlie at the Regent Hotel in Queen Street, Auckland. I believe he was given the tip about us by Martin Mansergh, Charlie's advisor and speech writer, as well as a nephew of some friends of ours. I accepted the invitation with pleasure on the condition that I could show Charlie our stallion.

He said, "No trouble. Bring him along to the hotel in Queen Street."

I said, "That is no good. I know the Regent Hotel, it has a revolving door and the stallion is seventeen hands."

So we hatched a scheme. Charlie would be brought from his plane to meet Kingsway Diamond at a small motel close to the airport, and then on to the Regent.

All went according to plan. We brought Kingsway Diamond to the motel, where I was astonished to find that a television crew and the press were there already. Word had got out about our scheme! Next the motorcycle escort and security chiefs turned up. Then Charlie and his wife were there, greeting us warmly.

Admiring Kingsway, Charlie said, "Thady, it looks as though you will beat us at our own game of breeding horses."

I said, "I intend to do so, but it will be with Irish horses."

Our little party with Kingsway was on television and in the papers next day—the best advertising I could wish for.

At the enjoyable reception I reminded Charlie an incident when Charlie had come down hunting with us. While I do not go along with his politics, we get on well in the hunting field. I think he was Minister for Finance at this time and was mounted on Jim Doherty's good grey hireling with the hard mouth. We came down from Cromhill Hill, hounds were flying, and the first fence was a small dry bank with bushes: Charlie went to jump between the bushes, but at the last minute the grey spotted a cattle track under a stiff blackthorn bush and ducked under it. Charlie had no time to lie forward on the horse's neck, so he had to lean right back instead. The thorn bush tore his face cruelly.

At the end of the run, his face covered in congealed blood, he said, "How can I attend the Dail (Parliament) tomorrow in this state?"

A year later when I was on Cromhill, out of interest, I went to see where Charlie had had his misfortune . . . only to find that the bush was dead. This is absolutely true!

Scarteen, New Zealand. Fox on letterbox is the only fox in N.Z. Anne with Chilli, Thady, Chips, and Darragh (by Kingsway Diamond). Kit Houghton photo

FIFTY

OUR NEW LIFE

Some parts of our first couple of years in our New Zealand home were not easy. I have to admit that I had left part of my heart in Ireland. Before leaving I had told our family and friends not to expect to see us back on a visit for at least five years. The trauma of parting had been so hurtful that I felt that if I returned, I would not be able to make the break all over again.

But then by chance, a year after we had left, our son John spotted an advertisement in an English paper. A company required a private courier to deliver some important documents to New Zealand, for which they would pay half the cost of the ticket. John jumped at the opportunity to visit us.

While there, he said to me, "Dad, you must take a trip home."

Reminding him of what I had said on leaving, I asked, "Do you really mean it?"

"Yes."

He was insistent, and the family would help with the cost of my ticket so I agreed to come. It was painful to leave Anne behind, but it was unavoidable. And it was wonderful to be "home" again staying with my sister Gwen and walking across the fields to spend the days with Chris, Sue, and our grandchildren Tadhg and Emma.

My visit did refresh a former hurt that had made it easier for me to leave Ireland in the first place. Back in the days when I was convalescing after my bypass, while I was following the hunt with Gwen, Chris found a brace of foxes in Ballinacree covert. Hounds divided: Chris and the field went with the body of the pack left-handed and two and a half couple went right-handed on their own. The latter checked after a few fields and I walked in hoping to keep them together until Chris returned to draw the covert again. I called the two and a half couple. They came to within twenty yards of me then stopped.

From the look in their eyes I could read their thoughts: "You are not our master." And they left me.

"You are dead right, lads", I thought. I broke down in tears.

Then during my visit, my former first whip Tommy Dwyer asked me, "Master, will you walk out hounds with me?"

"Tommy, I can't", I replied weakly. "They are not mine any more and I am not their master."

Tommy understood. Years on, however, the passage of years has eased the pain of handing over the horn to Chris. I can now enjoy the companionship of the pack.

I enjoyed driving around the country with Gwen, visiting old farming friends. Many of them made the same remark which gave me a great lift: "Ah, Master, things are not the same since you left us, but your son is doing great."

Gwen and Thady. My sister carries on for Chris as joint Honorary Secretary.

Since then, thanks to the generosity of relations and friends, I have been able to get home on several occasions. New Zealand and Ireland might be ten thousand miles apart, but modern transportation coupled with fax machines and an excellent telephone service, have brought the two countries closer together both, physically and psychologically. On earlier visits I was able to hunt Jacko occasionally. Latterly I have had to give up riding. But I have observed something else that has shamed me—my nerve has deteriorated and the ditches have become deeper and wider! All the same I have had a good innings.

On one occasion when I was home Fr Jack O'Connor, who had been our parish priest in Temuka, was in Ireland for a holiday. Gwen and I had planned to go on a pilgrimage to Medugorje, and Fr Jack was delighted to come with us. About eighty were in the group. We flew from Dublin to Split on the Adriatic Coast of Yugoslavia, then buses took us to Medugorje. We were billeted with a family in a comfortable house within walking distance from the beautiful church. Sadly the war in the Balkans was still going on and at times we could hear the guns near Mostar.

Every evening Mass was celebrated in the Croatian language, preceded by the Rosary. Halfway through the Rosary, there would be a pause. This was the moment when Our Lady appeared to one of the visionaries wherever she happened to be. Each day a group of young soldiers in battledress, unshaven and weary from the fighting, would come into the church, take out their Rosary beads, and prostrate themselves on the floor in prayer. One evening when Gwen and I were on our way to the Mass, we stopped in amazement.

We exclaimed, "Look at the sun!"

Normally in the clear sky the sun would be far too bright to look at it, but now we could watch it easily without blinking. It appeared to be boiling with a variety of brilliant colours. This strange spectacle lasted for a few minutes before the sun resumed its normal intense brightness. A similar behaviour of the sun often accompanies Our Lady's apparitions around the world.

Another day Gwen and I met up with Cindy, a charming young lady from the United States. She told us her story, which began when she and her husband and young son had been atheists. Diagnosed with terminal cancer, she was lying in bed watching a documentary on Medugorje and was struck with an urgent feeling that she must go there. Her husband protested that she would be dead before she got there but she insisted.

She survived the journey and joined the crowd going in to Mass. She had never been inside a church before and did not know what to expect. During the service she saw people "receiving a little biscuit," so she took one too. Soon she experienced a strange warmth going right through her body. Next she discovered that she could walk unaided and there was no more pain—she was cured. She hurried home and ran to meet her astonished husband and son. All three came without delay to Medugorje and soon were received into the Catholic church. I wish you also could meet Cindy; she just radiates happiness.

Our seven days at Medugorje were all too short. It was such an inspiring experience. Crowds are growing larger there every year. One can feel Our Lady's presence, and her message in all her apparitions is always the same: "Return to God." If only we would heed it,

Another time I was home in Ireland in early March for a heartbreak. John and Hugh had put together the makings of a beautiful milking herd of Friesians. Some of the paddocks had been reseeded and the grass was coming fast. John had installed a new milking parlour, using some of the latest ideas he had picked up in New Zealand. All was set for a promising milking season, when out of the blue, brucellosis (contagious abortion) struck. A test showed that many of the cows were infected. Government regulations required every female beast on the farm to be slaughtered.

I shall never forget the scene. Truck after truck being filled with beautiful cows and heifers, some recently calved and most on the point of calving, all off to the factory. I was in tears. John was wonderful and took the blow manfully. I think it was the Kiwi blood in him that gave him the resilience!

According to regulations no female beast was allowed onto a farm for three months after an outbreak. Maybe it was a blessing in disguise because it would have been totally impractical for Chris to run a dairy herd on top of his other responsibilities. Changing course, he decided on dry stock.

In the meantime John experimented with goats. With a friend milking a small herd, John went into partnership with him, adapting the milking parlour to handle goats. Prospects looked good as the market for goat's milk and cheese was improving.

John collected dairy goats around the country. He bought two from a small farmer up on the hills near Kilworth, Co. Cork. Chris and I went up one evening to collect them. The poor chap had just lost his wife and the goats had been her job. We found him sitting all alone in the small kitchen, a half bottle of vodka on the table beside him: He eyed us suspiciously at the start. Those goats were precious to him and must go to a good home.

He greeted us, "You don't mind, I do give myself a little trate occasionally."

My heart bled for him. We sat down.

"Dyd-dydjever drink the milk?" he asked me.

I replied that I had not drunk goat's milk for years.

"Hould on now an I'll get it out of the cooler."

He went to the fridge and filled two pint glasses. He put a glass in front of each of us and Chris's face went green, I told him he had to drink it!

Then I was dumbfounded: he asked me, "Dyd-dydjever read Plato?" There was an old book on the table beside the vodka. "Djuno ye aught to read it. 'Tis grate reading, I do read it regular."

Fancy, an old boy up on the side of a mountain reading Plato! Then I thought to myself, "We Irish must have brains, it is just a case of harnessing them. It is small wonder that Ireland is one of the leading manufacturers of computer software."

Chris and I downed the milk, collected the two fine goats, and we parted good friends.

Each time I return to Ireland I can scarcely recognise my own country. From being one of the poorest members of the European Union, Ireland now has a buoyant economy. The European Community funds poured into Ireland have transformed the country. I thought at first that the myriad of new main roads and huge bypasses were a waste of money, yet now they are crammed with traffic. There is an explosion of cars on the roads and queues of big container trucks with valuable sophisticated products heading for the European continent.

Traditionally an agricultural nation, we are now industrialised. This has brought huge changes in the family and social structure of Irish life. But have we lost more than we have gained?

FIFTY-ONE

SUNSET

Because those green hills are not highland hills
Or the island hills, they're not my land's hills
As fair as those green foreign hills may be
They are not the hills of home.

—"A Scottish Soldier," Andy Stewart

My sister Gwen and I are the last of our generation. My other sister Jean suffered a long and painful kidney illness that eventually claimed her life. Her husband Claude maintains a lively interest in hunting and in their son Geoffrey's successful thoroughbred breeding operation in Morning Star Stud at Rathcannon in Co. Limerick.

My brother John had lived at Burton Park, my mother's ancestral home. He had inherited from our Aunt Lulu Purcell and, as there was no male heir, John took the name Ryan-Purcell to perpetuate the family name. John worked hard with his herd of pedigree Jerseys. He and his wife Rosemary reared a wonderful family of six children. John was a far better man than I am. He was involved in many farming and parish activities, deeply religious and popular. He hunted when he could with the Duhallow hounds and Burton Wood was always a sure find.

Sadly, after much suffering, that dreaded cancer took its toll. His fortitude and patience up to the last were a shining example of a true Christian. At his huge funeral, it was a bitterly cold wet winter's day and yet, to everyone's astonishment, the big pile of flowers on the grave was swarming with bees. According to an old Irish tradition, this happens only at the grave of a saint.

My greatest joy on my visits to Ireland is being with Gwen. Kind and loving, formerly with red hair (now grey, like myself!), she has fresh and youthful features that belie her age. Like her father she has an uncanny knack of being in the right place to view hounds and, still blest with keen sight, she is always first to spot the fox.

To quote Jorrocks once again, "A good hunt secretary is a wery useful animal and a bad one is not worth hanging." My sister Gwen is surely the model hunt secretary and public relations officer. She is known and loved by farmers and their families throughout the hunt country, and her liaison with them has been invaluable to me in my time. In the 1968–1969 season Gwen joined Percy Harris as joint Hon. Sec. and is carrying on the good work for Chris as joint Hon. Sec. with James Purcell.

My son Hugh, Chris's twin brother, was an outstanding rugby player and, but for a serious injury, I'm sure he would have played for Ireland. He can turn his hand to anything. A couple of years ago he was co-driver with a group of about twenty adventure tourists in a big truck that had been adapted for camping. They drove overland from London to Kathmandu; their exploits could fill this book! Now self-employed, he is working hard importing and fitting the latest water-treatment plants in the Galway area, which has the fastest growth of new houses in the whole country.

My son John is farming in Galway. To our great delight he married into an old sporting family. His father-in-law is a brother to Micky Dempsey, long-time Master and huntsman of the Galway Blazers, and acts as honorary whipper-in. Martina, John's wife, is delightful and capable. She is also crazy on hunting, ironically, given that John originally relinquished the chance of hunting. Now he is wedded to it!

Scarteen is in great hands. Chris and Sue share an innate ability to spot superb young horses, the makings of high-class three-day eventers. After hunting, eventing is Chris's next love. With Sue also a brilliant horsewoman and instructor, they are making a name for themselves producing outstanding performers. On the farm their major activity is producing a high-class horse forage that he calls Equigrass, a sophisticated and scientifically produced form of haylage. His customers include some of the top trainers; several classic winners have been trained on this product.

Thady and Chris. I perceived in Chris from an early age a love and sensitivity for all animals, so I was confident in his natural ability to handle horses and hounds.

Chris and Sue have a grand young family. Tadhg (Irish for "Thady" and pronounced "Tighe"), taking after his mother, is brilliantly clever. He is already a "whiz-kid" with the computer and he enjoys his pony. His younger sister Emma might have been born on a horse, as she is a talented rider already. Being short, slight and wiry she takes after her father in build and character—she never walks if she can run!

In his stature, light build, finely chiselled features, character, weathered look (without the tan!), and twinkle in his eye, Chris resembles his grandfather John Peter. While quickly at home in any company, he is intense in all his activities. I could perceive in him from an early age his love and sensitivity for all animals, so I was confident in his natural ability to handle horses and hounds. His enthusiasm in farming, hunting, eventing, fishing, and all his other interests is infectious. In the hunting sphere I see Chris as a role model for all Masters and huntsmen; with his judgement, dedication, example, diplomacy, and leadership, I feel that hunting in Ireland has a long and bright future.

On the death of Arthur Moore, in 1995, John Harold-Barry took over the chairmanship of the hunt. A more competent and popular man for the job you could not imagine. He and his wife Dinky are the backbone of the hunt. John started as a partner of Willie Baker in the Bansha Veterinary Clinic and in time he took it over himself. His dedication and excellence in his practise endeared him to his vast number of clients.

Three Generations! right to left: Thady's grandson, Tadhg; Thady's son, Chris; Thady Ryan; Semon Wolf and Ian Hurst, Joint-MFHs.

I bought an expensive three-year-old gelding one time away in Co. Clare. It was a beautiful young horse and I had hopes of winning the Hunter Championship in the Royal Dublin Horse Show. I told the owner that I would send my vet to examine him. John reported that the horse had the smallest suspicion of a blemish on one tendon and as the price was so high, he could not recommend me to take him. The owner was real angry and insisted that his horse was perfectly sound. The following year I was judging the four-year-old hunter class in Ennis Show. My fine young horse came into the ring—lame. His owner and I looked in each other's eyes and not a word was said. John H-B had saved me a lot of money!

But I am slipping back into the Irish scene again. My apologies!

Anne and I are extremely happy living in her own country, all the more so for having Rachel and Mark and their families within seven hours' drive from Scarteen, New Zealand. Conveniently for us, they live only about ten minutes apart from each other and within half an hour from the city of Nelson, one of the sunniest spots in New Zealand.

Mark has a good job with one of the country's principal fish-processing companies, and is patiently trying to teach his father how to drive a computer! Rachel is happy lecturing in early childhood education in Nelson Polytechnic while her husband Grant is busy eel fishing. In Grant's off season they are building a fascinating wattle-and-daub house on their beautiful seaside site. Their two daughters Kiri, and Alice, along with Mark's daughter Claire, are musical. All are showing great talent in and love for Irish dancing. Mark's wife Ruth is artistic herself; no doubt her talents will pass on to their three lovely children.

I am so proud of all our family. God bless them.

Our "horse saga" has been a saga of success. I have *achieved* my ambition of seeing the Irish hunter blood spread throughout New Zealand. Progeny of both original sires (known as "Irish sporthorses") are proving their worth in all sports throughout the country. Now each one has sons and grandsons at stud (out of high-class thoroughbred mares), who are themselves outstanding showjumpers. Kingsway Diamond must have particularly strong genes as one can spot his progeny into the third generation. It is interesting that some show predominantly thoroughbred characteristics while others show more of their Irish pedigree.

As the breed has spread, so too has their popularity. In 1988 we formed the Irish Draught Horse Society (New Zealand). Membership is around 200 and rising. Recently, because of the confusion over the term "draught" (which conjures up the heavy Clydesdale breed, see chapter 33) we changed the organisation's name to The Irish Horse Society New Zealand. Its objectives are to promote and perpetuate the Irish Draught breed in New Zealand.

For some years the New Zealand Horse of the Year Show was held at the thoroughbred sales complex at Karaka, south of Auckland, where we mounted a display stand to promote the breed. In this connection John and Stef Hernon

Prize-winning trio by Kingsway Diamond. Michelle Thompson photo

gave so much through their help and hospitality. John is a big man in heart and build, a true Irishman from Co. Wicklow, who still has his brogue and an endless fund of stories. He has some outstanding young stock by Kingsway.

As the Horse of the Year Show coincided with St Patrick's Day, the Irish consul used to invite Anne and myself to his special feast day lunch on board a launch in Auckland Harbour—some party! Kingsway Diamond, still standing with Dr Ivan Bridge MVB at Drury, is still active at twenty years of age. Now with entire responsibility for the stallion, Ivan treats him as one of the family.

By clubbing together some friends bought another unrelated registered Irish Draught sire from England. Coalman's Touch, by the successful Irish Draught sire Touch of the Blues, is an outstanding example of a true Irish Draught with a colossal jump and an impeccable character. His first crop of foals are attractive. We have a filly by him, only the third pure Irish Draught female in New Zealand. She is awesome!

Coalman's Touch stands with Colin Price at Croftlea Stud near Oxford, North Canterbury. I am particularly pleased about this because Colin and his wife Raewyn are devoted to the Irish breeding, and their son Tim will produce and compete with their promising young stock. I am also happy that Colin agreed to take my place as chairman of the Irish Horse Society New Zealand when I retired last year. In his capable hands, the Irish Horse Society and the breed will have a bright future and will play a major role in the New Zealand sporthorse world. I wish Colin and his family every good fortune for years to come.

A couple of years ago the society organised a tour for breeders to the famous Dublin Horse Show, with me as their leader. About twenty-five of us flew to Dublin and revelled in the show by day and night. The following week, we hired a bus and toured the south, visiting stud farms, foxhound kennels, and fabulous scenery. It also involved a morning's cub hunting on foot with my son Chris; some adventurous members of the group sampled our banks and ditches on horseback. Our driver John gave us a running commentary on all points of interest. He had a lovely voice, though not always in tune, and we sang Irish and New Zealand songs incessantly.

At one point in Co. Galway we had to ask a local chap for directions. The conversation was as follows:

"Can you tell us the way to Mrs Deon's stud, please?"

"Now ye are on the right road but you're not. Go up to the four crossroads and turn left and ye'll be right and if ye're not right, there's something wrong wid ye."

We had to ask again, this time a lady in her car. "Can you tell us please how to get to Mrs Deon's place?"

"What d'ye want to go there for?"

"To see some horses."

"Oh is it horses ye're after? Are ye buying horses? I have a couple to sell, they might suit ye. Who's wid ye?"

"Thady Ryan."

"Oh, the hunt man. My horses would suit him."

Everyone dissolved in laughter. We were late for our appointment, but Mrs Deon had a lovely meal for us.

The tour had been a successful combination of activities. Members had feasted their eyes on the cream of Irish hunters at the show, and were then able to see the variety of hunting country, where our Irish horses have excelled themselves down the years. We hope to repeat the experience.

Anne and I are in partnership with Gerald and Sue Hargreaves and their daughter Belinda in the Galtymore Stud, at their beautiful home Kakahu (Maori for a laughing parrot), just ten miles from us in South Canterbury. We have yet to hit the jackpot—meaning produce a world-beater and sell him for huge money! But we have some promising young stock in the pipeline.

The Hargreaves are third-generation New Zealanders. Long before I met Anne, she used to look after Gerald and his sisters as children at Kakahu. Now we are "in harness" together, a happy coincidence. Gerald has one of the top herds of pedigree Aberdeen Angus in the country.

Like so many farmers, Gerald has a big problem with gorse infesting a big portion of his high land. It would be uneconomical to spray it. At one time he decided to graze it off with three hundred goats, which worked until the goats invaded all the neighbours. Then he had to employ marksmen to shoot them. I smile when I think of the lengths we used to go to at home in Ireland to *sow* gorse for fox coverts.

I never thought that I would miss my foxes so much. Frequently when catching sight of a big square of gorse, I automatically think, "What a great covert! I imagine I hear hounds find. What way is the wind? Which way will he break?" and I feel lonesome.

We live in the South Canterbury Hunt country. They have a small, but beautiful, pack of hounds that hunt well and regularly win championships in the National Hound Show. Their keen young huntsman shows good sport. They have a large open country, plenty of hares, wire fences (some panelled) and huge paddocks. Seldom do they hunt a given area more than once a season. All the ingredients are there for the top class sport that they have.

I enjoy following in the car, the company, the crack, and watching hounds working well, but to my shame I cannot get enthused hunting a hare. It is a terrible confession for a huntsman to make—hunting any quarry with hounds should satisfy—but having hunted a fox with my own hounds for forty seasons, I have been spoilt. A fox has a charisma that is hard to describe. There is a spellbinding urgency and a wild excitement in hunting a fox, sending the blood coursing in one's veins.

The other night I had a vivid dream: hounds were hunting hard in covert, Chris was at the far side. Charles, the elusive dog fox (chapter 20), broke covert just close to me.

I yelled "Tally-ho! Tally-ho!" and woke myself up.

Anne called to me, "For goodness sake shut up."

I cannot get it out of my system.

We live in the heart of a dairy area. Clandeboye Cheese Factory (close by) is the third largest in the southern hemisphere. Our nearest farming neighbour milks nine hundred Jersey cows in a large rotary parlour. Across the road another milks over four hundred in a new herring-bone forty-a-side parlour. It makes me feel quite at home!

We have great neighbours all round us. Temuka is the centre of an Irish colony; many families with Irish names settled here. We have a beautiful, big cut-limestone church, St Joseph's, and I have the great blessing of being able to get daily Mass. The Josephite sisters, an Australian order, have a convent school nearby.

The lovely town of Geraldine is only a short distance to the north of us. Among our many friends retired there are my first cousin Joan Hickley and her husband John. Joan (nee O'Connell) was from Lakeview on Killarney's Lower Lake in Co. Kerry, where we spent such happy times in days gone by. I have fished some of the local rivers, but without much success so far. Anyway I go fishing with a feeling of guilt because I should be working in the garden!

I am increasingly fond of Kiwi folk. I enjoy their warmhearted unsophistication and sincere friendship. Actually I found to my cost that this familiarity can be contagious. At a horse show with Anne, I spotted someone who I thought was a good friend walking from us.

Creeping up behind her, I hugged my arms around her and said, "How are ye me darlin?"

The lady turned round in disgust and said, "Who the hell are you?" It wasn't our friend at all!

Covered in confusion, I blurted out, "I am most frightfully sorry for the mistake. You are twice as good looking as the lady I thought you were." An absolutely lie.

Anne said to me, "It serves you bloody well right."

We get the most marvellous sunsets in our spot in South Canterbury. The extra bright-sun and dry atmosphere seem to create the intense contrast between the exquisite colours and cloud formations, unbelievably beautiful. They symbolise the love and happiness we enjoy in our little home in the second-best country in the world.

View of our New Zealand mountains. "They are not the hills of home."

My beloved Galtees.

As I write, I am looking out across the Canterbury Plains at the snow-capped peaks of Mount Peel, Four Peaks, and Fox's Peak. Behind them are the spectacular Southern Alps sheltering Lakes Tekapo and Pukaki, magical scenery. The majestic Aorangi (Mount Cook) towers above them all.

Yet, in the words of "The Scottish Soldier",

> Because those green hills are not highland hills or the island hills, they're not my land's hills. As far as these green foreign hills may be, they're not the hills of home.

Chris presents the brush to Thady. (l–r) Thady, Gwen, Chris, Tommy. Sketch by June Brilly

EPILOGUE

My readers, I hope that you have enjoyed sharing with me some memories of my truly privileged life as much as I have enjoyed reliving them all.

May God bless you.

Thady Ryan

GLOSSARY

bagman	bagged fox
banshee	fairy woman
bawn	old pasture
brace	two foxes
bread and scrape	thick slice of bread on which a little butter has been spread then scraped off again
brinkeen	a very small fish in freshwater streams, possibly salmon fry
butt car	a horse-drawn square cart that is capable of holding about one ton of gravel and can be tipped to empty
cadge a lift	get a ride in someone else's car for free
cock of hay	about eight hundredweight of hay
coombe	a deep wooded glen
corncrake	brownish bird about the size of a woodcock that lives in the meadows in summer and has a distinctive rasping call "Crake, crake, crake"; also known as a rail
cottier	farm worker
crack	fun
cuppa	cup of tea
drag	faint scent of a fox long gone
earthstopper	someone employed by the Master to close all known foxholes to stop a fox going to ground
entry	young hounds about eighteen months old starting their first season
flyer	a short, sharp, fast run on a good fox with a strong scent
gams	pigs' hocks or crubeens/trotters; delicious when barbecued!
harboured	located by professional gamekeepers
hunting topper	stiff top hat, which for years was the correct head gear for hunt members; also known as a silk hat
Joint-Master	one of two or more Masters of a pack of hounds who share with the senior Master the responsibilities of the hunt
leu in	a call from the huntsman to his hounds to encourage them to draw a covert
nate little hin	colloquial pronunciation of a neat little hen
owning the line	at a check when hounds are at fault and one hound finds the scent and speaks, he is said to "own the line"
oxer	spread
purler	heavy fall
rugger	rugby
Sí gaoite	(pronounced "shee geeha") fairy wind
silken thread	invisible contact between hounds and their huntsman
skelp	a stroke with a whip or a stick as a form of mild punishment

spuds	potatoes
stary coat	dry coat with the hair on end, as distinct from the sleek coat of a well-conditioned horse
stirk	shorthorn bullock aged one-and-a-half to two years
stooked	four or more sheaves of corn that have been tied by the reaper and binder, then stood on end together to dry out
sugán	a handmade twisted rope of hay
Tans	Scarteen Black and Tan hounds
tanning	corporal punishment
tenner	£10 note
thumbstick	a long walking stick with a forked branch on top to take the thumb
tilth	the upper layer of freshly ploughed sods that has been crumbed by a harrow to produce a good seedbed for corn or grass
trompe	French horn
tufter	steady old hound, too aged to keep up with the pack
veges	vegetables
la Venerie	the entire spectrum of stag hunting in France, including the long history, traditions, and rituals of *la chasse-à-cour* (hunting with hounds)
whipper-in	a member of the hunt staff who assists the huntsman by encouraging hounds to go to him
wynde	a large cock of hay of about eight hundredweight, shaped carefully to resist rain damage when left out in the meadow to season; no longer used since the advent of the baler

REFERENCES

Moore, Daphne. 1978. *Famous Foxhunters*. Surrey, Eng.: Spur Publications, Saiga Publishing Company.

Thomas, Joseph B. 1928. *Hounds and Hunting Through the Ages*. Lanham, Md.: Republished by The Derrydale Press.

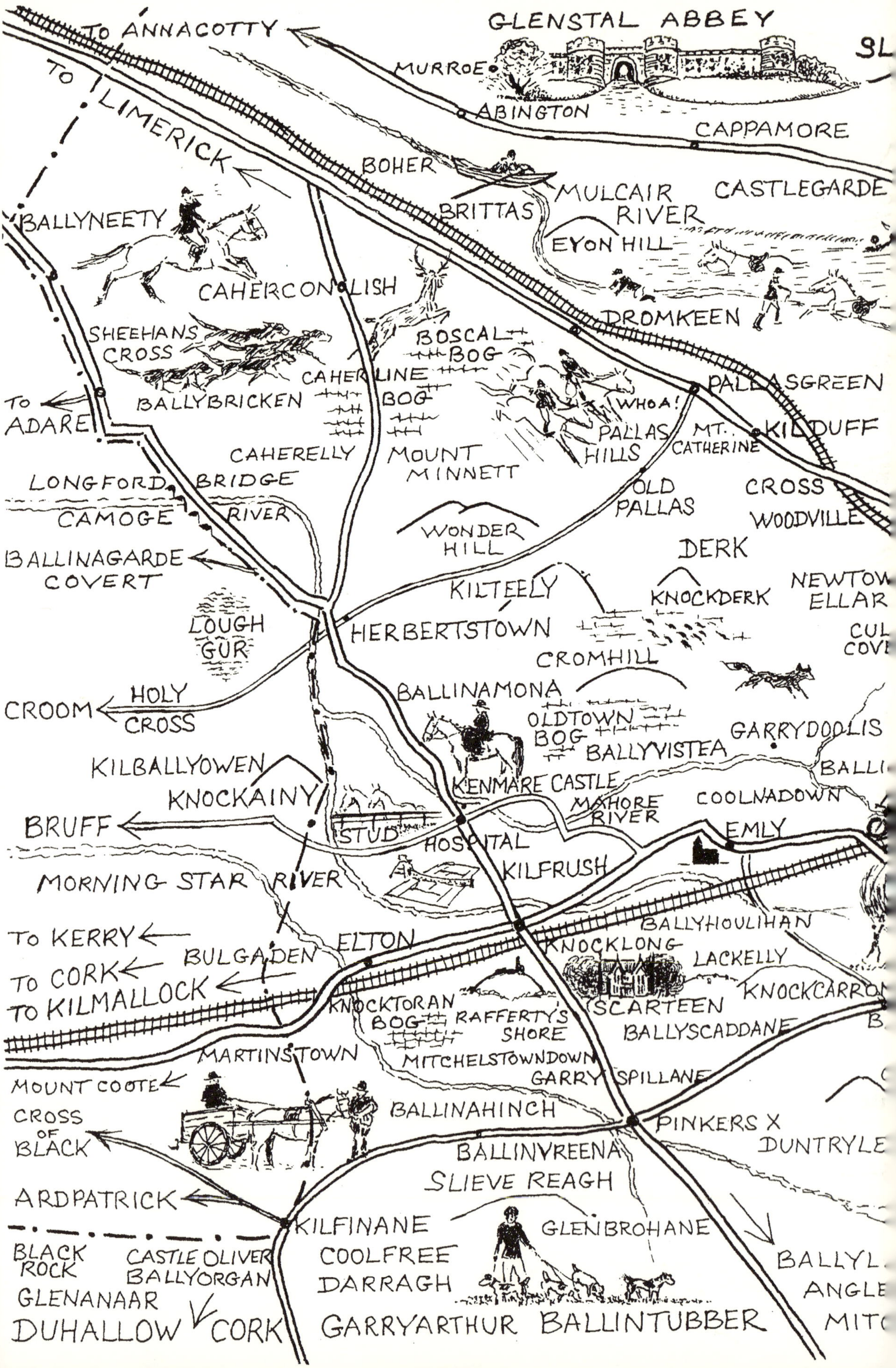

GLENSTAL ABBEY
TO ANNACOTTY
TO LIMERICK
MURROE
ABINGTON
CAPPAMORE
BOHER
MULCAIR RIVER
CASTLEGARDE
BRITTAS
EYON HILL
BALLYNEETY
CAHERCONLISH
DROMKEEN
SHEEHANS CROSS
BOSCAL BOG
CAHERLINE BOG
PALLASGREEN
TO ADARE
BALLYBRICKEN
WHOA!
PALLAS HILLS
MT. CATHERINE
KILDUFF
CAHERELLY
MOUNT MINNETT
LONGFORD BRIDGE
CAMOGE RIVER
OLD PALLAS
CROSS
WOODVILLE
WONDER HILL
BALLINAGARDE COVERT
DERK
KILTEELY
KNOCKDERK
LOUGH GUR
HERBERTSTOWN
CROMHILL
HOLY CROSS
CROOM
BALLINAMONA
OLDTOWN BOG
GARRYDOOLIS
BALLYVISTEA
KILBALLYOWEN
KNOCKAINY
KENMARE CASTLE
MAHORE RIVER
COOLNADOWN
BRUFF
STUD
HOSPITAL
EMLY
MORNING STAR RIVER
KILFRUSH
BALLYHOULIHAN
TO KERRY
ELTON
KNOCKLONG
BULGADEN
LACKELLY
TO CORK
TO KILMALLOCK
KNOCKCARRON
KNOCKTORAN BOG
RAFFERTY'S SHORE
SCARTEEN
BALLYSCADDANE
MARTINSTOWN
MITCHELSTOWNDOWN
GARRY SPILLANE
MOUNT COOTE
CROSS OF BLACK
BALLINAHINCH
PINKERS X
BALLINVREENA
DUNTRYLE
SLIEVE REAGH
ARDPATRICK
KILFINANE
GLENBROHANE
BLACK ROCK
CASTLE OLIVER
BALLYORGAN
COOLFREE
DARRAGH
GLENANAAR
DUHALLOW
CORK
GARRYARTHUR
BALLINTUBBER